Shakespeare and the Nature of Love

Rethinking Theory

GENERAL EDITOR

Gary Saul Morson

CONSULTING EDITORS

Robert Alter
Frederick Crews
John M. Ellis
Caryl Emerson

Shakespeare and the Nature of Love

Literature, Culture, Evolution

Marcus Nordlund

Northwestern University Press
Evanston, Illinois

Northwestern University Press
www.nupress.northwestern.edu

Printed in the United States of America

10   9   8   7   6   5   4   3   2   1

ISBN-13: 978-0-8101-2421-9 (cloth)
ISBN-10: 0-8101-2421-1 (cloth)
ISBN-13: 978-0-8101-2423-3 (paper)
ISBN-10: 0-8101-2423-8 (paper)

Library of Congress Cataloging-in-Publication Data

Nordlund, Marcus.
    Shakespeare and the nature of love : literature, culture, evolution / Marcus Nordlund.
        p. cm. — (Rethinking theory)
    Includes bibliographical references.
    ISBN-13: 978-0-8101-2421-9 (cloth : alk. paper)
    ISBN-10: 0-8101-2421-1 (cloth : alk. paper)
    ISBN-13: 978-0-8101-2423-3 (pbk. : alk. paper)
    ISBN-10: 0-8101-2423-8 (pbk. : alk. paper)
        1. Shakespeare, William, 1564–1616—Criticism and interpretation. 2. Love in literature.
    I. Title. II. Series.
    PR3069.L6N57 2007
    822.33—dc22

                                                                        2007012854

Material from the introduction and chapters 1, 4, and 5 has been taken from the following essays by Marcus Nordlund: "Theorising Early Modern Jealousy: A Biocultural Perspective on Shakespeare's *Othello*," *Studia Neophilologica* 74, no. 2 (2002): 146–60 and "The Problem of Romantic Love: Shakespeare and Evolutionary Psychology" in *The Literary Animal: Evolution and the Nature of Narrative,* edited by Jonathan Gottshall and David Sloan Wilson (Evanston, Ill.: Northwestern University Press, 2005), 107–25.

Contents

Acknowledgments

This is a book about love, about its roots in human nature and about its literary representation. Here is my feeble attempt to acknowledge some of the love, friendship, and generosity that surrounded me as I wrote it.

In Shakespeare's works, the word "love" is used in an extraordinary number of senses, one of which is a euphemism for "remuneration" or even "payment." I'm grateful to Uppsala University, Sweden, for the principal funding of my research, and to Göteborg University for granting me a generous leave of absence so that I could complete it. The final revision was performed when I finally returned to Göteborg and took up my position there, making my book a tale of two cities and universities.

While I was at Uppsala University, the chair of the English literature department, Monica Fryckstedt, was always keen to protect my research against the encroachments of other academic tasks, and I grew fond of more people than can be mentioned here. Let me single out four people: Donald MacQueen, one of the last true altruists; Richard Glover, who lent me some great books about love; and two very good friends of my own generation, Anna Swärdh and Christer Larsson.

Writing a book of this kind is mainly done in the company of other books, but academic research and publishing is also a collective endeavor. I want to thank my colleagues at the World Shakespeare Congress, the Annual Meeting of the Shakespeare Association of America, and the British Shakespeare Association Conference for their valuable feedback, both formal and informal. I've also had the wonderful fortune to have my book scrutinized and improved by several people who combine endemic generosity with deep discerning. Had it not been for Brian Boyd at the University of Auckland, New Zealand, Joseph Carroll at the University of Missouri at St. Louis, and Nancy Easterlin at the University of New Orleans, I would not only have written an inferior book, but without their own contributions to the field, and those of other fellow evolutionists such as Jon Gottschall and Ellen Dissanayake, my attempt to chip away at the literary-theoretical orthodoxy would have become a lonely struggle.

To my almost lifelong friend Jeremy Ray, I owe two things that are of particular importance to this book: an incentive in childhood to learn more English words like "fircone" and "adder," and the proverbial evolution bug. Thanks.

If there hadn't been "beggary in the love that can be reckoned"—and it may well be our rescue that there is—my final incalculable debt would have been to my family: to my partner, Anna, my son, Sam, and my daughter, Irma, without whom I would be pretty close to nothing. You said it, Sam, at the age of three: "I love you so much that you could melt."

SHAKESPEARE AND THE NATURE OF LOVE

Introduction

In 1898, Leo Tolstoy published a now-famous essay with the dual purpose of explaining the nature of art and of distinguishing good art from bad. He defined his object of study as a sincere transmission of individual feeling from the author to his audience and argued that its quality could be graded according to its impact or "infectiousness." Since simplicity was a virtue, and a good work should be intelligible to anyone, a masterpiece could be expected to command universal assent among its audience.[1] Today Tolstoy's art criticism is perhaps best known for its attacks on several Western artists who did not live up to his criteria, including William Shakespeare, who received a particularly scathing diatribe of his own in 1906:

> I remember the astonishment I felt when I first read Shakespeare. I expected to receive a great esthetic pleasure, but on reading, one after another, the works regarded as his best, *King Lear, Romeo and Juliet, Hamlet,* and *Macbeth,* not only did I not experience pleasure but I felt an insuperable repulsion and tedium, and a doubt whether I lacked sense, since I considered works insignificant and simply bad, which are regarded as the summit of perfection by the whole educated world; or whether the importance that educated world attributed to Shakespeare's works lacks sense. . . . I have again read the whole of Shakespeare . . . and have experienced the same feeling still more strongly, no longer with perplexity but with a firm indubitable conviction that the undisputed fame Shakespeare enjoys as a great genius . . . is a great evil—as every falsehood is.[2]

Given Tolstoy's assumption that a good work would always appeal to a wider audience than a bad work, Shakespeare's apparent badness and widespread recognition as a genius must have posed a major problem for him. Accusing the English dramatist of pretentiousness, shallowness, sensationalism, irreligiousness, and of having no identifiable artistic vision or convictions, he located the cause of Shakespeare's fame in his supposed pandering to the immoral leanings of the upper classes. Indeed, he was confident that Shakespeare would sooner or later be forgotten, sharing the fate of another illustrious figure who was now "beginning to be neglected"—Charles Darwin.[3]

With the benefit of historical hindsight, it cannot be denied that the Russian novelist was unfortunate in his choice of future "has-beens." In a recent poll conducted by the BBC, both Shakespeare and Darwin made it to the top-ten list of "Great Britons," eclipsed only by figures like Lord Brunel and Diana, Princess of Wales. Shakespeare remains the most celebrated author in world literature, and his plays have been transposed with commercial and artistic success into film (arguably the dominant artistic medium of our age). If you walk into the Library of Congress and consult their catalogues, you will find that there are more books on Shakespeare than on any other person, except Jesus.[4]

Darwin, for his part, cannot be said to have fared much worse. Almost 150 years after the first publication of *The Origin of Species*, we are still only beginning to grasp the full implications of his grand theory for human self-knowledge. At the beginning of the twenty-first century, an increasing number of academic disciplines concerned with human nature are slowly being transformed by the central insight offered by Darwin's legacy: that knowing where we come from can tell us important things about who we are.

I do not know if Darwin ever read Tolstoy, but for many years he was an avid and enthusiastic reader of Shakespeare. In 1881—the year before he died, and some twenty-five years before the great Russian novelist would predict his descent into anonymity—Darwin described a love of Shakespeare and the Romantic poets that had lasted from boyhood and well into his thirties. Then something had happened: "But now for many years I cannot endure to read a line of poetry: I have tried lately to read Shakespeare, and found it so intolerably dull that it nauseated me. I have also almost lost any taste for pictures or music." Looking back on a life spent in the service of science, Darwin regretted this development deeply and could not resist speculating about its potential causes:

> My mind seems to have become a kind of machine for grinding general laws out of large collections of facts, but why this should have caused the atrophy of that part of the brain alone, on which the higher tastes depend, I cannot conceive. A man with a mind more highly organised or better constituted than mine, would not I suppose have thus suffered; and if I had to live my life again I would have made a rule to read some poetry and listen to some music at least once every week; for perhaps the parts of my brain now atrophied could thus have been kept active through use. The loss of these tastes is a loss of happiness, and may possibly be injurious to the intellect, and more probably to the moral character, by enfeebling the emotional part of our nature.[5]

For Darwin, who was a modest man, the problem thus lay with himself and not with Shakespeare. Science and art were complementary aspects of a good life, and neglecting one of them could result in moral, intellectual, or emotional dysfunction.[6] While Darwin himself had produced a groundbreaking scientific work on the evolutionary origins of human emotions,[7] the special capacity of the arts to transmit and evoke human feeling seems to have been as clear to him as it was to Tolstoy. It would probably have warmed his heart to know that today an increasing number of people across the world are venturing into the no-man's-land between science and literature, seeking to bridge the divide between the Two Cultures described by C. P. Snow.

The purpose of this book is to explore Shakespeare's treatment of different forms of love: that between parents and children, between lovers, and the dark avatar known as jealousy. The chief novelty lies in my contention that the best conception of love, and hence the best framework for its literary analysis, must be a bicultural fusion of evolutionary and cultural/historical explanation. That is, we should not be content with reading Shakespeare the way most literary critics have read him recently—as a man of his time, determined by the specific historical conditions that attended the writing of his plays. We must also approach him as a member of the larger species whose origin Darwin finally managed to explain, seeking the advice of biologists, neuroscientists, and anthropologists, as well as philosophers and artists. Only then, when we begin to weigh human sameness against historical and cultural difference, will we give a more accurate picture of Shakespearean love.[8]

Most, if not all, imaginative works of fiction engage in a delicate balancing act where they alternately gratify and frustrate our expectations. Things mundane or predictable seldom attract our attention, but we soon lose interest in what is merely strange. In each of these plays, I will argue, Shakespeare deliberately violates a familiar aspect of human nature as a means of involving the audience emotionally and inviting us to reflect critically on the nature of love. This violation typically consists in the dramatic heightening or intensification of a human need or disposition—such as greed, integrity, jealousy, loyalty, or even a distorted form of love—that renders it lopsided, dysfunctional, and incompatible with human affection. From the interpreter's perspective, such a literary technique does not render human nature irrelevant but makes it a necessary reference point, since to define something as a *violation* of human nature presupposes an identifiable *concept* of human nature.

To assume a bicultural perspective—basing itself on the Darwinian interaction between genes and environments; seeking to recognize what is universal as well as particular to human beings; and rejecting the traditional dichotomy between nature and culture—is to enlist the most plausible account of human nature available. In this pursuit I align myself with a small but growing cadre of literary scholars who contend that the study of cultural artifacts like literature must ultimately be placed on an evolutionary foundation.[9] The humanities can no longer afford to ignore the wealth of evidence that emerges from outside traditional authorities like Marx, Freud, Nietzsche, and their more recent disciples.[10] This view is shared by Robin Headlam Wells, one of few experts on Shakespeare who have considered an evolutionary approach to human nature: if literary scholars are truly interested in "the mystery of human subjectivity" then they need to step out of their own "limited coterie" and familiarize themselves with the most recent developments in disciplines concerned with the mind and social behavior.[11]

In the current intellectual environment, such an interdisciplinary endeavor is bound to generate many questions and suspicions, especially of an ideological kind. Many of these will be addressed in chapter 1, where I discuss the nature and implications of my approach to love and literature. What does it mean, for example, to regard love as a material phenomenon that is rooted in an evolutionary process? What are the consequences if we accept that men and women have not evolved as identical emotional beings? For now, I will content myself with a few introductory remarks about the larger theoretical framework and disciplinary environment in which I situate my text.

Since this book is about love, it goes without saying that I find it misguided to associate Darwinism only with competition and a bloodthirsty survival of the fittest. If we accept that the human race has been tailored by an evolutionary process, then it seems likely that this process will not be responsible only for our tendencies toward, say, aggression or individualistic self-promotion. It will also underpin what we consider most beautiful and valuable about ourselves. Today there are few evolutionists who would dispute that our capacities for cooperation, trust, and affection have been equally instrumental in assuring our survival on the planet. And as I suggested earlier, when we study the nature of affection in any given culture, we must not stare ourselves blind at cultural differences.

In this context we can note another irony in Tolstoy's attack on the Bard from Stratford-upon-Avon. For Tolstoy, the chief hallmark of great art was precisely its universality, but what he meant was that the individual artist should project a unified moral vision whose truthfulness was such that it would win universal acceptance. Tolstoy was, in all likelihood, massively different in temperament and literary purpose from Shakespeare, who, in Harold Bloom's wonderful formulation, "truly seems to have become himself only by representing other selves."[12] Indeed, it is likely that this staggering capacity for empathy and identification—as opposed to Tolstoy's centrifugal projection of a moral vision—eventually contributed to Shakespeare's reputation as a universal dramatist.

The most frequently cited assertion of Shakespeare's universality is Samuel Johnson's eighteenth-century *Preface to Shakespeare*:

> Shakespeare is above all writers, at least above all modern writers, the poet of nature; the poet that holds up to his readers a faithful mirrour of manners and of life. His characters are not modified by the customs of particular places, unpractised by the rest of the world; by the peculiarities of studies

and professions, which can operate but upon small numbers; or by the accidents of transient fashions or temporary opinions: they are the genuine progeny of common humanity, such as the world will always supply, and observation will always find. His persons act and speak by the influence of those general passions and principles by which all minds are agitated, and the whole system of life is continued in motion. In the writings of other poets a character is too often an individual; in those of Shakespeare it is commonly a species.[13]

Like most people, Dr. Johnson was a child of his time. This passage is surrounded by an interesting historical paradox since the preference for the universal over the particular, for the species over the individual, is itself the expression of a historical attitude that we associate with the philosophical Enlightenment. The more Johnson stresses the universal, then, the more he reveals his own indebtedness to the values and ideals of a particular place and time. As I hope will become clear further on in this study, his concern with "the general passions of mankind" also causes him to overlook an important aspect of Shakespeare's achievement: the dramatist's interest in those cultural differences that he could glean from the material available to him. What Johnson gives us is one side of the coin, and the other side bears the imprint of our historical specificity.

During the last three decades or so, the discipline of literary studies underwent a drastic change that seriously undermined the claim for Shakespeare's universality. In the wake of a massive explosion of diverse theoretical currents it is now common practice—indeed, in many areas even a professional requirement—to scoff at Johnson's unchanging Shakespeare. By a monumental swing of the pendulum, the majority of literary critics have instead turned their attention to those particulars and differences that separate individuals and cultures from each other. For example, one of the chief tenets of the most influential school of criticism in the eighties and nineties—the New Historicism—was that "no discourse, imaginative or archival, gives access to unchanging truths nor expresses inalterable human nature."[14] One of the most recent developments, queer theory, takes this tendency to its extreme by celebrating almost *any* (politically acceptable) exception from *any* norm.

In this environment, the minority of critics who have continued to assert the timelessness of the Shakespearean passions have found it difficult to assert themselves because they have lacked a theoretical foundation of corresponding complexity. Allan Bloom's *Shakespeare on Love and Friendship* (2000) is a case in point. Although there is much to admire in this sensitive and illuminating study, Bloom's denial of the need for "an elaborate psychology to explain the miracle of deep involvement" seems to originate in a profound suspicion of science. Without really confronting his nemesis head-on, he asserts repeatedly that science cannot "dissolve the most powerful everyday experiences that men and women have," as if this were its chief objective.[15]

Bloom's view of scientific explanation and the phenomenology of experience as opposing rather than complementary approaches to the human affections is regrettable. Above all, it loses sight of one of the greatest virtues of science: that its systematic collective inquiry is intended to rescue us from the egocentric assumption that our own subjective "experience" is always representative of other people's experience. It is not enough to simply assert, as Bloom does in distinctly Johnsonian fashion, that "Shakespeare seems to be the mirror of nature and to present human beings just as they are."[16] It will also be difficult to argue convincingly for the universality of romantic love in *Romeo and Juliet* unless one has first made the same case for romantic love itself.

In the absence of such a framework it has been fairly easy for radical literary critics (who, ironically, share much of Bloom's conservative suspicion of biology)[17] to convince themselves that romantic love has nothing to do with universal human nature: it is only a heteronormative social construction specific to Western culture. In this way, the academic mainstream has produced an equally single-minded inversion of Johnson's Shakespeare: a writer who only deals in the "customs" of his own "particular place" and has little to tell us about our "common humanity."

There have, of course, been more moderate voices in this debate, even among those critics who have not considered the relevance of Darwin's perspective to literary study. In his masterful *Othello and Interpretive Traditions* (1999), Edward Pechter briefly considers why Shakespeare's play has managed to maintain its hold on so many different audiences throughout history. It might be "resonating on a universal register, transcending the partialities of particular audiences and appealing to an essential humanity shared across cultural differences. . . . Too many smart people have committed themselves to one version or another of Shakespeare's universality for us to dismiss it out of hand. But it doesn't seem to get us very far; once we declare it, what next?"[18]

The same question could, I suppose, be asked of virtually any proposition. Once we declare Shakespeare's profound historicity, what next? Once we have established that human beings have evolved from simpler life forms, what next? But the objection is definitely worth listening to, since the mere identification of human universals in literary works would seem like a trite affair. We must hope that the last decades of prescribed constructivism and particularism will not be replaced by an equally single-minded universalism of the following kind: *This essay will argue, in contrast to recent strong constructivist orthodoxy, that the characters in* Hamlet *live in a group, have a sense of self, engage in verbal humor and feasting, interpret intentions on the basis of behavior, do not like to defecate in public, have problems with incest, mourn their dead, and give each other gifts. I have not been able to verify if they have a standard time pattern for weaning.*[19]

So what should be the real function of human universals in literary study? In Shakespeare's *All's Well That Ends Well*, the French King delivers a line that could well serve as an anthem for the biocultural approach to literature:

> Strange is it that our bloods,
> Of colour, weight, and heat, pour'd all together,
> Would quite confound distinction, yet stands off
> In differences so mighty. (2.3.119–22)[20]

The gist of the King's meditation is that human nature is characterized by a *paradox of sameness and difference*. Among the learned in Shakespeare's own society, this paradox was most frequently understood in terms of Aristotle's traditional distinction between essentials (that are universal and define what something *is*) and mere accidentals. While the paradox remains as fascinating and relevant as ever, it is not an exaggeration to suggest that modern researchers in the life sciences have finally solved the fundamental conceptual problem that underlies it.

We know today that all humans, indeed all organisms on earth, are the result of an interaction between genes and environments. There is nothing that is absolutely "essential" about us, since even the most hardwired aspects of our nature require adequate environmental input—such as hormonal levels in the womb, nutrition, and some sort of social environment—in order to develop. In the same way, there are few things about us that are truly "accidental" in the sense that they have no connection to an evolved human nature; most human behaviors can sooner or later be traced back to their roots in evolved dispositions and needs. (This is very different from saying that they can be *reduced* to expressions of an evolved human nature. A tree is not reducible to its roots, but it can neither exist nor be understood fully without them).

As a result, the traditional dichotomy between nature and culture, between the innate and the acquired, becomes untenable. It is true, as we shall see further on, that such terms can still be useful in many contexts, especially when we weigh the relative contributions of genes and environments against each other. But to speak of a fusion between evolutionary and historical explanation is ultimately a tautology and a misnomer that pays more tribute to disciplinary boundaries than to reality. Evolution is itself a historical science—the history of life on earth—and spans millions, even billions of years, compared to the twelve thousand or so we have agreed to call "history."

When we zoom in to read Shakespeare from the perspective of historical time, he may well seem like a distant stranger, enveloped in his "dark backward and abysm of time" (*The Tempest*, 1.2.50). He has outdated ideas about sex and an incomplete grasp of democratic principles. But from the larger perspective of evolutionary time—where the human brain has undergone only minor alterations over the last hundred thousand years, and we are still raising children, admiring the landscape, and watching our loved ones die—he seems more like our next-door neighbor. This is the paradox of sameness and difference that any viable theory of human love must negotiate.

It may still not be entirely obvious why the idea of a universal human nature that generates cultural differences should be a paradox and not a blatant contradiction. How can people across the planet, by the most elementary rules of logic, be similar and different at the same time? Consider the philosopher Kenneth Bock's objection to evolutionary accounts of human nature: "To say that it is human nature to act in such and such a way, and then to say that people are not obliged to act in that way, is really to abandon any claim to natural law status for the generalization. There is a good deal of eating your cake and having it in this practice of explanation by appeal to a human nature that can break its own rules."[21] Kenneth Bock is not alone in demanding an absolute concept of human nature, or none at all. Gabriel Dover, a professor of genetics, raises a similar objection: since "there are no regularities of events from which universal and timeless laws can be drawn," he concludes, somewhat unexpectedly, that "all we have in biology are individuals."[22]

Once more we need to soften our rigid dichotomies slightly and consider the difference between an *absolute* and a *statistical* universal.[23] The universals employed here are of the latter kind (they are no more, and no less, than pervasive patterns across human populations) since biological systems are sufficiently imprecise and open-ended to become highly unpredictable on the level of individuals. This is a major difference between biological rules-of-thumb (in the form of gene-environment interactions) and the immutable "laws" that Bock and Dover demand.[24] Nor are we dealing with *normative* universals of Tolstoy's kind, expressing moral truths about how people should live their lives. Defined adequately, love can rightly be understood as a human universal, but this does not preclude individual, historical, or cultural variation in its form and expression.

A theory of human nature that does not respect this paradox of sameness and difference becomes lopsided and misleading. Of course, it is often necessary to delimit or emphasize one half of the equation—for example, geneticists focus on genes, while historians examine the impact of changing social structures—but it is incoherent and overly reductive to do so without bearing the other half in mind. Given the current proliferation of crude, quasi-evolutionary accounts of human nature in the media, one can easily get the impression that it is genes, rather than human beings, that fall in love with each other. (The male nose picks up a whiff of pheromones from an ovulating, sexually responsive female, and nine months later an offspring is born with just the right genetic combination.) But the postmodern rejection of biology and human nature is equally reductive, because it fails to consider that "if everything were caught up in the swirl of history, there would be no history at all."[25] A history without constants would not be a history *of* anything but a random and chaotic sequence of events.

As I write these words, it is hard to say in what direction the literary-theoretical winds are blowing. Will a new dominant paradigm emerge, and rescue literary studies from its increasing disenchantment with postmodern historicism (and other canonical, anthologized approaches)?[26] In a review essay on the state of Shakespeare criticism in 2005, Hugh Grady rightly submits that the "virtual monopoly on the field achieved by historicism over the last two decades has not been a good situation for a profession with ideas of free debate and intellectual independence."[27] But what Grady imagines should take its place sounds suspiciously like another swing of the literary-critical pendulum: we are now placed at a "crossroads" between a return to traditional forms of historical positivism and a forward-looking *presentism* that "takes as its point of origin the cultural present."[28]

In proposing presentism, Grady is far from suggesting that history is bunk; rather, he wants to emphasize the unobjectionable point that our engagement with the past is always shaped by the demands of the present. In fact, this perceived need for a critical presentism betrays Grady's continued commitment to a view of human beings as historically determined, fair and square. It is unintelligible unless the present is perceived as fundamentally different from the past, at which point a presentist perspective is called upon to rescue the past from modern-day irrelevance. So the pendulum may have swung back in the other direction, from the past and toward the present, but what is still lacking is a consideration of the manifold continuities and commonalities that come with membership in *Homo sapiens*.

What the biocultural perspective seeks, in contrast to a previously hegemonic historicism and an emergent presentism, is a more balanced account of the interaction between a slowly evolving genome and more rapidly changing environments. In other words, the present study does not offer an evolutionary "alternative" to historical explanation but a corrective for reductive historicism. "Part of the advantage of a bio-cultural approach to literature is that it makes it much less likely that we will reach for explanations at the wrong level."[29] What is at stake is the interaction between our common humanity and our historical contingency, as they are reflected, recast, transformed, or even suppressed in literary works. Shakespeare was both a *Homo sapiens* and an Elizabethan, and it is perfectly justified to study his works from either perspective, but the most interesting challenge is to see him as both.

Of course, the complexity of the relation between literature and human nature cannot be stressed enough. We cannot expect fictional products of make-believe to mirror the real world with complete faithfulness, not even when it is the author's manifest intention to do so, and some writers invent imaginative worlds that wage war on our conventional expectations. This makes the relationship

between literature and human nature even more uncertain than the aforementioned relationship between genes and environments.

If a theory of human nature cannot be validated by a literary text, then it
makes no sense to assume that the theory "works" or is "successful" just because
it achieves a symmetry or correspondence with said text. As I have argued elsewhere, this forces us to redefine human nature as a comparative, dialogical *reference
point* for literary analysis. Since our objective is not to reconcile literature and
human nature, but to map the relationship between them, it follows that human
nature can be equally illuminating when it is *at variance* with the work in question.[30] To return to my caricature of one-sided universalism, it would clearly be
more noteworthy if the characters in *Hamlet* did *not* have a sense of self, interpret
each other's actions, or mourn their dead.

Given the incomplete match between literature and human nature, the most
sophisticated form of biocultural interpretation aims for a sensitive, dialogical
approach that maintains the distinction between theory and text. The theoretical
framework, concerned with human nature, certainly makes a provisional claim for
truthfulness, and it will probably be relevant in one way or another to most literary texts. How could it not be, given its concern with human universals? But once
we accept that such a theory can never be more than a dialogical reference point,
we are freed (at least theoretically) from the urge to beat the object of study into
shape. The interactionist approach to human nature adds even more flexibility,
since it avoids the constraining bias of a rigid universalism or constructivism. The
same biocultural critic may stress the profound historicity of one text and then
focus on the universal dimensions of another.

Whether he or she succeeds in this endeavor is, of course, a different question, and this leads me to an area where my argument may conflict with some
widespread expectations. Today many literature professors—convinced of the
value-laden and political nature of all discourse—would flatly deny that human
beings or literary critics are ever capable of disinterested judgment, or that truth
can be a meaningful criterion at all. As a result, the distinction between descriptive and normative statements disappears altogether, and the act of interpretation
becomes little else than an expression of preexisting ideological convictions. It is
telling that the writer of a fine survey of Shakespearean love recently deemed it
necessary to *apologize* for having been guided by curiosity and fascination rather
than by a determinate set of ideological convictions: "I must confess that I don't
have any developed ideology from which I look at the text; this book is not 'committed' in any political sense."[31]

While I am far from suggesting that the relation between the normative and
the descriptive is uncomplicated, I believe this drive toward reductive ideologism
is both erroneous and damaging. It is one thing to accept that our descriptive
statements usually require some kind of motivation based on values—why else

would we bother to speak in the first place?—but it is quite another to proclaim that these statements themselves are mere functions of value, or that there is no meaningful difference between ideological contingency and propaganda.

The logical consequence of such intellectual absolutes—where we are all political beings, and we are therefore always being political all the time—would be the kind of flabbergasting response reported by the biologist Paul Ehrlich when he informed his students in the late sixties about the natural constraints on photosynthesis in plants: "That depends on whether you use fascist-capitalist photosynthesis or people's photosynthesis."[32] A sounder and more constructive attitude toward our human contingency is offered by the feminist anthropologist Sarah Hrdy, who recognizes and maintains her own ideological commitment but refuses to pander to it. "Precisely because I am aware of my bias, I consciously guard against distorted readings of such evidence for early hominid mating systems as would cause me to project on my ancestors—who lived under different circumstances—the same choices I have made."[33] Compared to disciplines like biology and primatology, the humanities certainly have a unique and important role to play in their concern with human values and ideals, including political ones, but this discussion will not be helped by reducing intellectual inquiry to ideological card-carrying.

Throughout this book I have also tried to keep things as accessible as possible, in the hope that this will promote enjoyment as well as critical assessment of my argument. I have tried to achieve what might be termed an informed common sense: that is, a mode of thinking that is theoretically informed and recognizes the provisional nature of all interpretations but that also prefers an unassuming truth to a fascinating falsehood. The same principle will also apply to my assessment of textual evidence and previous scholarship. Whenever I have been confronted with two rival explanations—for example, that King Lear invents the disastrous love-test (1) because he is afraid that his daughters do not love him, or (2) because he wants to push them away by asking them to love him—I have generally pulled out Occam's razor and preferred the simplest explanation, unless there has been good reason to think otherwise. My position presupposes that readings can be mutually exclusive, that it is our responsibility as critics to identify our points of convergence and disagreement, and that critical pluralism is by far preferable to relativism.

To turn to another disagreement of mine with some current critical practice, the reader will perhaps notice that I talk about Lear above as if he were a real person, endowed with a psychological depth and motivation that we can try to gauge using textual evidence. To some critics, this is a naive and unacceptable approach since Lear is a linguistic construct and not a real person. Some would add that he is merely a discursive nexus determined by sociohistorical forces and so cannot be discussed meaningfully in terms of individual motivation. Others still might object that the modern conception of "character" did not have an exact counterpart in Shakespeare's time and that the dramatist probably thought of his characters as "types" rather than as individualized human beings.

These are only the latest versions of a larger dislike for character-driven literary analysis that took many forms throughout the twentieth century, and that still appears to preoccupy professional Shakespeareans.[34] In my view, it has often been riddled with contradictions since it is actually very hard to talk about the meanings of dramatic works without also discussing the people in them. In my analyses of Shakespeare's plays, I will assume that his characters are fictional approximations of real human beings and that "very little is gained by reminding us that Hamlet is made up of and by words, that he is 'just' a grouping of marks upon a page."[35] In other words, I think we are *supposed* to explore Hamlet's motives and grapple with his actions with reference to what we (think we) know about real human beings in their various walks of life.[36]

It must also be stressed that biocultural exploration, if it is done right, will complicate rather than simplify the discussion of human behavior (and thus, indirectly, of literary characters). Since a framework that involves both biology and culture will naturally be more complex than a strictly cultural version, and since Darwinian explanations of animal behavior are themselves complex and multi-layered, it would be strange indeed if biocultural readings should become more simplistic, predictable, or reductive than their culturalist counterparts.

Consider, as an example, the well-known phenomenon of birdsong. As the philosopher Larry Arnhart explains, a Darwinian explanation of this behavior has at least four levels of analysis: *functional* (the song attracts mates and defends territory in spring), *phylogenetic* (the capacity for complex songs has developed from simpler sounds), *developmental* (young birds can learn to sing thanks to specialized neural structures), and *immediate* (the singing is induced by changes in hormonal levels).[37] The question "Why is the blackbird outside my office window singing?" can thus be answered in no less than four different ways, even though we are dealing with a behavior that can rightly be termed instinctive. This is, I hope, a humbling idea for anyone who puts forward cocksure accounts of why a particular human being (who is more psychologically complex and environmentally flexible than a blackbird), or a literary character (who is based on, but not bound by, human nature), behaves in this way or that.

In spite of these manifest complexities, the concern with universals—with what we share as readers of literature and as human beings—may still not cause restless literary academics to salivate. It gives a particular urgency to the inescapable question: what can *you* say about Shakespeare that has never been said before? But there comes a point when the cult of novelty and bold pronouncements makes us forget the virtues inherent in a cumulative research tradition that gradually replaces inspired but flawed ideas with more dependable ones. Though

I hope and believe this book will contribute valuable new insights into all of the plays under scrutiny, my most important question in writing it has not been, *is it new?* but *is it true?* My concern has been with what we can, and cannot, know about the plays in question, on the assumption that both these questions are vital. The chief contribution of the biocultural approach will be a novel *sense of perspective* as we retrace familiar Shakespearean ground, such as King Lear's motivation in the love test or the exact nature of Othello's jealous pangs.

In chapter 1, I will return to some of these fraught issues as I elaborate on the biocultural approach to love. Among other things, this chapter commits the ultimate heresy of seeking to define love in its various guises and component parts. I will also address what it means—and does not mean—to understand love as a material phenomenon that has roots in a common nature but that is also inflected by cultural factors. The chapter also examines the relationship between biology and gender, since this is an almost inescapable variable in any discussion of love.

Those who turn to my ensuing literary discussions looking for a straightforward celebration of love will perhaps be disappointed. For in spite of their substantial differences, the dark and brooding Shakespearean plays I discuss have one thing in common: love is under siege, and almost pushed to the brink of extinction. Each of these chapters explores a particular form of love and begins with a more focused theoretical discussion. They are also, with one necessary exception, genre-specific. The reason is that in the absence of a single, unified Shakespearean vision of love, someone who examines the tragedies may well conclude that love is always doomed, while a student of the comedies will rather conclude that love typically conquers all. While no study of Shakespeare's works can escape the proverbial situation faced by the four blind men poking an elephant, it is hoped that I will at least be poking the poor creature systematically.

Chapter 2 examines the vicissitudes of parental love in two Roman plays, *Titus Andronicus* and *Coriolanus*, where I argue that Shakespeare (and, in the former play, his coauthor George Peele) makes a sustained inquiry into the impact of culture and society on the natural human affections. Chapter 3 turns the tables on this relationship, and examines filial love in the tragedy of *King Lear*, with a particular eye to the conflicted relationship between love and duty. In chapter 4 I explore Shakespeare's conflicted view of romantic love in two problem plays, *Troilus and Cressida* and *All's Well That Ends Well*, where the tension between individual idiosyncrasies and social consensus becomes especially salient. The study ends on a dark note, with a chapter on jealousy in *Othello* and *The Winter's Tale*, but I hope that my conclusions will still be regarded as liberating.

Given the ambitious scope and purpose of my book, it is fitting to end this introduction on a note of humility. Since I have deliberately painted my subject in the broadest and most inclusive interdisciplinary strokes, it goes without saying that certain sacrifices have had to be made along the way. It has not always been possible to keep entirely abreast of recent developments in all the disciplines I depend on, and it has often been necessary to simplify issues of great underlying complexity. It is also likely that my broad sweep across the sciences will give rise to any number of errors, oversights, and distortions. But it is one of the great comforts of a collective and systematic inquiry that our errors, and not just our insights, can be useful to others as well as to ourselves. If the pages that follow can eventually serve as a footnote in the introduction to a prospectus for a future research program on Shakespeare and human nature, they will have served their purpose.

1

The Nature of Love

Nothing in Man is either worse or better for being shared with the beasts
C. S. Lewis, *The Four Loves*, 33

In 1957, Erich Fromm declared that any theory of love "must begin with a theory of man, of human existence."[1] Like most accounts of human nature, Fromm's own fusion of existentialism and psychoanalysis has its strengths and weaknesses, but he is certainly right that it is difficult to discuss the nature of love coherently without also discussing the nature of human beings. This holds just as true for those theorists who actively dispute the existence of an identifiable human nature, for what they are really saying is that human nature is extremely plastic and thus defies all forms of generalization.[2] Since there is no getting around the problem of human nature, the first challenge that faces the student of love is to understand the nature of the lover.

This is, however, easier said than done, and sometimes it is made more difficult than it should be. For many years it has been something of a commonplace among students of literature that human identity is a "construct" that is constituted historically, socially, and culturally and that any alternative modes of explanation can be grouped together conveniently under the rubric of "essentialism." Once they have been defined as essentialist, which basically denotes a belief that human nature is fixed and unchanging, these alternative views have typically been associated with a reactionary outlook (in spite of the dubious nature of such inferences) and then assigned to the critical dustbin.

This has been a regrettable development in many ways, not least because it has effectively closed the door on a fascinating array of evidence emerging from biology and the other life sciences.[3] In fact, the irony could hardly be greater, since it was Darwinism that delivered the deathblow to biological, philosophical, and religious essentialism in the nineteenth century by demonstrating that species are not unchanging creations. But if biological or evolutionary explanation entails constraints on cultural explanation, then it is obviously appealing for departments of culture or language to think that biology is irrelevant, that there is no human nature, and that the explanatory power of one's own theoretical framework is almost unlimited.

As Terry Eagleton puts it crisply in a recent book where he abjures some of his earlier post-structuralist leanings, anti-essentialism "is largely the product of philosophical amateurism and ignorance."[4] To be fair, there can be no doubt that the road has been paved with good intentions and that the repeated attacks on human universals by postmodernists have often been motivated by a respect for alternative lifestyles and the integrity of minority groups. It so happens that I share most of these ideals. But this shared ground does not preclude disagreement about how we should best understand human nature, and how such an understanding might best serve our ideals. It is by no means evident that the interests of marginalized groups are best defended by denying the existence of larger regularities, continuities, and even universals in human identity, experience, and values. In order to be consistent, a radical anti-universalist might even have to shelve the universal principle of human rights.

The most fundamental problem with the constructivist and post-structuralist heritage is that it has preserved an outmoded conflict between nature and nurture, now rewritten as a morality play involving a bad angel called Biological Essentialism (or "Biologism" for short) and a good angel called Cultural Constructivism. Time and again, literary critics presume to "deconstruct" the distinction between nature and culture when all they really do is turn nature into a form of culture (thus neatly discarding one half of the notorious dichotomy). This drama is often geared to a grim hermeneutics of suspicion, where love or beauty are described as artificial and unreal because they mask the workings of sinister social mechanisms and processes of subjection.

As Sue Laver and Mette Hjort have explained,[5] the central premise in the social constructivist account of the emotions is a commitment to cultural particularism and diversity. This diversity is then explained sociopolitically rather than psychologically, in that cultural variation is seen as the effect of differing social power structures and conceptual systems. People in different cultures have different emotions because they have internalized different social pressures to have these emotions. It is held that an emotion that exists in one culture can be completely absent from other cultures, or even that there are no universal emotions.

To say that this or that is a "construction" is to make an exceedingly vague statement. It has therefore become a commonplace in the social sciences to distinguish between two different kinds of constructivism. First, there is a *weak* version that does not dispute the agency of nonlinguistic realities and simply argues that human perceptions, emotions, and identities are *shaped* by particular languages, conceptual systems, social practices, and so forth. Since even a primal emotion like fear is dependent on cognitive appraisal (what *is* this thing before me? is it *dangerous?* should I *become afraid?*) this is something of a truism.[6] While I have the greatest respect for truisms (they are, after all, the necessary common ground that makes more controversial statements meaningful), they alone cannot make interesting (or even identifiable) theoretical perspectives.

This leaves us with a *strong* constructivism that is usually influenced by post-structuralist theory and that therefore regards conceptual systems as basically self-contained entities. According to this brand, which has usually been at work in literary and cultural studies,[7] emotions are constructed in the sense of being *social inventions:* "Societies can shape, mold, or construct as many different emotions as are functional with the social system."[8] This sense is what is usually intended when people say that something is "only a cultural construction." As internalized social inventions, emotions are arbitrary and can be expected to disappear if the dominant social and conceptual structure is altered significantly. This betrays the political motivation that often underpins the constructivist edifice: if everything is a social construction, then there is no human nature. If there is no human nature, then all humans are infinitely malleable, which is a good thing for those who think they have better constructions at hand.

It is in such a context that we must understand the distinguished literary theorist Jonathan Culler's claim that "romantic love . . . is arguably a massive literary creation."[9] For many literary and cultural theorists, the word "love" has become something of a professional embarrassment. It is true, of course, that earlier generations of Shakespeare critics were a little one-sided in their pursuit of aesthetic unity and timeless truths about the nature of love and spirit, but it is hard to see that the contributions of their recent successors—reared on oppressive "sexual economies," "sex-gender systems," and vaguely paranoid conceptions of language and identity—have really been a major improvement. As Kenan Malik points out, what most post-structuralists and other anti-essentialists have advanced is a sort of positivism-in-reverse that makes "difference" the absolute in human history.[10] How human beings might be characterized by total difference from each other and yet be recognizably human seems difficult to explain.

Fortunately, a critical paradigm never asserts itself at the total expense of all other perspectives—not even within its own discipline, and certainly not outside. In 1975, when literature professors were busy reading the latest works of Derrida, the anathema placed on biological and evolutionary explanations of human behavior was challenged by the publication of E. O. Wilson's *Sociobiology.* Wilson's ideas were provocative and his rhetoric quite uncongenial to the social and human sciences. In a now famous passage, he suggested nothing less than interdisciplinary *cannibalism* based on evolutionary principles, defining "sociology and the other social sciences, as well as the humanities" as "the last branches of biology waiting to be included in the Modern [Darwinian] Synthesis."[11] The humanities a mere *branch of biology?* The impact on the media and academia was huge, and the last three decades of the twentieth century saw a fierce debate about the scope and potentials of evolutionary explanation of human affairs. Too often, this debate has been dominated by propagandistic straw men and misrepresentations instead of by a balanced discussion of common ground and irreconcilable differences.[12]

In recent years, the tone in Wilson's writings has mellowed considerably. While he still thinks the social sciences need a major refurbishment to make them more scientific, he is now proposing something that sounds much more respectful with regard to literature. "There is only one way to unite the great branches of learning and end the culture wars. It is to view the boundary between the scientific and literary cultures not as a territorial line but as a broad and mostly unexplored terrain awaiting cooperative entry from both sides."[13] In the second half of the 1990s, a major step forward was taken in this area once a number of literary theorists and critics, most notably Joseph Carroll and Robert Storey, had realized that the only way forward was to attack the current constructivist orthodoxy from the outside. By placing the study of cultural artifacts like literature on a biological and evolutionary foundation, it might be possible to advance literary arguments that were theoretically consistent with the most promising developments in other disciplines.[14]

Given the historically conflicted relation between science and the humanities, it is important to stress that theoretical consistency does not mean subjection to alien methods or modes of inquiry. As Wilson points out, the ideal of conceptual integration between different disciplines is by no means opposed to the need for radically divergent methods and even objectives. Since the humanities operate on a different theoretical level than do the other sciences, they are also in a position to explore issues that are out of reach for biology or even psychology. The philosopher and psychologist Jon Elster even suggests that when it comes to emotions like romantic love, "we can learn more from moralists, novelists, and playwrights than from the cumulative findings of scientific psychology."[15] Whether or not he is right about this, it seems clear that philosophical and literary students of love have everything to gain from taking a converse interest in scientific explanation. In the words of another philosopher, Irving Singer, whose history of love in the West will figure prominently in this study: "After all the centuries of dispute and disagreement, we may soon be in a position to reconcile the divergent theories about love, to reach conceptions that will be defensible both as philosophy and as science."[16]

Can Love Be Defined?

Before I outline my biocultural perspective on love, it will be useful to specify more closely what is meant by this multifaceted and intriguing phenomenon. In the *Anatomy of Melancholy*, Robert Burton pointed out that love is "diverse, and varies as the object varies."[17] More recently, Irving Singer has listed some kinds of love that we habitually speak of:

> Love of self, of mankind, of nature, of God, of mother and father, of children, of tribe or nation, of sweetheart or spouse or sexual idol, of material possessions, of food or drink, of action and repose, of sports, of hobbies or engrossing pursuits, of justice, of science, of truth, of beauty, and so on endlessly. Each variety of love, involving its special object, has its own phenomenology, its own iridescence within the spectrum that delimits human experience.
>
> To be studied adequately, every type requires a separate analysis. From one to the other, their ingredients will often have little or nothing in common.[18]

It goes without saying that little progress will be made if we employ a concept that lends itself with equal readiness to erotic passion and, say, a special predilection for French fries. The first step must therefore be to narrow it down to "love of persons." This definition is sufficiently inclusive to incorporate parental love, romantic love, or any other strong emotional attachment, but also sufficiently narrow to exclude unrelated phenomena like love of football or material goods. It is also neutral to questions about sexual orientation.

To define love in terms of its object gets us some way toward a manageable definition, but we have of course only come halfway. Few people would probably disagree with the contention that love is an *emotion*, but when we take a closer look at what this actually means, things become very complicated. One problem is that the emotions are relatively recent objects of systematic study, at least partly because of a long heritage in Western thought that has separated passion from reason and then privileged the latter. As late as 1998, Robert C. Solomon declared that the emotions were "still on the defense in philosophy" and had "come into prominence in psychology in only the last decade or so."[19] As is often the case with a budding area of investigation, our understanding of the emotions may be progressing fast, but it is also fractured across a large number of competing perspectives and research programs: each with its own emphases and definitions of central terms.[20]

For example, the neuroscientist Antonio Damasio has argued persuasively for a distinction between *emotions* and *feelings*, where feelings denote private, conscious mental experiences, and emotions cover a broad collection of bodily responses—some of which may be unconscious and some publicly observable. For anyone who is interested in love this is an intriguing distinction, since the lover is sometimes the last to find out that he or she is in love. What is more, in one of the most constructive and incisive books on the subject to date, *What Emotions Really Are* (1997), the philosopher Paul Griffiths even suggests that the folk psychological concept of "emotion" is so unsatisfactory that it must be broken down and divided into several discrete categories.[21] This is enough to give anyone pause; if even "emotion" is an impossible concept, then how can we hope to talk meaningfully about love?

Things do not become any easier when we realize that love cannot even be contained within the already impossible category of "emotion." As a number of theorists have realized, it also includes behavioral tendencies or dispositions to act in certain ways. Love is not only about what we feel, but also about what we do, and depending on the quality of the relationship it can involve nurturing, caring, or sexual activity. This point becomes especially salient when we apply it to the study of dramatic works, since it would clearly be a very short study of Shakespearean love that bracketed the behavior of his protagonists and confined itself to direct evidence about their inward states of mind. Finally, according to the Darwinian emotions theorist Paul Ekman, love does not qualify as an emotion because of its duration in time: "Emotions come and go in a matter of seconds or minutes. Parental love or romantic love are not so transitory, and clearly different from momentary emotions. Love is an affective commitment, in which many emotions are felt."[22]

These vexing problems bring us right back to E. O. Wilson's description of the no-man's-land between literature and the other sciences, where radically different methods and objectives must somehow be weighed against the need for compatibility and coherence. While literary critics and theorists have everything to gain from approaching the other sciences and learning from them, it is also true that we have very little to gain from getting mired in technical debates that have only incidental relevance to our objects of study. The trick is to place emotions on an interdisciplinary foundation but also to allow for a degree of imprecision that would be intolerable at levels different from our own. By analogy, no one would expect chemistry to operate on the same analytical level as physics, but eyebrows *would* be raised if chemistry professors arrived at conclusions that contradicted the laws of physics.

As Aristotle pointed out more than two thousand years ago, "The same degree of precision is not to be sought in all discussions, any more than in works of craftsmanship. . . . It is a mark of an educated person to look in each area for only that degree of accuracy that the nature of the subject permits."[23] For the purposes of this study this means first defining love in its "broadest sense," which "brings together cognitions, evaluations, neurophysiological processes, somatic changes, subjective feelings, facial expressions, and behaviors."[24]

The virtue of this definition is that it is inclusive, but it is also so vague that it borders on meaninglessness. We can therefore go on from here to establish subsidiary distinctions among love as a *disposition*, as an *emotion*, and as an *action*. The capacity for love is an emotional *disposition* that can be realized as a concrete *emotion* (involving recognizable feelings and bodily states that make us want to act in certain ways); and the emotion, in turn, may be expressed in familiar *actions* (such as touching or caressing the other person). While emotions cannot arise without dispositions, there is no necessary link between emotion and action: an emotion can be felt but not acted on, and a person can act in ways that we would term "loving" without actually being emotionally involved. (This will be a central problem when we turn to plays like *King Lear* and *All's Well That Ends Well* in chapters 3 and 4).

At every step of the way from disposition to action, love is both dependent on favorable conditions and vulnerable to interference. A person who is *disposed* to love may never meet a suitable object of affection, and many societies have actively sought to restrict potential contacts with the opposite sex. The emotion of love, furthermore, can be experienced and expressed differently depending on a wide variety of factors. Love is often a source of joy, but it can also be a source of shame or suffering if it is felt for the wrong person, if it is not returned, or if the emotion itself is deemed socially unacceptable. Finally, it goes without saying that our capacity to translate the emotion into *action* will also be highly dependent on our situation.

Having established this overriding framework, we can now consider some more detailed definitions of love. Not surprisingly, the most useful conceptual tools for the literary study of love have come from philosophers and psychologists. In *Cupid's Arrow* (1998), the psychologist Robert Sternberg proposes a "love triangle" that I will draw on repeatedly in this study.[25] The love triangle draws together three components—intimacy, passion, and commitment—that may be present in various degrees in a relationship. *Intimacy* involves, among other things, a desire to promote the well-being of the loved one; the experience of happiness with that person; and holding him or her in high regard. Regarding *passion*, Sternberg draws on Elaine Hatfield's and Richard Rapson's definition of passionate love as a strong desire for union with another person. Their full definition, which exemplifies the "broad" concept of emotion I discussed above, runs as follows: "A state of intense longing for union with another. Passionate love is a complex functional whole including appraisals or appreciations, subjective feelings, expressions, patterned physiological processes, action tendencies, and instrumental behaviors. Reciprocated love (union with the other) is associated with fulfillment and ecstasy. Unrequited love (separation) is associated with emptiness, anxiety, or despair."[26] This is most likely the powerful emotion whose unrequited form was described vividly already in the sixth century B.C. by Sappho on the island of Lesbos:

Him I hold as happy as God in Heaven,
Who can sit and gaze on your face before him,
Who can sit and hear from your lips that sweetest
Music they utter—

Hear your lovely laughter, that sets a-tremble
All my heart with flutterings wild as terror.
For, when I behold you in an instant, straightway
All my words fail me . . . [27]

It has become common practice to distinguish passionate love from *companionate love*, which denotes an emotional relationship that is high on intimacy but less deeply passionate.[28] It is also a folk-psychological commonplace in the West that most relationships lose some of their passionate intensity over time and become increasingly companionate. In fact, this perception also appears to have been shared by a hunter-gatherer in the Kalahari: "When two people are first together, their hearts are on fire and their passion is very great. After a while, the fire cools and that's how it stays. . . . They continue to love each other, but it's in a different way—warm and dependable."[29]

Commitment, finally, is used by Sternberg to denote maintenance of the relationship over a period of time, and it is less closely tied to specific emotional states than the other two categories. While it is perfectly possible to be unfeeling and yet committed, it is obviously hard to be unfeeling and passionate about someone at the same time. Since actual commitment is something that can only unfold over time, it is also particularly dependent on favorable environmental conditions. While Sternberg thinks of love mainly as a relationship, and therefore regards commitment as a concrete phenomenon that unfolds over time, my own distinction between dispositions, emotions, and actions highlights the difference between a *desire* to commit and its potential *expression*.

One virtue of Sternberg's triadic scheme of passion, intimacy, and commitment is that it enables us to differentiate flexibly and clearly between different styles of loving among individuals as well as cultures. For example, some modern relationships in the West may be high on passion and intimacy but low on commitment, while others can be very different. In the same way, some cultures valorize passionate love while others stress commitment and regard both intimacy and passion as subordinate to this ideal (or, in the case of passion, even dangerous because it is socially subversive). In those cultures where marriage is not a matter of individual choice, passionate love may never have the chance to become either intimate or companionate.

The next item on the agenda, *romantic love*, is a more complicated issue, and I will return to it repeatedly in this chapter. Sternberg defines it strictly as a fusion of passion and intimacy,[30] preferring the term "consummate love" for the complete compound of passion, intimacy, and commitment. Since he thinks of love as a relationship that involves emotional experience, rather than as an emotion in a strict sense, he is consistent in regarding commitment as something that must unfold over time. But if we return to the aforementioned distinction among dispositions, emotions, and actions, I would suggest that the emotion of romantic love also involves commitment: that is, it involves a *desire* to commit, which may or may not be realized in concrete form. Someone who is experiencing intense passion and intimacy together with another person will find it difficult to accept separation and will want to be with that person for as long as possible. Once we distinguish in this way between emotions and actions, Sternberg's "consummate love" can be redefined as the concrete consummation of romantic love over time.

The nature of romantic passion can also be fleshed out in more detail, as the anthropologist Helen Harris has done in a very useful synthesis of previous definitions. In abbreviated form, the criteria for romantic passion include a desire for physical and emotional union; idealization of the beloved; a desire for exclusivity; intrusive thinking about the loved one; emotional dependency and strong empathy; and a reordering of one's life priorities to accommodate the beloved.[31] The latter criterion reminds us once more of the commitment component in romantic love. Most people assume that the desire for union in romantic love must involve sexual desire, but as we will see further on, this may not be a necessary criterion.

Romantic love is also the emotion that several influential writers have defined (somewhat problematically) as a Western invention. In *Medieval Misogyny and the Invention of Western Romantic Love* (1991), Howard Bloch puts forward a representative version of this claim:

> If the expression "invention of Western romantic love" seems like a contradiction, it is because we so often assume love as we know it to be natural, to exist in some essential sense, that is, always to have existed. Nothing, however, could be further from the truth. . . . The terms that serve to define, or mediate, what we consider to this day to constitute romantic involvement were put into place definitively—at least for the time being—sometime between the beginning and the middle of the twelfth century, first in southern and then in northern France.[32]

At first sight, this may sound more like the history of tennis (a twelfth-century French invention) than the origin of a human emotion. But since the idea has become so widespread, I will return to it further on in this chapter, when I discuss the interaction between evolved attachment structures with specific cultural environments. For now it is sufficient to note that Bloch equivocates in reading together *the existence of love* with *the existence of its definition*. To say that romantic love has been given a unique emphasis in the West, or that it has been conceptualized in special ways, is very different from saying that the emotion does not exist in other cultures or that it is not a natural phenomenon.

It would also be a poor theory of love that did not incorporate the proverbial idea that "love is blind"—or, more specifically, that it is in the nature of lovers to emphasize each other's positive traits and to downplay things that might not be quite as appealing. As we saw above, idealization is normally regarded as an important aspect of passionate involvement. In the seventeenth century, Robert Burton observed that "every Lover admires his mistris, though she bee very deformed of her selfe"—and then listed no less than a hundred potential imperfections, from stinky feet to a great nose, before he concluded that "if hee love her once, he admires her for all this, he takes no notice of such errors, or imperfections, of body or minde . . . he had rather have her than any woman in the world."[33] As we will see further on, this view even finds some support from recent neuroscientific findings.

But idealization, like blindness, is a problematic term, since it smuggles in the assumption that lovers lie to themselves about the true nature of their loved ones. In a survey of self-reports on passionate love, Dorothy Tennov found that lovers were not really "blind" because they were perfectly capable of detecting negative personality traits in their partners. The blindness of love, part of what Tennov (following Stendhal) termed "crystallization" to avoid the semantic connection between idealization and self-deception, was really more a matter of placing emotional *significance* on certain traits at the expense of others.[34]

A similar point is made by Irving Singer in his masterful account of the oscillation in Western philosophical and literary traditions between realist and idealist conceptions of love. As Singer observes, the "idealization" we associate with love is not simply a failure to be objective about another person's relative merit in the amorous marketplace. Even if love is not immune to such considerations—Singer calls them *appraisals*—it can also be characterized as *bestowal*, or "the making of ideals through the bestowing of value," which means that it cannot be reduced to a "mistaken belief."[35] This aspect of love is perhaps better described as a capacity to find others beautiful than a tendency to overlook their flaws. The tension between appraisal and bestowal—between love as a relational assessment and as a creative act—will be important in some of the literary chapters that follow.

So far, this terminological discussion has only touched on the question of historical differences between modern and early modern definitions of love. While the larger question of cultural and historical difference must be postponed until the final section of this chapter, I should mention that in Shakespeare's time the word "love" was more semantically flexible than it is today, covering a wide range of phenomena from friendship to even nonemotive phenomena. In Shakespeare's *Sonnets*, it is used in an extraordinary number of senses, from sexual passion and friendship to a euphemism for the financial remuneration that the poet seeks from his youthful patron.[36] In some cases, we will find that Shakespeare uses the word "love" to denote an *action* rather than an emotional state of mind.

This linguistic imprecision certainly prescribes some caution in the interpretation of early modern writers, but it would be wrong to conclude either that early modern "love" was an altogether different and more amorphous thing than ours or that Shakespeare's contemporaries did not differentiate subtly between different senses of this single word. As we saw above, Robert Burton was well aware that love was "diverse, and varied as the object varied." While the degree of conceptual precision a culture affords a phenomenon clearly says something about the latter's social significance, a period's mental or emotional world cannot be extrapolated from a dictionary.[37] In the chapters to come we will find several situations in Shakespeare's plays where love's historical ambiguity creates uncertainties, misunderstandings, and painful conflicts. These difficulties can arise in part because the same word means several different things in different contexts and so allows for conflicting interpretations. Am I expected to *feel* for this person, or simply to *act* in a loving way toward him or her?

The Three Boundaries of Love

Since Shakespeare and the theory of evolution have not been frequent bedfellows in literary criticism, the main emphasis of this chapter will lie on the evolutionary account of love and the relation between biology and culture. In order to make my discussion as accessible as possible, I will discuss love in terms of three theoretical boundaries as they have been outlined by the philosopher Janet Radcliffe Richards. The three boundaries are: Darwinism, materialism, and evolutionary psychology.[38] The focus will lie on the origins of the human *disposition* for love, rather than the concrete *emotion* or the *actions* we associate with it.

Let us begin with Darwinism. Although the word received some bad press in the previous century, at least partly because of a persistent association with social Darwinism and other objectionable relics of the past, this boundary is probably the least controversial of the three. Indeed, I anticipate that most enlightened readers will have crossed it already and are now waiting impatiently on the other side. To embrace Darwinism is simply to accept that the theory of evolution is correct in its broad outlines and that human beings have evolved from simpler life forms by means of natural selection.

The second boundary is that of materialism. It is one that normally stirs up a little more controversy, especially when it comes to the topic of love. Some of this controversy arises because of terminological confusion, since materialism can be used to denote anything from a crass obsession with material goods to certain brands of political philosophy. *Scientific materialism*, first of all, means that we are part of a physical universe and that Descartes was wrong to postulate a dualistic division between mind and matter. As I write these words, the electrochemical process that makes up my thought is just as physical as the word processor I am using to pass it on. There is no need for some spiritual substance or nonphysical process to make this possible, since even seemingly immaterial phenomena like consciousness or language can be attributed to incredibly complex combinations of elementary particles. Of course, this brand of materialism can be an ample source of anxiety in itself, since many people feel that an advancing scientific explanation threatens to rob the world of its mystery and meaning. "Science tells us that we are creatures of accident clinging to a ball of mud hurtling aimlessly through space. This is not a notion to warm hearts or rouse multitudes."[39]

It is true that the acceptance of scientific materialism has consequences for our understanding of practically everything around us as well as inside us. Since it is part of the physical world, even love—that most seemingly spiritual of phenomena—must ultimately be understood as matter. But the deep pessimism expressed by Paul Ehrlich above is by no means a natural outcome of the materialist perspective, which opens up a fascinating vista of its own:

> Whoever is prepared to accept this physicist's description of our world, and is not willing to add a belief in the existence of a mysterious force outside this created universe, necessarily also accepts the premise, and the challenge to explain it, that life itself, its evolution, its rich variety of form, the ever increasing complexity of structure and behavior—are all nothing but wondrous and supreme expressions of the behavior of the elementary particles. Life itself is nothing but matter. For there is nothing but the particles of the Big Bang in this space.[40]

To my mind, this account is an ample source of mystery and wonder. It is no less awe-inspiring than the spiritual transcendentalism that has often surrounded Western accounts of love. What is more, the widespread assumption that a materialist perspective will trivialize love or even destroy it is misguided, because it confuses two levels of explanation: the ontology of love (what it is made of) and its phenomenology (how it feels to love). The love I feel for my girlfriend is not trivialized by being a physical phenomenon, any more than my girlfriend herself is trivialized by being composed of atoms.

This distinction can be extended to the very idea of using science to explain love. On the one hand, it seems clear that if our minds are composed of matter, then we can expect an increase in knowledge about the brain to yield important insights into all sorts of mental phenomena, including love. Neuroscientists are now conducting exciting research into the physiological substrates of romantic love in the hope of understanding the material underpinnings of this powerful emotion. As we will see further on in this chapter, magnetic resonance scans have uncovered what may be a functional subsystem of activations and deactivations in the brain that is triggered when subjects view pictures of people with whom they profess to be in love. We are also getting a fairly good grasp of the biochemistry that is at work when people fall in love and when they feel deep affection.[41]

On the other hand, it should be apparent that such investigations can only provide individual pieces of a much larger puzzle and that there is an important difference between experiencing love and studying this experience from outside. It is only someone who already thinks of love merely as a delusion who has anything to lose from scientific investigation. Such a love—one that cannot withstand intellectual scrutiny and that must therefore be sheltered inside a cloud of dogmatic agnosticism—would be what Paul Griffiths calls a covert social construction.[42] As soon as we have explained its true nature, we cease to believe in it, like the Santa Claus who turns out to be Daddy wearing a false beard.

To say that love is matter (and not immaterial spirit) is not to suggest that spiritual *accounts* of love are irrelevant to a writer like Shakespeare. While Shakespeare was hardly the most spiritual of early modern writers—judging from his works, he may well have been one of the more secular—the predominantly Christian culture he belonged to typically associated the highest forms of love with spiritual transcendence of the body and defined the emotion as a religious virtue. To ignore this fact is to run the risk of secular anachronism. But it is essential to accept that we are dealing with two distinct levels of theory here: the perspective of the modern interpreter and the perspective of the author or period under scrutiny. One of the most frequent sources of bad literary research today is the inability (or, in some cases, the unwillingness) to distinguish one's own theoretical perspective analytically from that of one's object of study.

On the level of scientific materialism, to say that "love is matter" is not to dispute either its reality or its value but only to deny that it is composed of some transcendent substance that operates at one remove from the physical universe. This is an important conclusion, since it paves the way for a coherent integration of many different forms of inquiry, from science to philosophy. But just as there are many different forms of love, there are also different forms of materialism, and in literary studies the major fault line regarding love's supposed transcendence has been drawn on a different level than that of elementary particles. Over the last decades, the word "materialism" has become practically synonymous with various postmodern permutations of *historical materialism*, where all forms of human activity are regarded as determined by economic and other social arrangements. This raises an important question: to what extent is love caught up in, or even produced by, historically changing social structures and systems of belief?

In the early 1990s, a brief debate flared up in the radical journal *Textual Practice* between two literary critics—Linda Charnes and Richard Levin—about materialist versus transcendent love in Shakespeare. The debate began when Charnes published an article on Shakespeare's *Antony and Cleopatra* where she inveighed against a "liberal humanist" tendency to separate love from its social context and from politics. In these accounts, love was "universalized, naturalized, and more important, essentialized in its separation from the discourses that construct other kinds of experience." Even when liberal humanists did pay attention to political and social aspects, they still seemed to assume that *"in the last instance,* love (shared by autonomous human agents) is made of different stuff." By contrast, Charnes argued that "the forms of affective relations are inseparable from the specific material, political, and social conditions which they constitute and which constitute them." Love was a deeply political and decidedly nontranscendent phenomenon, and the love story was "one of the most effective smokescreens available in the politics of cultural production."[43]

There were at least two reasons why this article was bound to attract Richard Levin's attention. First, when Charnes built her argument around a sharp dichotomy between liberal humanism and materialism she employed a critical strategy that Levin had strongly criticized three years earlier in the same journal.[44] The second reason why Levin rose to the barricades was personal, since Charnes had singled him out in a footnote as a "quixotic" defender of the very perspective he had already dismissed as a polemical fiction.

The essence of Levin's critique of Charnes was that she had erected a liberal humanist straw man that she could then denounce programmatically. This time liberal humanists were charged with the assumption that love is a purely natural and unchanging phenomenon that happens between fully autonomous individuals, in splendid isolation from society and history:

> There certainly are people who believe this, but I do not think many of them are "educated middle-class liberals," a group to which I happen to belong. We know that what is called romantic love cannot be universal, natural, or essential because it is socially constructed, and we know this because it is constructed differently in different societies. So on that point I agree with her, despite my alleged "liberal humanism." I also agree with her contention that the love between Antony and Cleopatra is thoroughly "imbricated" with considerations of power and politics, even though this is supposed to contradict the "humanist scholarship" that I am supposed to be defending.

Having established this common ground at the expense of the liberal humanist straw man, Levin went on to disagree with Charnes about the consequences of taking a constructivist perspective on *Antony and Cleopatra:* "But the constructed and imbricated nature of their love does not devalue it because this is true of all human relations, which never exist in a pure state. Her criticism of their relationship implies that she is judging it against the very ideal of a transcendent-universal-natural-essential love that she attributes to 'liberal humanism.'"[45] In Levin's view, Charnes had become tangled up in a hopeless dichotomy between idealized transcendence and materialist contingency that prevented her from seeing romantic love as something more positive than an oppressive ideological apparatus or a political smoke screen. In her brief but thoughtful reply, Charnes repeated her claim that romantic love should not be declared innocent: "I don't know how Levin defines the term 'romantic love,' but if it played a role in eliminating arranged marriages [as he had suggested] it also played a major role in constructing the goddess/whore opposition, the virulent backlash of sexual misogyny, and the nuclear family in which the father/husband continued to reign supreme over wife and children."[46]

It will not have escaped my readers that much of the debate between Levin and Charnes was ideological in nature; they did not restrict themselves to a descriptive analysis of the nature of love; they also spent much of their energy assessing its *normative* dimensions. For Levin, who did his best to disentangle the descriptive and the normative, romantic love was mainly a positive phenomenon, while Charnes aligned herself implicitly with a long tradition—extending back to such illustrious figures as Friedrich Engels and Simone de Beauvoir—that has emphasized the dangers of inequality in romantic relationships.[47] While both perspectives on love have their merit, it is, I think, extremely important to try to disentangle the descriptive from the normative, the nature of love from the value of love, since premature fusions of the two are so particularly conducive to wishful thinking or ideological appropriation.

The most instructive point of convergence between these two critics, however, is that they embraced the same constructivist dichotomies in their discussion of love (and then, unsurprisingly, declared that love was "cultural" rather than "natural," "constructed" rather than "essential"). This somewhat unexpected consensus across the ideological divide brings us back to a major weakness with literary constructivism: that it is only meaningful as long as it is opposed to an absurd essentialist bogeyman. The term becomes so vague that it can cover anything from the truism that love "does not exist in a pure state" (Levin) to the radical claim that it is an artificial "ideological apparatus" or political "smokescreen" (Charnes). This is why the materialist account of love is insufficient in itself and needs to be anchored in a deeper understanding of human nature. We are not likely to understand the nature of love very well until we replace this vague framework with a better one, one in which cultural variation in a trait or behavior does not preclude a biological or evolutionary foundation.[48]

This brings us to the third boundary in our exploration of love—that of *evolutionary psychology*—which subsumes the previous boundaries of evolutionary theory and scientific materialism (and which is sometimes spelled with capital letters to distinguish the general approach from a specific school).[49] If love is matter, rather than some ghostly spiritual substance, and if it is rooted in material structures that have evolved across enormous lengths of time in response to selective pressures, then it becomes an open question to what extent—or rather, to what degree of specificity—the human affections have been tailored by an evolutionary process.

The Evolution of Love

To take an evolutionary perspective on the emotions is to seek their origin in the process of natural selection, where random mutations enable species to adapt in response to selective pressures in their environments. From a functional or adaptationist perspective, human beings have evolved a range of dispositions because these contributed to genetic fitness. What worked in the past got passed on, and what worked better got passed on more frequently. To take an example from the most rudimentary level of affective experience, it is not a coincidence that having sex or eating feels great, while stabbing yourself with a knife is considerably less pleasant. The typical degree of pleasantness or "hedonic tone" associated with these acts has obviously been selected for, since those of our ancestors who hated sex or food simply had less offspring.

There is now a growing consensus that a similar process resulted in the so-called primary emotions studied by the Darwinian emotion theorist Paul Ekman—surprise, fear, disgust, anger, happiness, and sadness—that correlate with distinct facial expressions in cultures across the world.[50] Again, the evolutionary rationale is fairly self-evident: those who liked food but who were also capable of being disgusted by inedible food, even when they were hungry, outlived and outreproduced those who were not. Admittedly, to look at love from the same functional perspective is far more complicated because of its staggering complexity. While both eating and having sex involve a wide range of appraisals that are environmentally contingent and dependent on learning, the emotion of love depends on more complex appraisals and, as I have already argued, must be understood as a complex nexus of feelings and behaviors.

The functional or adaptationist analysis of love is also constrained by the nature of the evolutionary process itself. Evolutionary theory tells us that "everything we do as a species, from our rituals to our sciences and arts, is part of a continuum with profound connections to the world out of which we evolved."[51] Since every species belongs to a small branch on the great tree of evolution, its development is always constrained by preexisting structures, which means that many basic elements of our mental equipment were singled out long before the rise of hominids. As a consequence, the human brain is structured in different evolutionary layers: the lower, subcortical regions exhibit considerable anatomical, functional, and neurochemical similarities with those of other mammals, while the higher cortical regions are more species-specific and account for many of our distinctive capacities (such as long-term planning and hypothetical thinking).

Crucially, our emotional experience is fueled by the lower region known as the limbic system, even if its impulses are always mediated and regulated by higher cortical regions. This constant interaction between older and more recent brain areas means that human love cannot be detached from our evolutionary past (even though natural selection obviously operates on all brain areas, and not just newer ones). Depending on what perspective you adopt, our evolved emotional dispositions can be seen as sophisticated adaptations or evolutionary hangovers:[52] we are capable of love because it was enormously adaptive for our recent ancestors to become emotionally entangled with each other, and we suffer the slings and arrows of unrequited love because our ancestors saw fit to dump a limbic system on us. It is all a question of perspective.

The main problem with our ancestors is, however, that they are all gone. It is hard to reconstruct their amorous passions from scattered pieces of fossilized bone, and this leaves us with our closest living relatives in the primate order. Humans and chimpanzees, for example, parted ways only six or seven million years ago, and our DNA exhibits only minor differences that are now being mapped in detail and with great promise. Some limited evidence about human love can also be derived indirectly from the interpretation of primate behavior, even if this activity, alluring as it may be, is fraught with difficulties.

Consider, as a particularly intriguing and vexing example, this description of typical courtship behavior in a relatively distant cousin, the baboon:

> First, the male and female looked at one another but avoided being caught looking. This phase was always accompanied by feigned indifference to the other, indicated by concentrated interest in grooming one's own fur or by staring intently at some imaginary object in the distance (both ploys are commonly used by baboons in a wide variety of socially discomfiting situations). Eventually, the coy glances were replaced by a more direct approach, usually initiated by the male. Grooming then followed. If the friendship "took," the couple would then sit together during daily rest periods, and eventually they would coordinate subsistence activities as well.[53]

It is difficult to read this passage without a strong sense of déjà vu. Except for the grooming that we no longer engage in for lack of fur—and that we might replace with fiddling with clothes (in the first instance above) and offering tender caresses (in the second)—the scene is hard to distinguish from human flirtation.

It is tempting to apply the principle of evolutionary parsimony: when faced with similar behavior in species that are closely related, assume similar mental processes unless you have good reason to think otherwise.[54]

But then, of course, we grow wary. What about the language that is used in this passage: can baboons really be described as "coy"? Isn't this a terribly anthropocentric notion that results from observer bias? Are they really capable of "feigning indifference," which would presuppose an advanced capacity to attribute thoughts and intentions to others and then subvert them strategically? Such claims have in fact been made recently about chimpanzees, but it would be even more astounding to find the same talents in such a distant relative. The problem is that "subjectivity, by its nature, is nontransferable. (Even the supposition that other *people* feel rests beyond the perimeter of verifiability and . . . that commonplace assumption is occasionally incorrect.)"[55] Therefore, researchers must always be careful not to posit homologies (the assumption of a shared nature) on the basis of loose analogies.[56]

The baboon behavior described above attracts our attention because it answers to shared evolutionary pressures—most important, mate attraction and social affiliation—and because it is fueled by brain regions and neurochemical processes that are markedly similar to ours. It would, of course, be very audacious to conclude from this that baboons or chimpanzees feel love in the same way that humans do. Even if their limbic systems probably foster emotions that we can translate roughly into human phenomena like "desire for union," "emotional dependency," and (at least among less promiscuous species) "desire for exclusivity," the extravagant human neocortex still endows our emotional experience with a richness and complexity that lies well beyond their grasp. Human love is filtered, consciously and subconsciously, through intricate conceptions of a past and a future; it is measured against hypothetical ideas about what could have been and what might happen; and it is drenched in assumptions and expectations about what we *should* be feeling (or, indeed, what we *think* we are feeling).

With these qualifiers in mind, let us now explore the nature of human love with an eye to its evolutionary origins. Evolutionary fitness can be subdivided roughly into two major problems, staying alive and reproducing, and these problems have been consistent for two billion years of multicellular life on earth. While life may not always have been "nasty, brutish, and short" in human prehistory, we must also remember that the human race has evolved in conditions where selective pressures were considerably harsher than they are in most affluent Western middle-class suburbs of today.

The first of these factors in natural selection is that of survival: to stay alive long enough to pass on your genes and to make sure that your progeny stays alive too.[57] Perhaps the most fruitful and influential application of this perspective to the human affections is John Bowlby's attachment theory. In the 1950s, Bowlby rejected the contemporary emphasis on interior fantasy-worlds in psychoanalytic theory and instead emphasized a very concrete problem that faces all primate infants: that their slow maturation process makes them totally dependent on the presence of a dependable caretaker with whom they can form a strong personal bond.

Linking Freud's original emphasis on the formative nature of childhood experience with the evolutionary problem of survival, Bowlby pointed to strong similarities in behavior between human infants and their primate relatives: "That the child's tie to his mother is the human version of behaviour seen commonly in many other species of animal now seems indisputable; and it is in this perspective that the nature of the tie is examined."[58] Just like the human child, a monkey infant will respond to prolonged separation from the mother with a fairly predictable sequence of protest, despair, and ultimately detachment, as the infant finally adjusts itself to the idea that mother may not be coming back.

Drawing on Bowlby's theoretical perspective, Mary Ainsworth conducted empirical studies that established different styles of attachment—secure, ambivalent/insecure, or avoidant—depending on how well the need for a dependable and nurturing primary caretaker was satisfied. For example, an "avoidant" child had been forced to dissociate itself so much from an undependable primary caretaker that it would respond with indifference or even cold hostility on the parent's return. Attachment theorists also postulated that this interaction between biological dispositions and environmental contingencies would have implications for an individual's future attachment behavior.

In the 1980s, Cindy Hazan and Philip Shaver developed Bowlby's intuitions about the lasting effects of childhood attachment into a theory of adult love. In their view, romantic love "has always and everywhere existed as a biological potential."[59] This would make it akin to most human traits that can be explained in evolutionary terms; that is, an emotional *disposition* that is attributable to an evolved genotype but that also requires favorable ecological conditions in order to emerge. They have also proposed that adult love involves three biologically based behavioral systems: attachment, care giving, and sexuality.[60]

Although the claim for a strong causal relationship between childhood attachment and adult love is still debated—will, for example, insecurely attached children tend to become jealous adults?—it is difficult to dispute that the two are intimately connected.[61] As Lisa Diamond points out, there is "increasing (albeit not universal) consensus and voluminous evidence from human and animal research that adult pair-bonds and infant-caregiver attachment involve the same basic emotions and behaviors."[62] To take just one simple example, it will hardly have escaped anyone's attention that there is a considerable similarity in the expression and experience of intimacy, since both types of relation involve caressing, kissing, smiling, and so forth.[63]

This connection between infant and adult attachment can be understood in different (but potentially complementary) ways. One approach is to side with the Freudians, who see adult romantic attachments more or less as outgrowths of the mother-infant interaction in infancy.[64] As we have seen, this view is also present in Bowlby's heritage, albeit in modified form. But the link between infant and adult love need not be as rigidly causal as the Freudians would have it: it could be that infantile and adult attachment are individual outgrowths of the same functional system, stemming from the same limbic blueprint, quite apart from the question of how far-reaching the effects of an individual's childhood experiences might be on adult love. "The evolution of the brain would have to be considered unparsimonious if it were not able to draw upon the same basic capacities of emotion and action in the various settings where strong attachment is called for."[65]

What the traditional psychoanalytic perspective overlooked, however, was the need to distinguish between sexuality and attachment. Lisa Diamond has marshaled considerable empirical evidence to suggest that "the evolved processes underlying sexual desire and affectional bonding are functionally independent," even if they tend to overlap in the case of adult sexual love. When I started working on this book I assumed, in keeping with traditional assumptions, that the definition of romantic love must somehow include a sexual component, but current research suggests that this is not the case. The desire for emotional and physical "union" it involves could be merely a matter of proximity or touch, and it is possible to feel romantic love for someone without wanting to have sex with him or her.

This "functionally independent" view of love and sex receives strong support from neuroscientific studies conducted by Andreas Bartels and Semir Zeki, who have used functional magnetic resonance scans (fMRI) to uncover a dopamine-rich "functionally specialized system" that is activated when people feel romantic love. When they went on to compare their findings to previous studies on sexual arousal, Bartels and Seki found that sexual arousal did not activate *overlapping* but *adjacent* areas in the brain.[66] A subsequent comparative study of romantic and maternal love, on the other hand, uncovered a more complex relationship with overlapping as well as discrete brain areas, all of which were saturated by the neurotransmitters oxytocin and vasopressin.[67]

Other recent neuroscientific studies seem to tease romantic attraction and attachment further apart while maintaining the rather firm distinction between love and sex. Helen Fisher, Arthur Aron, and associates have drawn on fMRI experiments in support of the view that humans come equipped with a primarily dopamine-driven romantic attraction system. This system, they argue, is distinct from the sex drive as well as attachment structures, and it also shows "behavioral and neural system similarities with other mammalian species." Like Hazan and Shaver, they regard human affection as involving three subsystems, but they propose a different triad composed of sexual desire, romantic attraction, and attachment.

(I must, however, admit to being bothered by a potential methodological circularity in their most recent study: can one's data really be said to indicate that "romantic love is distinct from the sex drive" if one has instructed one's fMRI subjects to "think about a nonsexual, euphoric experience with the beloved"?)[68]

It is still not clear, at least as far as I can gather, whether romantic love should be classified as a separate dopaminergic drive designed for mate selection that is then replaced by attachment once people have been brought together (as Helen Fisher et al. suggest), or whether it can still be defined usefully as a form of attachment (in the manner of Bartels and Seki or Hazan and Shaver). One problem with Fisher's theory is that the term "romantic love" comes to designate something much more specific (the initial flare of passion) than the full compound involving idealization, desire for union, empathy and concern, and so on, that other researchers have pieced together. It might be better to define this separate drive more strictly as "passionate love" (in keeping with the definition used in the first section of this chapter) and to treat it as a separable component of the emotion compound called "romantic love."

Whatever the future verdict may be, the general "functionally independent" view of our affections is highly plausible. For one thing, it may explain why people sometimes fall in love with members of their own sex in spite of having a heterosexual orientation. It could also tell us why children are capable of "maximally intense infatuations"[69] long before they reach puberty and sexual maturation. While Lisa Diamond does not draw this conclusion, the theory could also explain why people in some cultures have invested same-sex friendship with much of the same emotional intensity that other cultures reserve for sexual relationships.

Consider, as an example, the nature of adolescence in Shakespeare's England: "It was one of the peculiarities of Britain (and northwestern Europe generally) that young people initially experienced love as a form of polygamous play. . . . They spread their affections broadly, preferring to invest friendship with members of the same and opposite sex with the emotional intensity that we would reserve to our heterosexual relationships."[70] It seems plausible that this historical phenomenon will eventually be understood in terms of a complex interaction between (1) different functional systems involving sexuality, attachment, and romantic attraction, and (2) a culture that reserved sexual activity for a marital union that most people did not enter until their midtwenties. Such a system is bound to make young people emotionally inventive.

If these attachment theorists and neuroscientists are right about a universal disposition for romantic love, then we would clearly expect it to be a widespread phenomenon in human cultures (and not the Western construct it has been made out to be). Conversely, strong cross-cultural evidence that romantic love is *not* universal would seriously diminish the neuroscientific findings. According to the psychoanalyst E. S. Person, for example, the "best evidence that romantic love is not hard-wired into the emotional repertoire of humanity but is a cultural construct is the fact that there are so many cultures in which it is virtually absent."[71]

In 1992, the very same year that Person pronounced this "fact," the anthropologists William Jankowiak and Ted Fischer tested it empirically by examining a sample of 166 societies in the ethnographic record.[72] They found evidence of romantic love (defined as "any intense attraction that involves the idealization of the other, within an erotic context, with the expectation of enduring for some time into the future") in no less than 147, or 88.5 percent, of these societies. Jankowiak and Fischer added that this was a conservative estimate and that incomplete information about some cultures probably masked a much higher figure. Romantic love was in all likelihood a human universal or, at the very least, a near-universal.

This claim has since been given further corroboration by a number of field studies across the planet, and to my knowledge, no evidence has come forward that challenges it directly.[73] Patrick Hogan's recent empirical study of world literature has also identified "romantic union" as a universal prototype that suggests cross-cultural constants in emotional experience.[74] Most recently, a systematic, computer-assisted analysis of "seventy-nine folk tale collections from all inhabited continents, from different historical periods, and from societies vastly differing in ecology, geography, ethnic composition, religious beliefs, and degree of political organization" by Jon Gottschall and myself has given further support to romantic love's universality.[75]

In their original study, Jankowiak and Fischer were careful to stress that their claim was statistical in nature: they did not mean that everyone everywhere falls in love (or, one might add, that there is something wrong with people who never feel the slightest tinge of this emotion). This view is fully consistent with the idea of an evolved human nature, since all life forms are environmentally contingent to various degrees. Humans are far more plastic and cognitively sophisticated than land crabs, but in both cases evolved dispositions of varying intensity are enmeshed in unique life trajectories so that the life of an individual organism is not necessarily representative of broader species-specific patterns. Romantic love may be an evolved disposition, but it is also dependent on favorable conditions since nature and nurture are interdependent. There may be a thousand conjoining reasons why a biologically disposed individual does or does not fall in love, from cultural pressures to blind chance.

The most radical evolutionary view of romantic love—that it is an emotional adaptation, which may or may not be activated by the environment—leads us directly to a second question about its evolutionary function. The most widespread view is that it emerged as an emotional incentive for pair formation, keeping sexual partners together and securing parental investment for their children. At first sight, this idea may seem questionable since passion is often adulterous; indeed, in many cultures where marriage is not based on love, it might even be the chief nemesis of any lasting pair-bond. But this is really only a theoretical problem so long as we assume that the desire to commit must be synonymous with lifelong monogamy and that arranged marriages were also the rule in those ancestral environments where our current emotional dispositions were calibrated. It is quite conceivable that a tendency for serial relationships—where people are attracted to each other, stay together and have children, break up, and then form new relationships—would have contributed much more effectively to the evolutionary fitness of our ancestors.

Since Western culture is currently shifting from lifelong monogamy to serial monogamy, it may be tempting to write this off as sheer ethnocentrism. What a singularly convoluted way to convince ourselves that our own way of life is both natural and just! But this convergence between evolutionary pressures and Western social arrangements can be understood very differently. As I will emphasize in the last section of this chapter, there is a fundamental conflict at work in human nature: we are individual organisms as well as social animals, and we are constantly seeking to reconcile these two demands. It could well be that Western culture is currently engaged in a social experiment where individual desires —including the desire to leave your partner and start afresh once the passion has waned—are given free rein because our social organization permits this. From this perspective, Western culture is not being true to human nature: it is being true to the individual, and that is clearly not the same thing.

In the last section of this chapter, I will outline some other cultural factors that influence the experience of love, but we are not quite done with the evolutionary perspective yet. We still need to take account of that other aspect of evolutionary fitness whose centrality hardly needs defending: that one must also ensure reproductive access to the other sex. Here the second mechanism in human evolution comes into play: sexual selection.

Putting Sex Back in Gender

Sexual selection is a complicated process whose mechanisms are incompletely understood, but the general principle is fairly simple. Among all sexual species where individuals have some capacity to actively influence their choice of mates, the sexes become selective pressures for one another. This leads to *intrasexual* competition between members of the same sex (since they compete for the same mates) as well as *intersexual* competition (since the two sexes respond dynamically to each other's reproductive strategies). In this way, the sexes can be said to gradually sculpt each other's genotypes by means of an evolutionary arms race that is often wasteful and extravagant. A classic example is the ridiculously unpractical peacock's tail, which is directly detrimental to survival (it makes it harder to escape predators) and seems to have been selected for because the peahens like it.[76] Sexual selection introduces difficult tradeoffs into the evolutionary mechanism, not least because wild animals are highly vulnerable to predation when they are mating.

Competition for access to the other sex has had demonstrable physiological consequences in many species. For example, human males are roughly 15 percent larger than females, while our australopithecine ancestors may have been twice as large. Male elephant seals grow as much as four times the size of the opposite sex.[77] At least in the latter case, we are dealing with a particularly brutal example of intrasexual competition, where increased body weight and strength enables a minority of males to dominate large harems of females (to the exclusion of most other males). But as the awkwardly extravagant peacock reminds us, sexual selection can also be a more polite affair, wherever the sexes are forced to comply with each other's wishes and adjust to each other's actions. As early as the nineteenth century, Darwin realized that *female choice* was a crucial driving force in the evolution of different species.

With this in mind, let us now gnaw a little on the real bone of contention regarding love and sexuality: that of emotional and cognitive differences between men and women.[78] This is an important question for any study of love, and it is obvious that Shakespeare was interested in it. But since recent findings in neuroscience and related disciplines raise strong doubts about the dualistic wall between biological sex and cultural gender that still predominates in the humanities and some social sciences, there are few issues that are more controversial today. The evolutionary view clashes with traditional sensibilities that involve considerable ideological, emotional, and professional investment. For many people, the very idea of a biological basis for gender differences seems destined to destroy the advances we have made toward equity between men and women.

On a superficial level, this suspicion of evolutionary explanation is understandable. We know that human history has been characterized by a plethora of disturbing arrangements based on biological sex, from legally sanctioned double standards to claustration practices or even worse infringements on women's rights and interests.[79] Hence it is not surprising that the most frequent argument among opponents of biology is a historical one; that current biological arguments are ideologically suspect because similar arguments have served oppressive functions in the past.

The question is, however, whether we should really evaluate a theory merely on the basis of its superficial similarity to something that was proposed a hundred years ago. Like many others, I also find this form of argumentation problematic because there is no necessary connection between the contents of a theory and the multifarious, often conflicting uses it can be put to. As I suggested earlier in this chapter, the greatest obstacle to a serious, constructive, and hopefully enlightened discussion of such matters is the persistent tendency to confuse description (the nature of human beings) with moral or political prescription (what human beings ought to do).[80] It is likely that the relationship between the sexes will always be tense due to intra- and intersexual selection. But as long as we respect the analytical gap between what is natural and what is right, and as long as we avoid reducing our complex biology to a set of reified sex roles, it is possible that future generations will look back on our bitter gender debates and wonder what all the fuss was about.

Let us now turn briefly to the case for evolved differences. If we leave aside the question of cross-cultural comparison for a moment, the most compelling evidence for psychosexual dimorphism in humans comes from two interlaced areas of investigation: modern neuroscience and evolutionary theory. When it comes to the nature of the brain, researchers are finding sexual differences both in its structure and in its mode of operation. In the words of the neuroscientist Jaak Panksepp, "One of the spectacular revelations of modern behavioral neuroscience has been the organization of distinct neural systems that elaborate male and female sexuality in all mammalian species that have been studied."

For example, the epicenters of sexual impulses in males and females are located in unique sections of the hypothalamus, and sexuality is also regulated by distinct circuits involving different hormones. Panksepp's conclusion is emphatic: "Though human investigators are still prone to believe that gender identity is a matter of choice . . . the biological data affirm that there are strong evolutionary/biological constraints over such matters."[81] The fact that steroid hormones congregate in the limbic system and higher areas of the cerebral hemispheres also suggests some influence on emotional experience and even ways of thinking.[82]

In another neuroscientific review, published in 2006, Larry Cahill notes that "the past 5–10 years have witnessed a surge of findings from animals and humans concerning sex influences on many areas of brain and behaviour, including emotion, memory, vision, hearing, processing faces, pain perception, navigation, neurotransmitter levels, stress hormone action on the brain and disease states." It is therefore "evident that there are sex influences at all levels of the nervous system, from genetic to systems to behavioral levels. The picture of brain organization that emerges is of two complex mosaics—one male and one female—that are similar in many respects but very different in others."[83]

While such differences must have a strong genetic basis, it would be mistaken to see what happens in the brain as a direct expression of genes, or to exaggerate the differences between males and females for that matter. Every organism is the result of a complex interaction between many different factors, and genes alone cannot make a human brain. For the first six weeks of pregnancy human fetuses are identical, and they are then differentiated sexually by means of a delicate interaction between genetic information and sex hormones produced inside and outside the fetus. This introduces an environmentally contingent element into the developmental process, where different hormone levels can induce very different results in the mammalian brain even though the genetic recipe is fixed. Given the considerable environmental plasticity of the human brain, our life experiences will also have profound effects on its organization.

Whenever we talk about "male" and "female" we must also remember that we are talking about statistical averages, where individual women can exhibit typically "male" traits or behaviors and vice versa. As we know, most men are taller than most women, and the empirical fact that some women are taller than most men does not invalidate the generalization that "men are taller than women." The perception of complexity does not preclude broader generalizations about male and female, but it does rebut the assumption that individual men and women must be typical of their sex (or treated according to generalized expectations about what men and women are like).

Such insights about sexual dimorphism in the brain are an important piece of the sexual puzzle, but they also beg for an explanation. One important answer comes from prehistoric differences in selective pressures, where we have already seen that human size dimorphism can be explained partly as a response to sexual competition. In 1972, Robert Trivers improved on previous theories of sexual selection by formulating his theory of "parental investment," which predicted that animal courting patterns would correlate with the amount of effort each sex expended on raising the offspring.[84] A sex that typically made a great investment (time, resources, energy, and so on) in its young was likely to be more selective when it came to choosing partners, while a less biologically committed sex would increase its fitness by copulating with as many partners as possible.

As it turns out, this holds true for practically all species that have been studied. Females are generally more selective than males because they have the greatest reproductive burden, whereas males pursue females with more vigor and less discrimination. What is especially compelling is that parental investment theory is further corroborated by those rare species—such as sea horses, blowfish, and some bird species—where the typical sex roles are reversed so that males make the greatest contribution in nursing the offspring. Among these animals it is instead large, aggressive females that court choosy child-rearing males.

When Darwin first struck upon the concept of sexual selection in the nineteenth century he couched this female selectiveness in the Victorian terms that were immediately available to him: males of different species were ardent sexual rovers, and females were coy.[85] But being coy is not the same thing as being choosy, and it is certainly not the term I would apply to a female chimpanzee who solicits sex from males by sticking her swollen backside in their faces.[86] Today researchers in many different fields are piecing together a puzzle of increasing complexity and variation in reproductive strategies among our primate cousins, where females of the species often go on the sexual offensive if they have reason to do so. But the broader patterns predicted by parental investment theory still stand, and they appear to include human beings too: "Across a wide array of personal and behavioral attributes, except for age and physical attractiveness, women are generally more selective in their preferences for marriage partners than men are."[87] This is not surprising since the larger stakes in the mammalian mating game have been fairly consistent for nearly two hundred million years of evolution.

Even if we grant that the case for evolved gender differences is plausible, the question remains just how significant they are. This question really masks two distinct questions, and it is important to separate them. First, there is the *descriptive* problem: how much of our emotional experience and behavior can be attributed to biology? We are far from a comprehensive answer in this area, but there is growing evidence that many traditional clichés about men and women (for instance, regarding dispositions for risk taking, commitment, aggression, dominance, nurturing, and even differences in cognitive styles and capacities) are grounded in biological predispositions.[88] Such differences, however small, are bound to make themselves felt on a social and cultural level too. As numerous theorists have realized (some of whom are also feminists), we cannot understand a phenomenon like patriarchy fully without recourse to an evolutionary framework and parental investment theory.[89]

This leads us to the *normative* question of what practical consequences we might draw from biologically based gender differences. Should we act on them in some way? Such questions should not be dealt with lightly, and we have good reason to wait for more evidence before we even attempt to draw any normative— and necessarily indirect—conclusions. In the meantime, however, we will not be helped by sticking our heads into the sand and droning that sexual equality is the same thing as sexual sameness. As early as 1875, Antoinette Blackwell (1825–1921) drew this important distinction in the first feminist critique of Darwin. In Blackwell's formulation, which is sometimes passed over in feminist celebrations of her work,[90] the sexes are "always equivalents—equals but not identicals in development."[91] The anthropologist Melford Spiro chimes in more than a hundred years later: "That individuals and groups must be identical in order to be equal is surely one of the most pernicious dogmas of our time, and the fact that, ironically enough, it has become a liberal dogma does not make it any less so."[92] This is still a hard pill to swallow for many people, but it may well contain the cure for many a muddled theory of gender identity.

Since Shakespeare was such a notorious gender-bender there is yet another aspect of sexual difference that needs to be dealt with briefly before we turn to the relation between biology and culture. This study will not attempt to answer the currently unanswerable question of whether Shakespeare himself was heterosexual, homosexual, bisexual, or even intersexual for that matter, and the question of same-sex love is at best tangential to the plays that I consider in the follow-ing chapters. Nevertheless, the deliberate confusion or reversal of gender roles in many other Shakespearean works calls for a larger framework that does not restrict itself to heterosexual love. Here, of course, we wander into yet another academic minefield. In his study of Shakespearean love, Maurice Charney points out that the "issues of the homoerotic in Shakespeare are hopelessly entwined in academic controversy."[93]

While the last word has not been said concerning potential evolutionary or endocrinological explanations of homosexuality,[94] a wealth of evidence from the animal world has totally demolished the old pernicious argument that homosex-ual acts are somehow "against nature." The equivalents of homosexual activities have been documented in hundreds of species, from birds to apes, and among our closest primate cousins they even appear to have a number of social functions. As Helen Fisher observes, homosexual behavior is "so common in other species—and it occurs in such a variety of circumstances—that human homosexuality is striking not in its prevalence but in its rarity."[95]

It may be very tempting for the morally or sexually enlightened to conclude from this that homosexuality is natural and therefore right. But the hope for such a vindication involves yet another problematic confusion of the normative and the descriptive. The treacherous nature of such arguments becomes obvious if we apply the same thinking to disturbing phenomena like incest or physical violence, both of which are widespread in the animal world but can hardly be justified in civilized societies. Even more important, to seek to justify any sexual orientation by pointing to biology or the animal world is already to play into the hands of the homophobes by conceding too much ground. The real battle line should be drawn by means of moral and political principles, not natural theology.

Love and Culture

More than two thousand years ago, Aristotle made the simple observation that humans are social animals. A more recent philosopher, Mary Midgley, outlines some problematic consequences of our intricate forms of sociability and our ex-traordinary intelligence. As particularly advanced social animals we are often torn between our personal interests and the interests of the group:

> We want incompatible things, and want them badly. We are fairly aggres-sive, yet we want company and depend on long-term enterprises. We love those around us and need their love, yet we want independence and need to wander. We are restlessly curious and meddling, yet long for permanence. Unlike many primates, we do have a tendency to pair-formation, but it is

incomplete and gives us a lot of trouble. We cannot live without a culture, but it never quite satisfies us. All this is the commonplace of literature. It is also, to a degree, the problem of the other intelligent species too. . . . What is special about people is their power of understanding what is going on, and using that understanding to regulate it.[96]

While many literary critics have been conditioned to blame the Western capitalist ethos for all such tensions between the individual and the group, the problem not only predates our current social organization in the West but is older than mankind itself. The constant need to weigh our individual desires against the demands of the group, and very often to subordinate them to the interests of others, is something we share with our close relatives in the biosphere. In the novel *Enduring Love,* Ian McEwan's protagonist defines the problem as "our mammalian conflict—what to give to the others, and what to keep for yourself."[97]

What human culture adds to this predicament is, among other things, a complex symbolic regulation of the needs and desires of its members. This process necessarily involves both frustration and gratification, since individual and collective interests do not always overlap. Hence it would be erroneous to regard cultural systems either as direct expressions of natural dispositions or as arbitrary inventions. Take, for example, the currently conflicted relation between biological sexual dimorphism and cultural gender roles: "Among humans, conscious effort can minimise preexisting differences. More often, small initial differences in responsiveness are exaggerated by life experiences and then blown out of all proportion by cultural customs and norms."[98]

In the broadest sense, human culture can thus be characterized as "both an expression and a critique of what the species as a 'population' (or a set of sexually differentiated populations) is biologically disposed to do."[99] Our love lives are no exception to this rule. As we have seen, romantic love is most likely a universal biological potential in *Homo sapiens,* but as readers of *Romeo and Juliet* are keenly aware, society also has important stakes in the mating game. In the words of the emotion theorists Richard and Bernice Lazarus, attitudes to love and commitment "vary with the culture and historical period. Society is concerned with marital records, protecting the rights of the partners, maintaining their mutual obligations, making sure that they remain in predictable and functional social and work niches, facilitating childrearing, and upholding the values to which the society is dedicated."[100] These are problems that every society or social group must tackle on the basis of its material situation and its traditions, and it will do so with varying degrees of flexibility or collective influence.

Depending on the capacity of the larger social group (the family, the clan, or the state) to subordinate the amorous desires of individuals to the larger good, we can distinguish usefully (following Harry Triandis et al.) between

"individualist" and "collectivist" cultures. In brief, the former place a strong premium on individual goals, and their members are usually adept at meeting new
people and forming new groups. The latter subordinate personal interests to group
interests, draw a sharp distinction between the in-group and the out-group, and
place a firm emphasis on hierarchy.[101] Of course, such a distinction can only be a
matter of degrees. All cultures demand an enormous amount of conformity from
their members—including, in Western culture, a somewhat paradoxical demand
for group conformity with an individualist ethos—and any advanced civilization
can also be characterized by major differences between different social levels.

In early modern England, for example, it seems that arranged marriages were
more or less the exclusive province of the ruling elite. The common folk, or at
least those who had sufficient funds to set up a new household, were typically
expected to consult their parents but were otherwise free to follow their hearts.
Forced marriages were rare.[102] In other words, the mating pattern in early modern
England appears to have been largely individualist with a small collectivist clique
at the top.

The individualist/collectivist distinction also gives us some clues about how
the members of different cultures will respond to the idea of romantic love. In a
modern cross-cultural survey that compared self-reports from the United States,
Italy, and China,[103] Philip Shaver and his research associates found that people
in all three cultures could readily identify the emotion, like all other emotions
that were tested, but they differed on one significant point. While Italians and
Americans associated romantic love with happiness, the Chinese tended to see
it as something more negative. This is not surprising since Chinese culture has a
long tradition of arranged marriages rather than love matches. For anyone whose
choice of marriage partners is subordinated to larger social interests, falling madly
in love with another person is bound to be a problematic idea. In the language of
emotion theory we can say that love's potential for realization necessarily influences its hedonic tone; we saw earlier that unrequited love is characterized by
feelings of emptiness, anxiety, and despair. Human nature always interacts with
human expectations, and our expectations are always environmental in nature.

If one important role of culture is to suppress, inhibit, redirect, or transform
behavior whenever it is deemed inappropriate, and to intensify and channel those
tendencies that are deemed socially desirable, the same goes for its treatment of
an emotion like love. "In some cultures romantic passion is rejected as an evil and
frighteningly emotional experience. In others it is tolerated but not celebrated
or asserted, and, in still others, romantic passion is praised as an important and
cherished cultural ideal."[104] Depending on its social status, it can be expected to
be valorized or classified differently, talked about more or less frequently, and
accorded greater or lesser social significance in different sociocultural contexts.

In Paul Heelas's useful formulation, emotions in general are subject to *hypercognition* or *hypocognition*, where "hypercognized emotions are those which are culturally identified, hypocognized being those which receive much less conceptual attention."[105]

It is likely that an increasingly individualistic Western culture has hypercognized many pleasurable personal emotional states at the expense of collectivist ideals, and this is especially probable when it comes to love. We are, on average, much more prone to stress the importance of being "true to our feelings" and to base our choice of partners on love than people are in other cultures. If we switch briefly to a normative angle on the subject, it is hard not to see this as a major step forward since it has enabled more and more people to pursue their heart's desire and thus improve their quality of life. But such hypercognition also has a price. It may entail a potential loosening of social bonds and an unprecedented pressure on individuals as isolated agents of their own fortunes and misfortunes. I have often wondered just how "liberated" those Western individuals feel who scour singles bars looking for someone to love, only to face repeated rejection.

To see the distinctly Western obsession with romantic love as an instance of hypercognition rather than as a cultural invention enables us to modify the tendency of numerous theorists to exaggerate the role of historical ruptures and contingencies. For example, ever since Denis de Rougemont and C. S. Lewis expounded their influential views on the subject, and Michel Foucault added that history is a long chain of discontinuous thought systems, many people have believed that romantic love is a specific Western phenomenon whose origin lies in the medieval tradition of courtly love. As we have seen, there are strong reasons to suppose that this assumption is incorrect. It is true that something important did happen in France in the twelfth century that would have great consequences for our Western conception of love, but as Irving Singer points out in his monumental study of the Western love tradition, we must not confuse the emotion with the ideal. In his definition, courtly love was based on the assumption that: "(1) Sexual love between men and women is *in itself* something splendid, an ideal worth striving for; (2) love ennobles both the lover and the beloved; (3) being an ethical and aesthetic attainment, sexual love cannot be reduced to a mere libidinal impulse; (4) love pertains to courtesy but is not necessarily related to the institution of marriage; (5) love is an intense, passionate relationship that establishes a holy oneness between man and woman."[106]

What the tradition of courtly love affirmed was that sexual love is both authentic and valuable and that it has an aesthetic or even religious value. It was first and foremost the valorization of a universal human need in a cultural milieu that seemed diametrically opposed to its very existence. Originally a response among the ruling elite to the political reality of arranged marriages, it gradually freed the amorous passion from its denigrated role in Christian culture and became "West-ern man's first great attempt to demonstrate that the noble aspirations of idealism need not be incompatible with a joyful acceptance of sexual reality."[107]

What was culturally specific about courtly love and its later offshoots was that romantic passion, understood as a spiritual phenomenon, was fused with a central aspect of Judeo-Christian religion. "In general, courtly love attacked pro-miscuity as the church also attacked polytheism. As there was only one God, so was there only one man and only one woman who could satisfy their ideal long-ings."[108] If we want, we can perhaps describe this institutionalized version of the exclusivity that we have already associated with passionate love (that people gen-erally do not feel it for more than one person at a time, and that they will normally want to reserve that person for themselves) as a historical "construction." But this is a far cry from saying that the basic emotion was a newfangled historical inven-tion and that Sappho gave expression to something entirely different on Lesbos in the sixth century B.C. Courtly love seized upon a universal human potential, invested it with social significance, and placed it within a normative framework as a laudable spiritual connection between two unique souls. As such it also had to be unchanging, as Shakespeare suggests in his famous sonnet: "Love is not love / Which alters when it alteration finds."

As an institutionalized tradition, courtly love gradually took on a life of its own and would exert a powerful influence on Western styles of loving, to the point where many people today regard the absence of passionate love in their lives as a social or personal failure.[109] By the fifteenth century, much of the origi-nal sexual dimension in the courtly love tradition had been downplayed as the church renewed its onslaught on sexual passion, and Petrarch's poetry in par-ticular would immortalize the irreconcilable conflict between spiritual and sexual passion. From there, the road of literary influence leads directly to Shakespeare, who satirized Petrarch and yet shared a good deal of his ambivalence. Like his literary predecessor, Shakespeare shows us a perspective on human affection that is alternatively detached and conflicted, idealistic and realistic. He also adds an important component that is absent in Petrarch: a sense of humor.

Seen in this way, the story of courtly love is the story of a tug-of-war be-tween evolved needs and cultural constraints that eventually produced an ideal that had been harmonized with a culture's official system of belief. To take a bio-cultural view of human nature and love enables us to discard the view that human beings are basically products of their cultural and historical environments (or genetic robots, for that matter). All humans are the inheritors of numerous needs and desires that have been tailored by an evolutionary process to interact with specific environments. As Mary Midgley puts it succinctly: "Our basic repertoire of wants is given. We are not free to create or annihilate wants, either by private invention or by culture. . . . Thus, if twentieth-century people want supersonic planes, they do so because of wants they have in common with Eskimos and Bush-men. They want to move fast, to do their business quickly, to be honored, feared, and admired, to solve puzzles, and to have something bright and shiny."[110] And most of them, one might add, want someone to love, to care for, and to be cared for by. As we have seen, the disposition for love and affection is by no means unresponsive to the environment, since most evolved dispositions are designed to interact with the environment and to produce cultural variation in the face of variable life conditions. In some situations, such as social deprivation, the innate disposition for love may be totally suppressed. But there will also be constraints on the capacity of any culture to regulate or vanquish those rudimentary needs and desires whose history lies buried deep inside the human genome.

This interactionist framework illustrates why humans are not always happily or successfully socialized by their cultures, not even when smooth compliance with societal norms might actually be in their best interest. Take, for example, the Fulbe of North Cameroon, a sedentary Islamic tribe where mastery of the emo-tions is accorded paramount importance. In this culture the existence of romantic love is recognized, but "it has no legitimate place in the community. The Fulbe therefore have a tremendous incentive *not* to fall in love . . . yet time and again they fail."[111] In all likelihood, the Fulbe succumb to these forbidden passions for the same reason that Westerners sometimes find themselves completely swept away by desire; because it was adaptive for our ancestors to do so.

As Melford Spiro points out usefully, we need to distinguish between *learn-ing a culture* (to acquire its propositions) and *becoming enculturated* (internalizing its propositions as personal beliefs about what is right or true).[112] For example, the Wiltshire gentleman who declared in 1622 that "there was no God, and no Res-urrection, and that men died a death like beasts"[113] had clearly mastered the of-ficial norms of his culture, but he had also refused to become enculturated by them. Of course, since cultures are never totally homogeneous entities and can comprise many different perspectives and ideas, it can always be argued that this particular villager had simply been enculturated differently than most of his contemporaries, perhaps by some underground sect of atheists. We can also de-bate the extent to which the "official" or "dominant" doctrines of a culture can be identified with any real certainty. But the main purpose of Spiro's distinction is not to provide a cultural taxonomy but to remind us of the incomplete correla-tion between official culture, on the one hand, and individual belief, experience, or behavior on the other.

For similar reasons, the historian of emotion Peter Stearns distinguishes be-tween the "emotional standards" or "feeling rules" of a particular culture—that is, what people are generally expected to feel—and their actual feelings.[114] In the following chapters, we will find many Shakespearean examples of the con-flict between cultural expectations and a deeper human propensity for love, but we will also find examples of a culturally motivated love that is less *felt* than *adhered to.*

I would like to end this chapter with a final attempt to clarify the special virtues of the theoretical perspective that I have been advancing. To avoid the impression that I have been flogging a dead horse (I am, after all, arguing for the universality of my subject!) I will do so by contrasting my views with a fairly recent argument by Ann Beall and Robert Sternberg that love is a "social construction that reflects its time period because it serves an important function in a culture." [115] (For your information, Sternberg is the same person who has constructed the valuable "love triangle" involving passion, intimacy, and commitment.)

In their article, Beall and Sternberg address the question of love's potential universality by means of four theoretical hypotheses, choosing to side with the following view: "Love is not a universal experience. It changes according to its cultural milieu and is viewed differently in numerous cultures" (418). They base this claim on a broad, but necessarily rhapsodic, account of historical and cultural differences in the conceptualization of love. They show how love can vary in terms of its object as well as function in a society, and they rightly point out that "an essential part of one's experience of love is one's conceptualization of it" (419). The latter point is also supported by means of a brief but exemplary discussion of the cognitive component in love, where our beliefs and expectations affect our experience.

In other words, there are many important points of agreement between their argument and the biocultural perspective I have adopted here. But then we get to the central premise that "love is a social construction"—that is, that it is not everywhere the same. From a biocultural perspective, this perception of cultural and historical variation can only serve as the starting point for a deeper and more sophisticated analysis. Indeed, Beall and Sternberg do not appear to consider a rather obvious rejoinder to their argument: that the very notion of love as something that is experienced and conceptualized differently in various cultures necessarily presupposes that it is precisely a *single* phenomenon (rather than a random set of phenomena that happen to have been grouped together).

This is not a mere play on words. So far as I can tell, Beall and Sternberg can respond to my complaint in two different ways. One is to emphasize the aspect of difference even further, so that different cultures and forms of love are seen as truly incommensurate. But in that case they should really stop talking about "love" altogether and write it off as an unfortunate remnant of folk psychology. As we saw earlier, a similar case has been made by Paul Griffiths regarding the concept of emotion, which he deems too imprecise to be of any academic use. But at least in their present form, Beall and Sternberg's repeated references to love in the singular seem to preclude such an option: "Although we believe that love is an idea that reflects its culture, we believe that it has an enormous impact on how people think and feel about themselves and others" (434).

The other alternative is, of course, to attempt to reconcile the idea of love as a single, universal phenomenon with the evidence for its cultural and historical variation. To venture a potentially misleading but hopefully illustrative analogy, we can consider the much simpler act of *eating*, which is universal but also varies substantially between different cultures. People eat different things, they eat in different ways, at different times, using different utensils; some cultures eat more than others; some make a virtue of not eating at certain times; and eating has different social functions in different places. But we all recognize that these are cultural variations on a single universal theme and that that this theme, in turn, answers to a basic human need.

So far as I can tell, Beall's and Sternberg's dismissal of a similar universality in the case of love stems primarily from the absence of a "definition that describes love throughout the ages or across cultures" (433). But if they ever hoped to find such a universal definition—one that would be mirrored by the official concepts of ancient Greeks, Aztecs, Kalahari bushmen, and modern Westerners alike—then this hope must have been optimistic on the verge of misguided. There is a plethora of human phenomena that can safely be termed universal to human cultures —such as religion, or culture itself for that matter—in spite of our demonstrable incapacity to arrive at neat and unshakeable definitions of their exact nature.

What is more, we have seen that a culture's dominant "definition" or attitude toward love (to the extent that it is even recognized officially) is not always representative of its actual experience or practice. For example, how can we ever hope to find an adequate definition of romantic love in a culture that regards individual passion as a social evil and therefore refuses to talk about it? For this reason, we also need an empirical approach that is not entirely dependent on a culture's conception of itself. We have seen that in one such study of the ethnographic record romantic passion turned out to be *at least* a near-universal, found in more than 88 percent of the 166 societies studied, and that other studies appear to corroborate this picture.

As I have argued in this chapter, the question of love's universality will also sooner or later need to be restated below the immediate level of cultural differences and similarities. We must also consider the biological dispositions that enable people to feel for each other in the first place. Like most social constructivists, Beall and Sternberg do not actively dispute the idea of a biological foundation for love, they just deem it irrelevant: "We can presume that love includes such a component" (423). End of story. By contrast, I hope to have demonstrated that the biocultural alternative is better equipped to address love's paradox of sameness and difference. Its concern with evolutionary as well as historical time makes it an excellent reference point for the works of a dramatist who is sometimes our next-door neighbor and sometimes seems light years away.

2

Parental Love in Two Roman Tragedies

Nature is Often Hidden, Sometimes Overcome, Seldome Extinguished.
Francis Bacon, "Of Nature in Men." *Essayes,* 119

The overarching purpose of this first literary chapter will be to explore the treatment of parental affection in two of Shakespeare's Roman plays: *Titus Andronicus* (c. 1594) and *Coriolanus* (c. 1608). These plays are excellent examples of the biocultural paradox, where a universal human nature generates cultural diversity. Taken together, they demonstrate that Shakespeare (and, in *Titus,* his coauthor George Peele) not only saw substantial differences between classical Roman and early modern English culture, but that he also systematically explored the potential effects of such a different cultural environment in his writing. Both plays attest to the disastrous impact of an exaggerated Roman concern with honor on parental love, to the point of the latter's near-extinction. However, such cultural norms do not appear to be omnipotent, for in both plays the onslaught on parental love also reaches a series of breaking points where nurturing impulses are vindicated.

Those who believe that such an awareness of cultural or historical difference is the exclusive province of an enlightened modernity will quite naturally regard my claims as anachronistic. Others may object that Shakespeare was a dramatist and not a historical anthropologist. I am fairly confident that my argument will answer both objections, thus lending textual support to as well as laying a theoretical foundation for Tom McAlindon's contention that Shakespeare's tragic worlds are "culturally distinctive" and yet "grounded on a construction of reality which his contemporaries considered to have a timeless validity."[1] For now, it is enough to point out that the very word "anachronism" was actually invented during the Renaissance as a response to an increasing awareness of historical difference and that the old distinction between "nature" and "art" did more or less the same work as the twentieth-century dichotomy between nature and culture.[2]

In *The Winter's Tale,* Shakespeare expresses a basic insight that our contemporary intellectual world is still struggling to incorporate on a broad level—namely, that all such dichotomies are ultimately misleading because one term really sub-sumes the other: "Yet nature is made better by no mean / But nature makes that mean. . . . The art itself is nature" (4.4.89–90, 97). This can be compared with Joseph Carroll's remarks on how the evolutionary account of the nature/culture distinction outranks all other twentieth-century models, from structuralism on-ward: "This dichotomy has been intensively scrutinized and ultimately aban-doned by all contemporary evolutionary thinkers. It is now clear that nature and culture are neither antithetical nor identical. Culture is a subordinate term *within* nature; culture is that form of nature that has been regulated and elaborated by collective human efforts."[3] Four hundred years may have passed, but we are still only catching up with Shakespeare [4]

Parenting Old and New

Before we turn to Shakespeare's treatment of parental love, we must consider a question whose answer will have major consequences for what follows: is parental love a universal aspect of human nature that can be attributed to an evolutionary process? That is, when we enter into dialogue with Shakespeare about this sub-ject, can we expect to be talking about at least roughly the same thing?

Let us perform a brutal act of reductive exclusion and think away all the personal and cultural meanings that human beings attribute to their all too brief sojourn on earth: that life is about being happy, doing the right thing, or going to heaven. Once we have stripped life down to its bare essentials in this way, it becomes a ludicrously circular argument. Its purpose, indeed its very nature, is simply to produce more life; the capacity for *replication* is a central criterion for distinguishing between life and inanimate matter.

From such a bird's-eye perspective, where humans and beetles and bacteria share the same tasks of survival and reproduction, an organism's activities can be divided into *somatic* and *reproductive* effort. The former term covers anything the organism does to stay alive long enough to ensure the second objective, which is the production of surviving offspring. Since human babies mature very slowly after birth and are uniquely dependent on parental care, the need for prolonged reproductive effort becomes very great in our species. Wherever such strong se-lective pressures remain constant or even invariant over long periods of time, the process of natural selection has a tendency to provide species with built-in mecha-nisms to help them along. It is simply so much more efficient if humans come into this world with some sort of built-in dispositions than if each generation has to convince the next that loving and caring for your children is a good thing.

The problem with such sweeping statements, however, is that they hardly do justice to the considerable variation and complexity that characterizes human cultures and epochs, not to mention individuals. As we all know, humans are not unthinking reproductive machines, and we arrived at our neat equation above precisely by ignoring the *meanings* that humans assign to their existence. We reflect in complex ways on our options and our experience, and many who have the opportunity to choose parenthood decide to forego this option, spending their energy and resources on other pursuits. In rich societies, some people positively revel in somatic effort and pamper themselves in the same way that others spoil their children, while others become abusive parents.

Does this mean that there are *no* dispositions for parental love? Hardly, since evolved psychological characteristics are not hardwired or inflexible and usually require adequate environmental input. What is more, even if we should assume that a genetic disposition for nurturing has spread universally across human populations, then we can always expect to find individual exceptions to this rule. Nor do different styles of parenting necessarily constitute evidence to the contrary, for as we saw in chapter 1, it is a categorical mistake to conclude that cultural variation in a trait is opposed to its potential universality. So what shall we make of this theoretical quagmire? I suggest we make a strategic retreat from these accelerating abstractions and complexities and turn to an early modern philosopher who seems to have shared our confusion.

Toward the end of the sixteenth century, when Shakespeare had probably just arrived in London and taken up work in the theater, Michel de Montaigne gave the question of parental instincts some thought in his *Essays*. The result was, unsurprisingly, bewildering. On the one hand, he was firmly convinced that there were deep impulses at work in human nature. To use modern biological parlance, he concluded in the essay "On the Affection of Parents to Their Children" that the *reproductive* impulse was second only to the *somatic*: "If there be any truly-naturall law, that is to say, any instinct, universally and perpetually imprinted, both in beasts and us, (which is not without controversie) I may, according to mine own opinion, say, that next to the care, which each living creature hath to his preservation, and to flie what doth hurt him; the affection which the engenderer beareth his offspring, holds second place in this ranke."[5] But Montaigne also had two other distinguishing characteristics that tended to undermine such broad generalizations; he liked to change his mind halfway through an argument, and he was intensely aware of how powerfully culture (or "custom," as he called it) could shape human identity. Like Francis Bacon in England, he was also well aware that parental love varies in intensity and can be distributed unevenly.

A little further on in the same essay, Montaigne gives every sign of being a loving parent, but he also confesses that he finds small infants troublesome and irritating. In short, he prefers to hand them over to their mother. On closer inspection, even mother love seems to have a "weake foundation," for how else could his country have arrived at its widespread system of wet-nursing where women routinely hand over their newborns to strangers? To complicate things even more, Montaigne notes that wet-nurses often develop maternal feelings that are "more vehement than the naturall, and to be much more tender and carefull for the welfare and preservation of other mens children, than for their owne." His conclusion is that beasts and humans alike "doe soon alter, and easily bastardise their naturall affection" (84–85). He leaves us with the paradox of a strong innate impulse that is deeply vulnerable to cultural interference.

The confusion generated by widespread cultural practices like wet-nursing— not to mention darker facts like child abuse and even systematic infanticide in some cultures—has led many modern social scientists and humanities professors to conclude that humans do not have parental instincts. Instead, we are looking at a series of cultural constructions where even parental affection is the product of a modern sentimental age. The overall picture presented by scholars like Philippe Ariès, Lawrence Stone, Lloyd De Mause, and Michel Foucault is one of massive historical change where premodern Westerners did not even have recourse to a concept of childhood (or even a concept of "man") and were either cruel or indifferent toward their offspring.

As David Cressy demonstrated in 1991, these ideas have been adhered to by many literary critics in spite of powerful criticism from other historians.[6] That Michel Foucault and Lawrence Stone have been particularly popular among New Historicists and cultural materialists is only to be expected, since it is in the nature of a radical historicism to stress the role of history at the expense of other factors. But since these ideas have become an academic commonplace that continues to assert itself in the most unlikely places—most recently, in a book by the conservative cultural critic Neil Postman[7]—they must be dealt with at some length here.

As early as 1983, the historian Linda Pollock examined the widely disseminated notion "that there was no concept of childhood in the past and that parents were, at best, indifferent to their offspring and, at worst, cruel to them."[8] The main evidence put forward to support the former claim was that children were portrayed as miniature adults in paintings or referred to as "it" by their parents, and that parents freely recycled the names of dead children when new ones arrived. As for the supposed cruelty and indifference of premodern parents, scholars pointed to infanticide, abandonment, wet-nursing, swaddling, and early apprenticeships as illuminating examples, as well as a parental need to dissociate oneself psychologically from newborn children in societies with high infant mortality.

Even at first sight, one need not be a professional historian to see that there is something dodgy about some of these arguments. For example, it seems dubious on principle to draw such direct historical inferences from pictorial art to reality. Just imagine what extravagant theories might be concocted from the work of the Renaissance painter Giotto—who paints humans so large that they do not fit inside their own castles—if we did not have surviving architecture from the fourteenth century! What we are dealing with is no more than a pictorial convention or technique that has, at best, an indirect relation to other aspects of historical reality.[9]

As for the "no concept" argument, even someone who believes (mistakenly) that there can be no nonlinguistic concepts—and therefore no thinking without language, which would mean that human babies cannot think at all until they acquire it—will want to be careful not to equate linguistic concepts with historical realities. After all, this amounts to a full-blown linguistic idealism. It is perfectly possible to recognize that children are different from adults even if one does not have recourse to a fully developed concept of "childhood." Among our fellow primates the chimpanzees, adults routinely adjust their rough-and-tumble games to the needs of infants, even though they have no words for what they do. What is more, is it really convincing to claim that infant mortality must have caused parents to dissociate themselves from their offspring? It seems at least equally plausible to suggest the obverse: that in an environment where children cannot be expected to live beyond the age of one, parents will shower even more attention and love on them because they cannot be taken for granted.[10]

Without questioning that children had often suffered in the past, Pollock challenged these widespread ideas on both theoretical and empirical grounds. What she found in premodern and early modern accounts of children was a marked awareness among parents that their children were special creatures who went through different developmental phases, indulged in play, and needed care and protection as well as guidance and discipline. Nor was there any support in her sources for severe whipping as the usual fare for children. Instead, seventeenth-century parents used various strategies to discipline their children, from physical punishment to remonstrations and simple advice, and many "found it difficult to be as stern as they intended with their offspring" (149).

Pollock was also struck by the depth of paternal affection and involvement in children's upbringing. While women obviously had the main responsibility for the care of young children, she found many examples of men who rose in the night to comfort their sick or frightened children, or helped them through the difficult weaning period. There was "no denying the depth of their involvement with their offspring, the anxiety which the 17th-century fathers felt for their children's future and the amount of pleasure which these fathers derived from their children" (103). Such affections could also turn to unthinkable grief at the death of a child, as in Nehemiah Wallington's moving response to the death of his daughter: "The grief for this child was so great that I did offend God in it; for I broke all my purposes, promises, and covenants with my God, for I was much distracted in my mind, and could not be comforted, although my friends speak so comfortably unto me" (135). It is difficult not to connect this with Polixenes' description of his son in *The Winter's Tale* as "all my exercise, my mirth, my matter."[11]

For Pollock, these results pointed historical research in an important direction· "Instead of trying to explain the supposed changes in the parent-child relationship, historians would do well to ponder just why parental care is a variable so curiously resistant to change" (271). Although her strong views on the historical continuity in parental affections did not meet with immediate approval,[12] historians like Nicholas Orme, Sally Crawford, and Shulamith Shahar have since fleshed out our knowledge further concerning the Middle Ages. They have "gathered copious evidence to show that adults regarded childhood as a distinct phase or phases of life, that parents treated children like children as well as like adults, that they did so with care and sympathy, and that children had cultural activities and possessions of their own. . . . Medieval people, especially (but not only) after the twelfth century, had concepts of what childhood was, and when it began and ended."[13]

Of course, this strong corrective does not preclude more subtle historical changes in the relationship between parents and children. From the evolutionary perspective I have adopted here, we can expect not only strong parental dispositions to love children and cater to their needs, but also flexible responses on the part of parents to changes in the environment. These might include historical changes in emotional standards and child-rearing practices, as well as other social contingencies. The important point is that such historical differences, where they exist, do not lend themselves to extravagant slogans about massive historical change.

What we have arrived at again is the need for a framework that approaches any human emotion—including parental love—from a decisively *interactionist* perspective. The first thing we must do is discard the ingrown tendency to think in terms of mutually exclusive oppositions between nature and nurture, continuity and change: "Properly understood, evolutionary accounts of human behavior are far from deterministic. A Darwinian approach calls attention to the constant interaction between nature and nurture, doing so, moreover, within a developmental framework."[14] Biological predispositions for parental love cannot be instincts in the sense of fixed, hardwired action patterns that operate with little or no concern for environmental contingencies.

We know from other animals how extremely dependent such dispositions can be on social learning and experience, and it would clearly be strange if humans turned out to be less flexible in this respect than monkeys. In Harry Harlow's famous and gruesome experiments in the 1960s, female rhesus macaques that had been isolated at birth became totally incapable of caring for their own offspring. Instead of nurturing their young they became indifferent or even hostile toward them. (It would seem, then, that Lawrence Stone picked the wrong subject for his analysis of parental affections. If we replace "the early modern parent" with "the socially deprived rhesus macaque," then the theory fits the facts quite nicely.) The bright side of the picture is that these monkeys actually became better at nurturing their young the second time around, which demonstrates how later social learning can at least partially overcome poor beginnings for the primate brain.[15]

With this in mind, let us now return to the question of universal parental love with which I began this discussion and break it down into smaller and more manageable questions. For example, is there an evolved panhuman desire to have children, in spite of all demonstrable exceptions to this rule? In principle, there is no evolutionary need for such an imperative since the desire to engage in heterosexual intercourse would have solved the problem for most members of *Homo sapiens*, at least prior to the age of contraception. The famous "biological clock" could just as well be the result of learning (for example, being told that parenthood feels great or is a social duty or having had contact with young children), combined with a unique human self-awareness that one's reproductive years are numbered. It is when humans are actually confronted with a newborn life that requires their nurture and protection that we can expect the most salient evolved dispositions to kick in.

Perhaps unsurprisingly, there are a number of cross-cultural patterns in maternal behavior toward young infants. As Ellen Dissanayake explains, decades of developmental research have shown that mothers across the planet respond to their infants using rhythmic and repetitious vocalizations, facial expressions, and gestures. Adults, and especially mothers, talk to infants in special vocal registers, and the activities of child and parent are synchronized with astounding precision.[16] A wide number of endocrinological studies have also established connections between certain hormones and parental involvement, but the links between hormones, cognition, and behavior are extremely complicated and defy simple characterization in a study of this kind.

In Sarah Hrdy's view, human mothers do appear to have strong evolved dispositions to care for their offspring, but this assertion comes with at least two important qualifications. First, "there is probably no mammal in which maternal commitment does not emerge piecemeal and chronically sensitive to external cues. Nurturing has to be teased out, reinforced, maintained. Nurturing itself needs to be nurtured" (174). Second, it may be difficult for well-fed Westerners to fathom just how harsh life has been for the most part of our history as a species. The result may be a failure in both empathy and understanding when we consider those who live or have lived under vastly different conditions. With greater intelligence and capacities for reflection than other animals comes greater choice, including the horrendous option of giving up on a child in the face of hopeless conditions. Whether we like it or not, this tendency to discriminate flexibly between offspring on the basis of their attributes or environmental factors is something that distinguishes humans from all our primate cousins.

There is a Swedish saying that translates into something like this: "My children, and other people's brats." Since natural selection will favor any behavior that contributes to an individual's inclusive fitness, evolutionary theory predicts that humans will care more readily for their own offspring or close relatives than for other people's children. But as Shakespeare pointed out in *All's Well That Ends Well*, "'Tis often seen / Adoption strives with nature" (1.3.141–42), and the world is full of adoptive parents who are paragons of parental love. So if the predictions of evolutionary theory are correct in this area, one might ask how these people can be so genetically suicidal as to devote all their parenting efforts to biologically unrelated children. Doesn't this question the association of parental love with evolutionary fitness?

According to Sarah Hrdy, the solution to this crux lies in the pragmatic natural engineering that underpins our nurturing impulses:

> In the environments in which most humans evolved, there was no possibility that another woman's baby would *accidentally* be substituted for a woman's own. If a woman adopted an infant to replace her own, chances were that foster-baby would be a relative—far and away the most common circumstance for adoption in both human and nonhuman primate societies. This is why adoption—especially of very young infants, or when the infant is a substitute for her own rather than in addition to it—often works so well and results in relationships between mothers and adopted infants indistinguishable from those of mothers and offspring they gave birth to.[17]

Since there has been no need for evolutionary safeguards in this area (let's say, a genetic radar that would establish the degree of kinship between mother and child) it is instead *early and prolonged intimacy* with the infant that has become the most important elicitor of nurturing behavior. Again a comparison with the animal world may be helpful, since it underscores the importance of such psychological sensitization, even in relatively lowly beasts. A virgin rat (Hrdy calls her "the au pair from hell") who encounters a stray pup will often try to kill it, but given enough exposure to pups, the rat can switch to nurturing them as if they were her own. As with the socially deprived rhesus above, life experience can fundamentally alter the rodent's behavior.

In the case of humans, a long evolutionary process has infused us with a capacity for love that is ultimately and originally in the service of our genetic fitness but is not strictly bound to it. Even though our love is naturally geared toward a genetic nepotism whose excessive expressions every egalitarian society must curb, it also spreads in ways that the blind process of natural selection could not possibly have anticipated.

This interdependence between evolved dispositions for parental love and the need for early quality time also throws light on Montaigne's observation about sixteenth-century wet-nurses, who felt intense affection for infants who were not their own. As a species that is highly dependent on social learning and whose brain restructures itself continually to accommodate new experiences, we are shaped as much by our actions and experiences as by our innate dispositions. (This is especially true of nursing, which triggers an encouraging hormonal cocktail that promotes maternal feelings.)

As her book title suggests, Sarah Hrdy's *Mother Nature* is mainly about the evolution of motherhood rather than fatherhood, and I suspect that some readers will be wondering impatiently what happened to *paternal* love in this discussion. From an evolutionary perspective, this question is complicated by differences in selective pressures between men and women. In the words of Franz de Waal, the active nurturing of offspring has been a consistent scenario for every single female parent during "nearly two hundred million years of mammalian evolution,"[18] while the males of around 95 percent of mammalian species have mostly concerned themselves with other tasks. Among most of our primate relatives, routine male parental involvement in the care of infants is typically rare or nonexistent,[19] and Sarah Hrdy lists three conditions for parental care to be elicited most easily from a male primate:

1. long-standing familiarity with the immature;
2. the nearby infant is urgently in need of rescue; and especially
3. the male has a relationship with the mother.[20]

While human males belong to the small minority that makes substantial contributions to its offspring, we saw in the discussion of parental investment theory that the basic reproductive stakes have still been very different for men (with their minimum contribution of five minutes of fun) than they have been for women (who are looking at a minimum of nine months, and usually much more). Since women have had much less to gain from indiscriminate matings, and their inclusive fitness has been more closely tied to individual offspring, we can expect more powerful selective pressures to have operated in favor of nurturing impulses in women than in men. Concerning item three above, it is interesting that a "pattern of relatively little parental involvement with children after separation from the children's mother" is found in both industrial and preindustrial societies.[21]

More generally, the "cross-cultural pattern of sex differences in parental care is consistent with the view that human parental investment follows the general pattern found in most mammalian species; that is, mothers are relatively more invested, on average, in the well-being and development of their children than fathers are."[22] From an evolutionary perspective, this asymmetry in parental investment may also offer a partial explanation of why men are usually more prone to risk taking, status-seeking, and competition: "Men hold their lives less tightly in their hands because they have been more marginal than women in ensuring the successful survival of their offspring."[23]

It is, however, important to distinguish here between different forms of parental investment: direct parental *care* of children (e.g., nursing, feeding, and comforting them) and more *indirect* investment in the form of acquiring resources. It is not obviously true that a modern, progressive father who stays at home with his kids makes a greater contribution than his grandfather who slaved in the coal mine to support ten children. We must not confuse historical differences in the division of labor with differences in actual investment.

Since the very mention of emotional or cognitive differences between the sexes always causes something of a stir, let me elaborate a little on this subject. I am far from suggesting that there is a direct, linear link between biological differences and childrearing practices. In *Evolution and Literary Theory*, Joseph Carroll argues that "traditional sex roles codified relations that were grounded in antecedent biological and economic conditions."

> Sex roles have now changed primarily because biological and economic conditions have changed [. . . and] the one consideration that is of the most overwhelming importance is that medical knowledge has fundamentally altered the conditions of reproduction. Together with technological advances that reduce labor for the whole population, birth control and increasing life-expectancy have radically changed the proportion of women's lives that is devoted primarily to reproductive activity [24]

From a present-day perspective, there is no denying that those women whose ambitions lie elsewhere than in the cradle have suffered a tremendous injustice in the past and that considerable talents were lost to the world because of unequal arrangements. It would also require substantial analytical acrobatics to deny that women have been, and continue to be, systematically oppressed by men in many parts of the world. Nor would anyone argue that biological or economic conditions have led *directly* to a change in sex roles, since everyone knows that this has been a long and arduous political struggle. But as Carroll argues, an awareness of the dilemmas faced by our ancestors should "prevent us from reconstructing this history too crudely as a simple, melodramatic narrative in which the main characters are female victims, heroic female liberators, and wicked male oppressors. The proportion of historical truth in this commonplace is, I think, something less than half" (362–63).

When it comes to parental instincts, we may well have to tolerate that the average woman will always have an edge on the average man in understanding children's needs and responding to them, especially with small infants. Admittedly, two hundred million years of mammalian evolution is a very long time compared to one hundred years of radical sexual politics. What we must avoid strenuously, on the other hand, is allowing such humbling perceptions to harden into the kind of simplistic and oppressive dichotomies that have characterized so much of human history. Too often, relatively small biological differences have been magnified out of all proportion and then turned into metaphysical and political dogma. Men may well be somewhat less disposed than women to find small babies fascinating, less adept at reading and responding to their signals, and downright useless at breastfeeding, but this is hardly a reason to throw up our hands and return to the olden ways. To my knowledge, there is no genetic safeguard that prevents men from changing diapers or staying home to nurse their young.

Titus Andronicus

"How Roman are the Roman plays of Shakespeare?"[25] That is, to what extent did Shakespeare try to capture a historically authentic Rome? This is a crucial question for anyone who wants to explore these texts with an eye to the interaction between human nature and culture. In *Shakespeare's Rome* (1983), Robert Miola asserts that "the prevailing attitude toward the classics in England was enthusiastically acquisitive and undiscriminating. . . . For Elizabethans, ancient authors provided a treasury of practical information on everything from the raising of bees to the attaining of wisdom." But for Shakespeare this utilitarian impulse appears to have been tempered by a genuine attempt to portray Rome as a distinct culture with its own ideals and practices. In Miola's view, his Roman plays explore "the thematic implications of three Roman ideals: constancy, honor, and *pietas* (the loving respect owed to family, country, and gods)."[26]

Other critics have provided equally valuable perspectives on this subject. A. D. Nuttall stresses that we must not let occasional anachronistic details obscure the knowledge that Shakespeare would have derived from his reading in the classics: "While he will blunder in the physical detail of daily life—that is, over things like clocks and spectacles—when he comes to deal with a Roman suicide, as distinct from an English suicide, he leaves the average modern student light-years behind."[27] Clifford Ronan also reminds us in his excellent study of English Roman plays (1995) that the Renaissance was a period of growing historical awareness that actually invented the term "anachronism." An author like Giraldo Cinthio, whom Shakespeare used as a source for *Othello*, even defended the deliberate use of anachronisms whenever contemporary aesthetic sensibilities required harmonization between the past and the present.[28] Coppélia Kahn sums up the current critical situation admirably: "The question of Shakespeare's 'accuracy' has now been superseded by the question of how his conception of Rome differed from any prevailing notions of it in Tudor-Stuart culture."[29]

The following discussions of *Titus Andronicus* and *Coriolanus* will subsume these insights about Shakespeare's historical awareness and place them on a biocultural foundation. As I hope to show, these plays are as close as Shakespeare ever got to a kind of dramatic anthropology: that is, a systematic exploration of the impact of a specific culture on a central aspect of human nature. What is more, in one of the two plays under consideration here, Shakespeare was not left to his own devices but could lean on another dramatist whose classical learning and knowledge of Roman customs probably outshone his own. A century of painstaking textual scholarship, culminating in Brian Vickers's recent *Shakespeare, Co-Author* (2002),[30] has finally placed George Peele's coauthorship of *Titus Andronicus* beyond reasonable doubt. The first act, peppered with very specific references to Roman customs and traditions, is definitely Peele's creation, and the claim also seems strong for act 2, scene 1, and act 4, scene 1.

We must bear in mind, however, that dual authorship is not synonymous with dual authorial intention. Intention can be shared, and two writers writing individual parts of the same play can be expected to share at least a vague conception not only of the plot but also of its overriding theme. As we will see, there are powerful tensions between Peele's and Shakespeare's sections of the play —not least regarding parental instincts—but we are still dealing with a *single* work written by two collaborators.

Titus Andronicus is without question one of the most curious plays in the Shakespeare canon, and I am tempted to apologize for beginning with such a gruesome piece in a chapter about parental love. Frequently written off as either a Senecan-Ovidian potboiler designed to please the Elizabethan masses or as an illegitimate child in Shakespeare's collected works, it revels in murder, rape, mutilation, and even cannibalism. The violence is so exaggerated and extreme that spectatorial horror easily shades into nervous laughter, and many attempts have been made to make sense of the authorial intentions behind it. Most recently, the discovery of certain subtexts and allusions in the play suggests an intriguing topical commentary on the religious strife in Shakespeare's England.[31] Such aspects need not contradict an active dramatic interest in Rome itself, since a historical play will quite naturally "reflect language, beliefs, and customs not just of the age during which it is set but also of the age when the dramatist and the audience are living."[32]

In the first scene of *Titus*, George Peele establishes the common denominator in the atrocities that he and Shakespeare will portray in their play: that they typically involve a brutal attack on the bond between parent and child. When Titus Andronicus returns victorious to Rome with his Goth captives, he follows Roman custom in ordering a sacrifice. His sons are given permission to take the life of Queen Tamora's eldest son, and having done the deed Lucius returns with a graphic account of his activities:

See, lord and father, how we have performed
Our Roman rites: Alarbus' limbs are lopped

And entrails feed the sacrificing fire,
Whose smoke like incense doth perfume the sky. (1.1.145–48)

The captive Tamora, who has pleaded desperately for her son's life, is present on stage and hears the description of his death. It is not surprising, therefore, that her revenge on Titus in the ensuing acts will be directed principally against his own children.

But in the first scene, this actually appears to be a misguided stratagem since Titus's callous treatment of Alarbus is matched by a remarkable indifference to the survival of his own offspring. It is true that he refers once to his daughter Lavinia as "the cordial of mine age to glad my heart" (169), but we also learn that he has gladly forfeited the lives of more than twenty sons in previous wars against the Goths (1.1.193; cf. 3.1.24). Later in the same scene he even improves on these figures single-handedly by killing his son Mutius in hot blood. The reason is that the latter has stood in his way and defended the clandestine betrothal of his sister Lavinia to Bassianus, which is a major source of embarrassment to their father. Somehow this romantic tryst seems to worry Titus much more than having slain his own son. As Robert Miola puts it succinctly, the "audience must squint especially hard to determine which shape it sees when Titus, his dead son lying on the stage, complains about not being invited to the royal wedding and about his fallen status in the city."[33]

As Brian Boyd has argued recently, this dramatic incoherence may have a simple explanation. It exists because Peele simply inserted the death of Mutius into the first act as a kind of spectacular afterthought, without making sufficient alterations to the surrounding text. He also suggests that Peele made this late addition without notifying Shakespeare, who either wrote his own sections without waiting for Peele or using an earlier draft of the first act. As a result, Boyd finds that the Peelean Titus cannot be reconciled with the compassionate father depicted by Shakespeare. There is "ample justification for critics to treat the play as it appears to have been designed and written by Shakespeare, *without* the killing of Mutius, since such a version of *Titus Andronicus* offers coherence in place of the contradictions of the *textus receptus*."[34]

While Boyd's argument for a willful Peelean "insert" is thought-provoking, I am less inclined than he is to purge poor Mutius from the text as it now stands. Even if Peele did go ahead and insert the passage without consulting Shakespeare, he could still have based this rash decision on a shared understanding of the protagonist. As I hope to demonstrate further on, the Titus depicted in Shakespeare's sections of the play is a more troubling character—and therefore much closer to Peele's version—than Boyd would allow. But let us now look more closely at the unexpurgated Mutius, who dies at the hands of his own father for what appears to be nothing more than a minor offence. What could possibly inspire such callousness in a parent?

A closer look at Peele's language in the first scene gives us an important clue. In its first 482 lines, he uses six variations on the root word "honor"—honor, honors, honorable, honored, dishonor, dishonored—no less than thirty-five times.[35] This means that on average, honor and dishonor are referred to explicitly every thirteen or fourteen lines. Furthermore, there is not a single character in this scene that does not refer to honor at least once, and none of them expresses any doubts about its importance or validity in the manner of, say, Shakespeare's Falstaff. The repetition of "honor" in this scene thus echoes the Elizabethan perception of Rome as a culture where honor was the single most important determinant in human life.

It may be an empirical fact that the use of the word "honor" here is excessive, to say the least, and that the concept it denoted was seen by the Elizabethans as a crucial element in Roman culture. But honor, one might object, was clearly integral to life in early modern England too,[36] and this raises the question of whether the play is really exploring the codes of a different culture. Isn't this rather an example of how Shakespeare holds up his mirror to nature, only to see his own face reflected in it?

A rough frequency analysis of the word "honor" does not show an unusual incidence in either *Titus Andronicus* or *Coriolanus*, considered in their entirety, and Shakespeare's 788 usages of the word are spread out quite evenly across the forty-two works that are usually attributed to him. But in early modern England, there was honor, and then there was honor: the word did not only denote strictly interpersonal or social attributes like social rank, status, esteem, fame, good name, and so forth, but also personality attributes like elevation of mind or virtue.[37] It could be used not only to acknowledge a person's status in society but also to characterize his personality in positive terms, especially among the noble classes that Shakespeare normally portrays in his plays. In *All's Well That Ends Well*, the French King draws precisely this distinction between *social standing* and *personal characteristics* as he attempts to convince Bertram of Helena's individual worth (2.3.126–45).

The same ambiguity does not characterize the word's negation, "dishonor," whose usage was more strictly concerned with a fall from social grace, with all the shame, humiliation, or insults this entailed (regardless of whether the person was "intrinsically" honorable or not). We can thus expect dishonor to be referred to more frequently in plays where the fear of embarrassment is acute. Interestingly, *Titus* and *Coriolanus*, two out of forty-two works attributed at least in part to Shakespeare, account for almost 30 percent of the total usage of this word. In the case of "dishonored" and its variant spelling "dishonor'd," the figures peak even more dramatically. There are twenty-three instances of these words throughout Shakespeare's works, and no less than ten (or 43 percent) of these are to be found in *Titus* and *Coriolanus*. This is, of course, an extremely high figure.

Let us now turn back to the first scene of *Titus Andronicus* and add a final piece to this linguistic puzzle before we evaluate its significance. Brian Boyd, who has noted the preponderance of "honor" in this scene, also demonstrates that the word "Rome" and its variants occur no less than sixty-eight times in 495 lines, "or once every 7 lines." Even "excessive repetition" would thus seem to be a relative term in this first scene! According to Boyd, the "lazy repetition of a few common words the author has retrieved from his workbox" is an unmistakable example of George Peele's "inattention to his own repetitiveness" (301, 302).[38]

But even if it now seems indubitable that George Peele infected *Titus* with his notorious repetitiousness, there is still good reason to regard this remarkable staccato of "Rome" and "honor" as thematically significant. For taken as a whole, *Titus* is not unique among the Roman plays in its excessive reference to *place*: "Loconominative terms, a reflection of setting, appear an amazing 123 times in Shakespeare's *Titus Andronicus*, and in his *Caesar* and *Coriolanus*, a still gigantic 68 and 106 times respectively."[39] What act 1 pounds into the minds of its audience—regardless of who did most of the pounding, and on whose instigation—is not only a horrifying lack of parental concern for children, but also an inextricable connection between "Rome" and "honor." It seems reasonable to assume that these extravagances are causally related: Peele is not repeating any old words, but words that are intimately connected with the play's setting in classical Rome.

At this point it may be tempting to cry "social construction!" and to declare that Shakespeare and Peele are dealing with "culture" rather than "nature" in their play. But this is to fall straight into the kind of false dichotomy that any serious student of human nature and literature must avoid. On the most basic level, all aspects of human experience or behavior are biologically determined, and even the most complex system of belief can ultimately be traced back to—but not reduced to, or predicted from—biological needs and dispositions. On a different analytical level, which necessarily subsumes this basic insight, we can sometimes speak meaningfully of a conflict between nature and culture, or even suggest that a specific social arrangement is "unnatural." What we are really saying is that a particular culture has become so lopsided and extreme that certain rudimentary needs have been elaborated and emphasized at the expense of others. In E. O. Wilson's terminology, they have become subject to *hypertrophy*, which he defines as "the extreme growth of pre-existing structures."[40]

In such a Darwinian account, the traditional opposition between nature and culture does not disappear, but it is reconceptualized so that culture rests on a biological foundation that it can only express or modify selectively (and never escape). What we describe in shorthand as a conflict between nature and culture is really a matter of a cultural emphasis that produces conflicts between different aspects of human nature.

There are probably few human inventions that are totally arbitrary in the sense of having no ground whatsoever in an evolved human nature, and honor (Roman, English, or otherwise) is certainly not one of them. Human ideas about honor arise from a universal need among social animals to regulate the relationship between the individual and the group. Such regulation is equally necessary for both sides, in that it not only ensures group cohesion but also protects the individual from being ostracized or victimized. While most animals handle this problem by means of relatively straightforward impulses, our closest primate relatives even appear to have elementary social rules—or at the very least, ritualized expectations about the behavior of other individuals—the violation of which typically gives rise to considerable in-group hostility.

What *Homo sapiens* adds to this predicament is a unique capacity to imagine ourselves as others see us, coupled with an equally unique ability to codify our experience symbolically and over time in the form of social norms. As Frank Henderson Stewart suggests in his excellent book on the subject, the cross-cultural phenomenon of personal honor is probably best understood as a *right*, or more specifically, "the right to be treated as having a certain worth."[41] In any given society, there will be rules for the allocation as well as the loss of honor, and the content of these rules will naturally shift in accordance with the cultural and social environment. For example, in his study of the concept of honor in English Renaissance literature, C. L. Barber detects a gradual change of emphasis in the seventeenth century from an externalist definition (concerned with reputation) to an internalist definition (based on the intrinsic properties of the person).[42] This is roughly the same distinction I pointed to above, and that Shakespeare brings to the forefront in *All's Well That Ends Well.*

We can also speculate about why the concept of honor has been downplayed so considerably in the modern West compared to other neighboring cultures. One likely reason is that increasingly efficient legal and fiscal institutions have relieved individuals from the need to avenge themselves on others (and also barred them from doing so by means of legislation). Stewart suggests that an increasingly *moral* conception of honor may also have paved the way for this development: "Once the shift is made from basing honor on a certain kind of behavior . . . or on the possession of certain external qualities . . . then the way is open for the whole notion of honor to be undermined."[43] But the disappearance of a clearly identifiable *code* of honor—where an honorable man is one who does A and B but does not engage in X, Y, and Z—is not synonymous with the disappearance of honor itself. There have so far been few reports about human cultures that have no concept of honor or personal integrity whatsoever, or where the majority of people could not care less what other people think of them. What we are looking at in *Titus Andronicus*, therefore, is not an arbitrary social construction but a hypertrophic and destructive variant on a human universal.

At the end of act 1, Titus has not only lost favor with the newly elected Emperor Saturninus; he has only four children left, and Tamora will see it as her task in the following act to decimate his kin even further. Following the advice of Tamora's clandestine lover, Aaron, her sons Chiron and Demetrius first kill Lavinia's husband Bassianus. Lavinia is then raped and mutilated so that she will not be able to tell her father what has happened. Through Aaron's careful machinations, two of Titus's remaining sons, Quintus and Martius, are charged with the murder of Bassianus and sentenced to death.

The indifference that Titus has so far exhibited toward the health of his children is not matched by the Goths, however evil they may be in other respects. When Tamora goads her sons to kill Bassianus she invokes the bond between parent and child, and Demetrius responds dutifully:

> Revenge it as you love your mother's life,
> Or be ye not henceforth called my children.
> DEMETRIUS: This is a witness I am thy son. [*Stabs him.*] (2.2.114–16)

When they turn their attention to the helpless and desperate Lavinia, the latter has only one chance: she must untangle their close-knit familial tie. She first turns to Demetrius and argues that the tyrannous wrath he feels has been inculcated in him by his mother. It is not his own; it has been taught to him; he has quite literally sucked it from his mother's breast (143–44). To try to please his mother is therefore as backward as if the "tiger's young ones [should] teach the dam" (142). What is more, there is no natural reason why he must obey Tamora since "every mother breeds not sons alike" (146). When Demetrius perversely interprets the last assertion as an accusation of bastardy, Lavinia turns to Chiron with another argument taken from nature. She gives examples of animals that forego their normal habits of violence or indifference to take pity on offspring other than theirs, sometimes even at the expense of their own kin (149–54). Why cannot Chiron do the same?

It is probably not a coincidence that Lavinia takes her examples from nature rather than from human customs, or that Shakespeare does so frequently in other works. As Keith Thomas points out in *Man and the Natural World*, humans have always turned to nature in search of categories by which we might describe ourselves. In early modern England, where animal fables and other observations were readily employed as instructive mirror images of human society, such arguments probably had a stronger normative force than they do today. One of Shakespeare's contemporaries, the Elizabethan preacher Thomas Wilcox, even declared that animals had been created by God to serve as moral examples, so "that even in them we might be provoked to virtue and deterred from vice."[44] Earlier in *Titus*

Andronicus, when Marcus and one of his nephews implore Titus to let them bury Mutius in the family tomb, they "naturalize" their kinship with Titus in order to deepen its normative weight:

> MARCUS: Brother, for in that name doth nature plead—
> 2 SON: Father, and in that name doth nature speak— (1.1.375–76)

What is interesting about Lavinia's supplication, by contrast, is that it turns to nature not for *confirmation* of the familial bond but for its *dissolution*. Nature, in other words, has other normative functions in this play than only to instill a proper respect for one's kin, just as Elizabethan attitudes toward the natural world were both complex and variable. Lavinia's plea gives us a more complicated angle on the natural bond between parents and children since it suggests that virtue may well consist in the rejection of this relation. Couched in terms of Roman *pietas*, her entreaty shows how loving respect for family and nation may not always be compatible with respect for the gods.

As the violence directed at the younger generation continues in the second act, we are thus treated to new and increasingly diversified perspectives on the parent-child relation. But in the following act, when Shakespeare has clearly taken over the pen, the treatment of the parental bond enters a distinctly new phase—one of affirmation—that continues for almost the entire rest of the play. The beginning of act 3 finds Titus in Tamora's earlier position as he pleads movingly to the tribunes for the lives of the two sons who have been sentenced to death. At first sight, this might seem to bear out the historicist analysis of early modern parental affections as a kind of "zero-sum game" where love was portioned out differentially depending on the amount of offspring and the likelihood of their survival. Since Titus now only has three sons left, we might expect the loss of another two to be much more upsetting. But his own analysis of the profound change that is taking place inside him does not accord with such a view:

> For two-and-twenty sons I never wept,
> Because they died in honour's lofty bed.
> > [ANDRONICUS *lieth down, and the judges pass by him.*]
> For these two, tribunes, in the dust I write
> My heart's deep languor and my soul's sad tears.
> Let my tears staunch the earth's dry appetite;
> My sons' sweet blood will make it shame and blush. (3.1.10–15)

The ideal of honor, which was repeated so obsessively by Peele in the first scene of the play, has enabled Shakespeare's Titus to cope with the loss of twenty-two sons because it made their deaths *meaningful*. Now, when there is no ideal to which he can cling but only meaningless savagery and death, he also encounters his mutilated and ravished daughter for the first time. He immediately renounces the remaining fractions of the duty that has so far guided his life: "Give me a sword, I'll chop off my hands too, / For they have fought for Rome, and all in vain" (3.1.73–75). He then gives in to a self-pity so intense that he only gradually awakens to his daughter's agony and seeks to ameliorate her suffering: "Gentle Lavinia, let me kiss thy lips / Or make some sign how I may do thee ease" (121–22).

In most Shakespeare plays, this is about as bad as it gets. But Titus has not even had time to dry his tears when his parental affections are given another jolt by Aaron's grotesque ultimatum: if you love your sons, you will ransom them by sending the Emperor a severed hand (3.1.151–57). This is, of course, a perverse parental love test: How far-reaching is your love for your children? What costs to the self are you prepared to incur to save them? What follows is an extended and almost farcical deliberation among Titus, Marcus, and Lucius about who should do the honors:

> LUCIUS: Sweet father, if I shall be thought thy son,
>   Let me redeem my brothers both from death.
> MARCUS: And for our father's sake and mother's care,
>   Now let me show a brother's love to thee. (180–83)

Titus finally severs his own hand, only to see it returned together with the severed heads of his two sons. So much for parental love and good intentions.

As often in Shakespeare, suffering is a great teacher for Titus. Now that he has hit rock bottom, the cultural ideals he has lived by start to disintegrate and give way to parental impulses that they had previously quelled. In the following scene (3.2), which was only printed in the Folio version, this pattern culminates in what can only be described as a complete volte-face with respect to the first act. The increasingly distracted Titus and his remaining family have gathered for a meal when Marcus, to his brother's surprise, stabs his own dinner plate:

> What dost thou strike at, Marcus, with thy knife?
> MARCUS: At that which I have killed, my lord—a fly.
> TITUS: Out on thee, murderer. Thou kill'st my heart.
>   Mine eyes are cloyed with view of tyranny;
>   A deed of death done on the innocent
>   Becomes not Titus' brother. Get thee gone;
>   I see thou art not for my company.
> MARCUS: Alas, my lord, I have but killed a fly.
> TITUS: "But"?
>   *How if that fly had a father and a mother?*

How would he hang his slender gilded wings
And buzz lamenting doings in the air.
Poor harmless fly,
That with his pretty buzzing melody
Came here to make us merry, and thou hast killed him. (3.2.52–66;
italics mine)

It is difficult to imagine a more far-reaching personality change than this: a fear-less martial hero who has previously sacrificed and even killed his own children without remorse and who now objects even to the killing of a fly because he imag-ines it has parents. Perhaps the passage is best thought of as a somewhat cruder prototype for *Lear*, in that suffering and madness enables the tragic protagonist to reach deep into himself and expose what he previously deemed important as shal-low fabrications. At such a tragic nadir, which never quite becomes tragic in this curious play, cultural ideals and beliefs are peeled off like a thin veneer and give way to a deeper humanity.

It is only when Marcus rescues the situation by suggesting that the fly looked like Aaron the Moor that his brother's aggression is rekindled in the name of re-venge: another universal impulse built into human nature, in spite of considerable cultural variation in its form and expression.[45] At first sight, it may look as if one human instinct is ousting another. But given the function of revenge as the up-holder of personal honor and integrity, we are really witnessing the unification of the two contradictory impulses—honor worship and love of kin—that have so far proven irreconcilable for Shakespeare's main protagonist. In seeking to avenge the lives of his loved ones and to defend his own reputation and integrity, Titus is finally at one with himself; beyond qualms, doubts, and second thoughts.

Interestingly, Titus is not the only character who travels the road from cal-lousness to parental concern when Shakespeare takes over from Peele. The new perspective we get on Aaron the Moor in act 4, scene 2, is perhaps even more remarkable since he is one of those extravagant Shakespearean villains who take delight in making other people suffer.[46] As Aaron puts it unrepentantly toward the end of the play: "Even now I curse the day—and yet I think / Few come within the compass of my curse— / Wherein I did not some notorious ill" (5.1.125–27). In act 4, it turns out that his frolicking with Queen Tamora has resulted in an illegiti-mate child whose skin color will be difficult to explain to her husband Saturnine. Tamora and her sons are of one mind—the baby must be put to death before the scandal is unravelled—but Aaron is not easily persuaded:

Stay, murderous villains, will you kill your brother?
Now, by the burning tapers of the sky
That shone so brightly when this boy was got,

He dies upon my scimitar's sharp point
That touches this, my first-born son and heir. (4.2.90–94)

When Chiron and Demetrius object that this amounts to a betrayal of his noble mistress, Aaron's response is telling: "My mistress is my mistress, this myself, / The vigour and the picture of my youth. / This before all the world do I prefer" (4.2.109–10). Such a stance is in keeping with broad evolutionary predictions, for when push comes to shove we would expect most parents to be more deeply devoted to their children than to their mates—unless they have a long reproductive career ahead of them. But this is no more than a broad generalization, and it does not even do justice to the scene we are exploring. For why does Tamora, who seems to have a strong emotional bond to her sons, choose to sacrifice her child in this way?

As I suggested in the introduction, it is a mistake to suppose that any theory of human nature can ever be more than a reference point in the study of literary texts. To apply evolutionary principles directly to literary texts will often prove either uninteresting or reductive, and usually both. But if we do want to make sense of this difference between Aaron and Tamora, then the most likely solution lies in the different environmental pressures they are facing. Unlike Aaron, who is a mere dependent in her household, Tamora is a queen who has everything to lose from the discovery of her adultery. As the Nurse points out immediately (116), the saturnine emperor is likely to put Tamora to death for this infringement, and he will hardly relish the new addition to his household. Tamora has, in other words, put herself in one of the most terrible dilemmas that parents have faced throughout our history as a species: that it can be necessary to give up on one's child in the face of impossible odds.

Aaron's ingenious remedy for this crisis raises new questions about parental love in this play. He proposes to deliver the infant to one of his countrymen whose wife has just given birth to a baby with a fair complexion. The idea is to bring some gold and propose an exchange where "their child shall be advanced / And be received for the emperor's heir, / And substituted in the place of mine" (4.2.157–61). Since Aaron's embassy is intercepted by Lucius, we never find out whether this stratagem would have been successful, but it nevertheless invites reflection. Does he expect these parents to simply sell their child in exchange for gold? Or does he project his own parental feelings and expect them to give up their child for *its* sake, since becoming the emperor's son means enjoying a life that they themselves can only dream of? In short, does he expect egotism or a considerable emotional sacrifice on their part? There is no way to resolve this ambiguity except by vague inferences, and the question must therefore remain open.

When it comes to the strength of Aaron's own parental feelings, however, there can be no doubt about their depth and authenticity. When he and the infant boy are captured by Lucius in act 5, Aaron appears to have no concern whatsoever for his own safety as long as the boy survives. He promises to confess everything—which, of course, will bring down a death sentence or something even worse on his own head—as long as Lucius promises to look after his son. It is telling that it takes no less than thirty-three lines for Lucius to convince Aaron that his word is good and that the boy will survive (5.1.53–86).

It is, I think, profoundly moving that a man who has delighted in other people's misfortunes and identified himself so closely with his capacity for evil should feel such deep concern for his child. Human sympathy is always most touching where it is least to be expected, and Aaron's newfound parental impulse also fits in nicely with the larger thematic development we have been exploring. The first scene of the play has treated us to a massive onslaught on the parent-child bond, where the natural impulse to nurture one's children proves quite defenseless against the cultural ideal of honor. Such cultural dominance does appear to have its limits, however, for when Shakespeare takes over the pen from Peele he treats us to a fairly consistent reaffirmation of the parental bond. A man who has not shed a single tear at the deaths of more than twenty children suddenly complains about the killing of a fly because it might have parents. Another who has prided himself on being totally evil now sacrifices his own life in order to save his infant son.

It might be tempting to conclude at this point that Shakespeare's sections of the play simply give us a universalist counterpoint or riposte to Peele's cultural constructivism regarding parental affections. But true to the essential strangeness of this play, Shakespeare's fifth act brings yet another reversal as the play returns to its filicidal ways—and with a vengeance.

I will spare the reader the most gruesome details of the play's denouement and relate them in selective shorthand: having put Chiron and Demetrius to death, Titus feeds them to their mother in a pie and then kills his own daughter because she must not outlive the shame produced by her rape. Significantly, Titus first addresses the emperor—who is unaware of what has happened to the veiled Lavinia—with what appears to be an abstract moral question based on the legend of Philomel:

> My lord the emperor, resolve me this:
> Was it well done of rash Virginius
> To slay his own daughter with his own right hand,
> Because she was enforced, stained and deflowered?
> SATURNINUS: It was, Andronicus.
> TITUS: Your reason, mighty lord?
> SATURNINUS: Because the girl should not survive her shame,
> And by her presence still renew his sorrows. (5.3.35–41)

Saturninus may be a somewhat unlikely source of moral guidance, but Titus is looking for some sort of cultural or legal sanction for his deed: is it *right* for me to kill my own child because she has been dishonored? By formulating this question without reference to his own situation, he is more likely to receive an impartial answer that grounds itself in the larger scheme of things, in regulative social principles rather than in empathy with the suffering individual. The emperor has given him precisely what he was looking for:

> TITUS: A reason mighty, strong, and effectual;
>   A pattern, precedent, and lively warrant
>   For me, most wretched, to perform the like.
>   [*Unveils* LAVINIA.]
>   Die, die, Lavinia, and thy shame with thee,
>   And with thy shame thy father's sorrow die.
>   [*He kills her.*] (42–46)

With this grotesque execution of his only daughter, the recently unified Titus collapses as a person. Honor and nurturing impulses once again prove incompatible for him, and his response is to immediately swerve back to the callous honor worship that dominated the first act. Once again, parental love proves highly vulnerable when pitted against the shaming force of custom. What is particularly remarkable here is that Shakespeare almost surgically removes the possibility for his audience to exonerate Titus by defining the murder as an act of mercy. As we have seen, both Saturninus and Titus understand the killing of a ravished child as a legitimate attempt to end one's own grief, and after the deed Titus even professes to have "killed her for whom my tears have made me blind" (48). This can be read as a remarkable and horrifying self-recognition: he has not killed his own daughter out of sympathy with her distress but because her shame is so painful to him that he can no longer allow himself to feel for her.

If the play had ended here, its treatment of parental love would have come full circle: from oppressive honor worship to renewed parental instincts and unification of self, and then back again. Apparently, Shakespeare could not resist giving his parental pendulum one last swing with the appearance of Titus's only surviving son and his grandchild. Even in death, the Titus we had just diagnosed as a culturally determined filicide—a patriarch who quite deliberately exchanged his daughter's life for some peace of mind—is transformed once more into an affectionate being:

> LUCIUS [*to his son*]: Come hither, boy, come, come and learn of us
>   To melt in showers. Thy grandsire loved thee well:
>   Many a time he danced thee on his knee,

> Sung thee asleep, his loving breast thy pillow;
> Many a story hath he told to thee,
> And bid thee bear his pretty tales in mind
> And talk of them when he was dead and gone.
> MARCUS: How many thousand times hath these poor lips,
> When they were living, warmed themselves on thine! (159–67)

This is a beautifully crafted passage where the unassuming details of everyday life combine simplicity with depth of feeling. It is also a fitting conclusion to a play that has moved rapidly between two extremes: just when we think that honor will conquer all we are treated to an equally radical assertion of parental love, and vice versa. As in Montaigne, parental love appears to be an easily bastardized universal instinct, but it may not be a coincidence that Shakespeare finally comes down on the side of flesh and blood.

Parental love and personal honor may be universal impulses, but the contradiction that Shakespeare and Peele stage in *Titus Andronicus* goes right to the heart of a distinctive Roman *pietas*. How can I love my country and my children when love of the former requires me to sacrifice the latter? What is presented in this play is not a mirror image of sixteenth-century England, but an exotic and unsettling example of cultural hypertrophy: how biologically grounded ideals that would have been instantly recognizable to early modern Englishmen are taken to devastating, even horrifying lengths. In *Coriolanus*, which was probably written some fifteen years after *Titus*, Shakespeare returned to this Roman predicament from a slightly different perspective.

Coriolanus

Written around 1608, Shakespeare's *Coriolanus* tells the story of the military superhero Caius Martius—dubbed "Coriolanus" after his victory against the Volscians at Corioles—whose excessive individualism, pride, and contempt for the masses leads to his rejection as consul and banishment from Rome. Devastated by this humiliation, Coriolanus sides with his former enemies and marches on his native city to exact bloody revenge, but he finally wavers at the gates of Rome. As a result, he is branded a traitor and put to death by his new allies.

This political tragedy is Shakespeare's only portrayal of "an open class struggle for control of the state,"[47] and more than one critic has seen intriguing connections between the uprising in the opening scene and the English corn riots of 1607.[48] Robin Headlam Wells has also linked the main protagonist suggestively to Prince Henry of Wales, the figurehead of English militant Protestantism.[49] Such historical allusions certainly enrich our understanding of the play and may even give us some clues about Shakespeare's ulterior motives in writing it. But they can also be taken too far, so that the play is turned into a sociopolitical allegory wherein Romans are reduced to thinly disguised versions of early modern Englishmen. In my view, the appropriate term for the relation between England and Rome in *Coriolanus* is *analogy* and not *allegory*.

In *Coriolanus*, I will argue, the mature Shakespeare returns one last time to Rome and fleshes out its conflict between parental love and honor worship in two important ways. First, he grounds the clash between instincts and injunctions in the unique life history of an individual, thus adding another important factor in the making of a human being. Secondly, his treatment of honor becomes more focused and precise as he dissects one of its component parts: the classical ideal of *constancy* that was enjoying a powerful revival in early modern Europe. As a consequence of these developments, what we term *innate* and *acquired*, *natural* and *cultural*, become even more tightly interwoven.

Like *Titus Andronicus*, this play is centered on a family where one parent is dead or at least missing. Such broken families "are for Shakespeare typically charged with the most electric emotions,"[50] and we will find yet another example when we turn to *King Lear*. What makes *Coriolanus* a special case among these plays, and perhaps a more intensive psychological study than the other two, is that there is only one child in the family. While Titus has spawned no less than twenty-five sons and scattered most of them across the battlefield, Coriolanus's mother Volumnia has been "fond of no other brood" (5.3.164) and entertains a more convoluted relation to her only son.

As Coppélia Kahn observes, Shakespeare "follows Plutarch in leaving the father's place vacant, but enlarges the mother's role considerably to make her pertinent at every moment to the tragic action."[51] Barred of any real access to official power, Volumnia invests all her hopes and ambitions in her son's career, and this Roman obsession with martial honor runs so deep that it has the paradoxical effect of nullifying her concern for his safety. In a remarkable and chilling passage she explains to her daughter-in-law Virgilia—who is worried that her husband might not return safely from the war—how she went about raising her son. When Caius was "but tender-bodied" and "a mother should not sell him an hour from her beholding" she

> was pleased to let him seek danger where he was like to find fame. To a cruel war I sent him, from whence he returned, his brows bound with oak. I tell thee, daughter, I sprang not more in joy at first hearing he was a man-child, than now in first seeing he had proved himself a man.
> VIRGILIA: But had he died in the business, madam, how then?
> VOLUMNIA: Then his good report would have been my son, I therein would have found issue.

She concludes with an assertion that cannot fail to remind us of *Titus Andronicus* in its almost total— and unnervingly quantitative—renunciation of nurture in the Roman quest for martial honor: "Hear me profess sincerely: had I a dozen sons, each in my love alike, and none less dear than thine and my good Martius, I had rather had eleven die nobly for their country, than one voluptuously surfeit out of action" (1.3.11–25). When Virgilia expresses her fears that her husband might return bloody from the battlefield, Volumnia states bluntly that the "breasts of Hecuba / When she did suckle Hector, look'd not lovelier / Than Hector's forehead when it spit forth blood / At Grecian sword contemning" (1.3.41–44). Since her son's wounds are effective advertisements of his military service to Rome —and thus pave the way for his becoming consul—Volumnia even rejoices perversely in his physical damage. "Oh, he is wounded; I thank the gods for't . . . there will be large cicatrices to show the people when he shall stand for his place" (2.1.120, 146–48).

In her study of fathers and daughters in Shakespeare (1986), Diane Dreher argues that possessive fathers are "by far the most common" in his plays. They are typically "egocentric, perceiving their daughters as parts of themselves, projections of their own animas."[52] Titus is an obvious candidate here, but Volumnia's attitude toward her son raises the question of whether we are really dealing with a gendered trait, or with a more general tendency among Shakespeare's parents. Given the logic of evolutionary fitness, we can expect strong dispositions in women as well as men toward seeing their children as parts of themselves, and it may not always be easy to isolate that precise point where a mother's concern for her children gives way to personal wish fulfillment. This is Volumnia's telling response to her son's latest triumph:

VOLUMNIA: I have liv'd
    To see inherited my very wishes,
    And the buildings of my fancy: only
    There's one thing wanting, which I doubt not but
    Our Rome will cast upon thee. (2.1.198–202)

In other words, this Shakespearean mother seems just as egocentric and possessively projective as any father. The complicating factor is that Shakespeare does not describe Volumnia as a typical woman, but as an Amazon who loves nothing more than battles and blood. When accused of behaving like a man rather than a woman, she retorts boldly: "Ay, fool; is that a shame? . . . Was not a man my father?" (4.2.16–18). As Margaret Bryan points out, this is a major modification of Shakespeare's source character in Plutarch, and a complete inversion of the ideal Renaissance housewife.[53]

Few readers and spectators fail to notice that Volumnia exerts a tremendous influence over her son: "Guided by her desire for honor she dominates Coriolanus by his desire for honor."[54] As early as the first scene, a citizen sneers that Caius Martius is less interested in serving his country than in pleasing his mother (1.1.35–39). Whenever Volumnia wants to manipulate or dominate her son, she resorts to the rhetorical tactic of disowning him emotionally, saying either that he is not her son or that he is not like her (3.2.129–32, 5.3.177–80, 5.3.158–69). As several commentators have noted, this fearless warrior has never quite shaken off his identity as a small boy, and he even dies protesting against this epithet when it is hurled at him by Aufidius in the final scene.

A. D. Nuttall sees the relationship between Coriolanus and Volumnia as an example of "the wholly remarkable sense Shakespeare displays of the possible formative tyranny of the parent" which is "astonishing in a pre-Freudian writer."[55] This miraculous preemptiveness on the part of Shakespeare can perhaps be overstated, since pre-Freudian societies would hardly have expended so much energy on teaching and disciplining their young if it did not have any perceptible effect. But there can be no doubt about the psychological incisiveness with which Shakespeare presents this claustrophobic relationship between an autocratic parent and a child who was never allowed to grow up.

As an outgrowth of psychoanalysis that places formative childhood experience on an evolutionary foundation, attachment theory certainly posits that early infancy can have profound, if not irreversible, effects on personality. How much influence parents typically have over their children as they grow older depends on so many factors that it defies even the most basic overview. It is, however, becoming clear to modern investigators in various fields that our upbringing is far from everything: partly since many personality traits have a strong heritable component, and partly since social factors other than upbringing (such as peer groups) may have strong effects on personality.[56]

In one account, which is fully in keeping with the predictions of parental investment theory, the family functions like an ecological system where children "cultivate distinct niches" for themselves.[57] What we find in Shakespeare's play, by contrast, is a family without niches, where one parent appears to have had complete power over a single child. Volumnia has sculpted Coriolanus into the figurine she wanted, and she remains the overarching presence in his life even after he has married. As she puts it herself, there is "no man in the world / More bound to's mother" (5.4.160–61). As a consequence, this angry, sulking hero "has no inside. All he has was given him by his mother and confirmed in him in the physical stress of battle."[58]

Consequently, there is both irony and pathos in Coriolanus's objection when Volumnia expects him to kneel before the crowds in the marketplace so that they will accept him as consul.

> I muse my mother
> Does not approve me further, who was wont

> To call them woollen vassals, things created
> To buy and sell with groats. . . Why did you wish me milder?
>   Would you have me
> False to my nature? (3.2.7–8, 14–15)

In response, Volumnia takes credit for her son's valor but acknowledges nothing else: "Do as thou list. / Thy valiantness was mine, thou suck'st it from me, / But owe thy pride thyself" (3.2.128–30). This is an argument that really ought to be unsuccessful, since her son has just outlined her own attitudes toward the citizens, but Coriolanus will rather yield than endure more remonstrations from his primary caretaker: "Pray be content. / Mother, I am going to the market-place: / Chide me no more" (130–32).

Like many other Shakespearean characters (or real human beings for that matter), Coriolanus is a paradox in human clothing. Just as he combines the roles of magnificent warrior and small boy, this deep dependence on his mother's approval coexists with a profound incapacity to acknowledge *need* of any kind, including his obvious need of his mother's approval. One of those horribly needful things he cannot stand is simple praise. When Volumnia revels in his exploits on the battlefield, he mutters, "My mother, / Who has a charter to extol her blood, / When she does praise me, grieves me" (1.9.13–15). The same thing happens when the crowds greet him after the triumph at Corioles: "No more of this; it does offend my heart. / Pray now, no more" (2.1.168–69). And when Cominius begins to celebrate his martial exploits so that the Roman leaders can mete out a rightful reward, he becomes very uncomfortable and leaves the room (2.2). As we have seen, he also refuses to humble himself before the citizens of Rome, whose approval is required if he is to become consul.

There are two kinds of people who cannot stand praise—those who are very modest, and those who are very proud—and Shakespeare leaves us no doubt about what category Coriolanus belongs to. He cannot express need because that would make him less than self-sufficient, but the problem is that the individual honor he seeks is dependent on the perceptions of other people. "The dilemma, of seeking independence in something which depends on others, is the dilemma of honor itself."[59] Once again we are reminded of the fundamental conflict involved in being an individual organism and a social animal at the same time. It is impossible to deduce from the play just how old the "tender-bodied" Coriolanus was when his mother first decided that danger was a better nurse than security or affection, but we know at least from Menenius that "he has been bred i'th' wars / Since a could draw a sword" (3.1.319–20). From the perspective of attachment theory, at any rate, an insecure early infancy will typically result in an "ambivalent" or even "avoidant" personality, afraid to acknowledge need or dependence.

It is frequently argued that the main theme of *Coriolanus* is that of an uncompromising individualism. Richard Ide defines the main protagonist in terms of a "titanic individualism," and Thomas McFarland even suggests that the play dem-onstrates "Shakespeare's wizard grasp of the depth of the eternal struggle between individual and society. Coriolanus is a play about that struggle; it is about noth-ing else."[60] It is certainly true that this conflict is a central issue in the play, and it is also endemic to all social mammals. But we must not forget that such conflict is naturally intertwined with a need for community, sharing, and belonging. As McFarland puts it himself, Coriolanus's attempt to become fully independent of his society "makes his nobility seem instead a kind of stupidity" (131). Or in the words of Richard Ide, the problem with Coriolanus's "titanic individualism" is that "no matter the distance he puts between himself and society by his peculiar kind of negative definition, he still remains dependent on it for his heroic identity. Shake-speare is at pains to make this clear."[61] Since Coriolanus's banishment from Rome is the consequence of a failure to adjust his own behavior to the expectations of the group—something all humans must do—it would be just as true to say that this play is about our eternal need for group conformity (which may not sound quite as sexy to modern Westerners).

The most fundamental reason why a rampant individualism creates anxi-eties, then, is not that it contradicts the teachings of Marx. It is rather that ostra-cism from the group has been a disastrous—and often fatal—event for most of our evolutionary history. Just as the Empedoclean cosmology that informs Shake-speare's works explains the world in terms of two opposing forces, Love and Strife, a modern Darwinian perspective sees the life of any social animal (including hu-mans) as a balancing act between conflict and cooperation. In this context it is interesting to note that Shakespeare not only presents his supreme individualist as larger than life but even as larger than *nature*. When Coriolanus marches on Rome with his new allies, the Volsces, Cominius admits that he "leads them like a thing / Made by some other deity than nature, / That shapes men better" (4.6.91–93). And as we shall see shortly, Coriolanus's individualistic quest for social transcendence finally culminates in an explicit attempt to renounce his natural "instincts"—or more specifically the very parental impulses that have so far been given almost as short shrift as in *Titus Andronicus*.

Before we are ready to explore this development in Shakespeare's play, how-ever, we must first examine the main protagonist's proud individualism from yet another perspective. Richard Ide sees Coriolanus as a remarkably static character who "undergoes no essential change" and "moves through the plot rather than with it."[62] If this is a complaint about incomplete characterization, I think it misses Shakespeare's point, at least as far as it can be deduced from the play. *Coriolanus* is *about* an unchanging man. It is about the price paid by someone who only wor-ships his own integrity and will not let his surroundings affect him. Some readers and theatergoers may well admire a character with total integrity who does not stoop to the demands of other people, and such tragic identification is, of course, one of Shakespeare's literary objectives. But he also reminds us that a person of this kind will most likely become very lonely.

More specifically, it can be argued that Shakespeare shrewdly puts his finger on how the ideal of constancy—which enjoyed a powerful vogue in his time through the Neostoicism of Justus Lipsius—can shade into individualistic pride. It is yet another instance of a specific Roman ideal that was readily intelligible to many early modern Englishmen. That Shakespeare must have intended Coriolanus to be a singularly unchanging man receives support from perceptions by other characters in the play. We saw earlier that Coriolanus reacts against the changing directives from his mother by protesting his constancy "Would you have me / False to my nature?" (3.2.14–15). Toward the end of the play, in a scene we will soon examine more closely, Aufidius is impressed by Coriolanus's capacity to keep his word at the expense of his emotions: "You keep a constant temper" (5.2.93). In the previous act, the same Aufidius has reacted to his excessive pride with the following observation: "Yet his nature / In that's no changeling, and I must excuse / What cannot be amended" (4.7.10–12). We find a similar element of exoneration in the first scene when the Second Citizen defends Coriolanus: "What he cannot help in his nature, you / account a vice in him" (1.1.40–41).

While many Shakespearean villains like to declare that "they are not what they are," the message that emerges from this tragic protagonist is something like this: *I am what I am, and I cannot be otherwise.* This dramatic stance is, of course, the literary equivalent of a tower of playing cards. When Coriolanus finally *does change his ways,* as we will see shortly, it is because his desire for integrity or constancy gives way to stronger impulses that transcend the immediate interests of the honorable self. As in *Titus Andronicus,* Shakespeare paints a vivid example of how hypertrophic honor worship can undermine a parent's concern for his or her offspring— provided that these pressures are accepted as meaningful by the individual. At the moment of deepest crisis, such heartlessness gives way to a powerful vindication of parental love because one Stoic ideal (constancy) has proved irreconcilable with, and ultimately powerless against, another (*sequere naturam,* follow nature).

In the last act, Coriolanus has reached the gates of Rome with his Volscian army and is about to destroy his native city. That his own mother, wife, and son will probably perish in the process seems of less concern to him than the imminent restoration of his Roman honor. When the consul Cominius returns from a fruitless embassy that has convinced him of Coriolanus's steely resolve, it is decided that the next ambassador will be Menenius, the former general who entertains a special relationship to Coriolanus. His love for the younger man is everywhere apparent in the play, and it is also couched significantly in terms of "father" and "son." That Shakespeare has added this "quasi-paternal relationship" to the story he took from Plutarch[63] gives us further evidence about his interest in family dynamics, and about the care with which he elaborates his Roman theme of honor versus familial love: "The glorious gods sit in hourly synod about thy particular prosperity, and love thee no worse than thy old father Menenius does! O my son, my son, thou art preparing fire for us: look thee, here's water to quench it" (5.2.68–72). We know from an earlier passage that Coriolanus has called Menenius "father" (5.1.3) at some point in his life, but the exact nature of their relationship is rendered enigmatic by Shakespeare. We can only speculate that Menenius, who is a general, may have served as a father surrogate in the army for the emotionally crippled young man. But now, when Coriolanus brushes off the desperate old man like so much dandruff from his shoulder, his refusal is clearly a deliberate act of exclusion: "Wife, mother, child, I know not. My affairs / Are servanted to others" (5.2.81–82). There is no mention of fathers, either biological or otherwise. When Menenius has left, Coriolanus acknowledges the love between them to Aufidius but still distinguishes himself from its paternal implications:

> This last old man,
> Whom with a crack'd heart I have sent to Rome,
> Lov'd me above the measure of a father,
> Nay, godded me indeed (5.3.8–10)

As Aufidius realizes, Coriolanus has made up his mind to "keep a constant temper" (92) that does not stoop to such sentimental concerns.

After this harrowing encounter, Coriolanus decides that he will admit no more embassies from Rome. But in an almost inescapable instance of stage irony he is immediately confronted with a new embassy, this time from his own flesh and blood, as Volumnia, Virgilia, Valeria, and his little son arrive in the Volscian camp. This dramatic juxtaposition between quasi-paternal relations and genuine biological kinship returns us to the opposition between individualism and the demands of nature, and this time with a vengeance. What emerges in this passage is a sharp conflict between the ideal of constancy and a natural disposition to love one's kin:

> My wife comes foremost; then the honour'd mould
> Wherein this trunk was fram'd, and in her hand
> The grandchild to her blood. But out, affection!
> All bond and privilege of nature break!
> Let it be virtuous to be obstinate.
> What is that curtsy worth? or those doves' eyes,
> Which can make gods forsworn? I melt, and am not
> Of stronger earth than others. My mother bows,
> As if Olympus to a molehill should
> In supplication nod; and my young boy
> Hath an aspect of intercession which

Great nature cries, "Deny not." Let the Volsces
Plough Rome and harrow Italy; I'll never
Be such a gosling to obey instinct, but stand
As if a man were author of himself
And knew no other kin. (5.3.22–37)

Since Coriolanus has just rejected his honorary "father" Menenius in a brutal manner—"Away!" (5.2.79)—it is difficult to avoid the impression that blood is still somewhat thicker than water. Confronted with his own flesh and blood, he now finds himself in a painful tug-of-war between natural kinship and a hardened individualism that, as I have remarked already, is inextricably intertwined with the ideal of constancy.

After a long plea from his mother, Coriolanus finally gives up and renounces his campaign against Rome. It is significant that Volumnia ends her speech with an argument that goes to the roots of her son's nurturing impulses:

Nay, behold's,
This boy that cannot tell what he would have,
But kneels, and holds up hands for fellowship,
Does reason our petition with more strength
Than thou hast to deny't. Come, let us go:
This fellow had a Volscian to his mother;
His wife is in Corioles, and his child
Like him by chance. (175–82)

When Coriolanus gives up, the impression that "great nature" has finally triumphed over cultural extremism is given further support by Aufidius's remark that Coriolanus has set "his mercy and [his] honour / At difference" (5.3.204–5). In this subtle aside, Shakespeare crystallizes the opposition we have traced between natural love and Roman honor. A previous line also clarifies the connection between honor worship and the distinctly masculine values that have been Coriolanus's only fare since childhood: "Not of a woman's tenderness to be, / Requires nor child nor woman's face to see" (5.3.130–31). This gives us some idea of how much he has had to repress in order to qualify as a real man.

Coriolanus's insight that babies and women are dangerous for military superheroes is more than a matter of constricting gender roles, for it brings us back to Volumnia's recognition that words, arguments, or remonstrations are ultimately weak instruments in the elicitation of nurturing behavior. After all, it was possible for Coriolanus to sacrifice his family as long as he did not *see* them: "To see sad sights moves more than hear them told" (*The Rape of Lucrece*, 1324). This is an example of how context-dependent human empathy can be, since it is triggered more easily by concrete situations than by abstract reasoning about moral principles. As Anthony O'Hear puts it, "There may be something inherently utopian, and in the real world even tragic about our moral sense. It is practicable and workable and fully motivating only within limited environments, particular communities, and well-understood circumstances."[64]

So far I have argued that the reunion of Coriolanus with his family vindicates a repressed aspect of human nature. But what does this mean exactly? This is a complicated question, not least because Shakespeare suggested in another play that culture is ultimately subsumed by nature and cannot be simply opposed to it. On the other hand, I have also suggested that it can be meaningful to speak of an opposition between nature and culture provided that we define the statement more closely. We saw that Titus was seized by powerful parental feelings when the cultural ideals that had guided his life suddenly lost their meaning. This spoke strongly for the emergence of impulses that could no longer be suppressed in honor's name. But we also saw that the concept of honor is far from an arbitrary cultural invention since it responds to fundamental human needs. In other words, one aspect of human nature—the need to regulate the relation between individual and group—had been exaggerated by Titus's culture to the point where it became hypertrophic and dysfunctional. The conflict between nature and culture in *Titus* is best understood as a culturally inspired conflict between different aspects of human nature.

As we have seen, Shakespeare gives us good reason to perceive a similar conflict between nature and culture when Coriolanus is reunited with his family. He refuses to be a gosling and follow instinct; his encounter with his biological kin is juxtaposed tellingly with his rejection of Menenius; and he describes his inner conflict as a battle against "great nature." It is not misguided to suggest, therefore, that Coriolanus finally surrenders to natural impulses that can no longer be quelled. In *The Winter's Tale*, where another powerful male refuses to acknowledge his kinship with his child, Paulina draws the following conclusion:

> We do not know
> How he may soften at the sight o'th' child:
> The silence often of pure innocence
> Persuades, when speaking fails. (*The Winter's Tale*, 2.2.39–42)

As we saw earlier in this chapter, the biological salience of this scene—a helpless child in distress—is such that even the males of nonhuman primate species are prone to step in and rescue infants for whom they would normally display minimal interest.

This is not to say, however, that Coriolanus's volte-face can be understood as a straightforward triumph of nature over culture (not even in the qualified sense discussed above). As some critics have suggested, it could also be argued that Coriolanus really only continues to do what he is told by his mother, who once again resorts to emotional blackmail and pushes every guilt button she can find:

> Thou hast never in thy life
> Show'd thy mother any courtesy,
> When she, poor hen, fond of no second brood,
> Has cluck'd thee to the wars, and safely home,
> Loaden with honour. (5.3.162–66)

We have seen that unlike the sweeping dramatic panorama of *Titus Andronicus*, with its central conflict between parental love and honor, *Coriolanus* also gives us detailed insights into the environmental conditions that have contributed to making the protagonist who he is. Shakespeare leaves us little doubt that Coriolanus has been raised in a claustrophobic domestic ecology, a family without niches, where he was fully exposed to the demands of a parent who systematically chiseled him into an instrument for her own agenda. Volumnia, in turn, is presented by Shakespeare as the embodiment of larger cultural norms such as the Roman obsession with martial honor.

Coriolanus's change of heart becomes even less opposed to culture when we consider his first response to Volumnia in the Volscian camp: "My mother bows, / As if Olympus to a molehill should / In supplication nod" (29–31). In his view, the idea of a mother who bows to her son is simply *unnatural*. The following exchange is also accompanied by a considerable amount of kneeling, as both son and mother engage in what they consider to be unseemly behavior:

> Sink, my knee, i'th'earth: [*Kneels.*]
> Of thy deep duty more impression show
> Than that of common sons.
> VOLUMNIA: Oh, stand up bless'd!
> Whilst, with no softer cushion than the flint,
> I kneel before thee, and unproperly
> Show duty as mistaken all this while
> Between the child and parent. [*Kneels.*]
> CORIOLANUS: What's this?
> Your knees to me? to your corrected son? (50–57)

As we all know, kneeling is not a hardwired action pattern that rises from the depths of the human genome. If there were a strong genetic disposition for this behavior we could rather be expected to show our backsides to each other, as other primates do whenever they wish to subordinate themselves (the action is called "presenting"). Even if human kneeling performs a similar function in that the kneeling person places himself in a vulnerable position and thus acknowledges his inferiority and dependence, we are obviously dealing with cultural symbolism rather than instinctive behavior. My simple point is that the vindication of parental love in *Coriolanus* is never purely "natural" in the sense of being unfettered by cultural assumptions about what is right and true. On the contrary, it is replete with normative ideas about the proper nature of familial relations; ideas that we will explore more closely from the child's perspective in the next chapter. The word "duty," which is used twice in the passage above, will be of great importance in the next chapter when we consider filial love in *King Lear*.

When Coriolanus finally refuses to attack his native city, he knows that this amounts to a death sentence from his new allies who will not take treason lightly. It can perhaps be debated whether this acceptance really constitutes a major change of orientation, since Coriolanus is used to risking his life in the battlefield. The difference is, however, that his former actions have been geared to an individualistic honor worship that accepted risk in exchange for personal glory, and such an explanation no longer applies here. What Shakespeare presents us with is a former individualist who now consciously decides to save his family at the expense of his own life, belying Montaigne's assumption that the reproductive instinct is second to the somatic.

This raises an intriguing final question that was only touched on earlier when we considered Aaron the Moor: under what circumstances can we expect these nurturing impulses to become so strong that someone will die for his family? I would like to end this reading by using this question to briefly consider the limitations (and not just the strengths) of evolutionary explanation. After all, a theoretical perspective that fails to consider or recognize its own limitations is seldom worth the paper it is written on.

When the famous evolutionist J. B. Haldane was asked whether he would lay down his life for his brother, he responded jokingly that he would do so for two brothers or eight cousins. He was referring to the evolutionary logic of *inclusive fitness* that predicts altruistic behavior whenever the benefits to genetic kin exceed the costs to the self. Since the fitness benefits in Haldane's example were equally balanced, he was really being quite generous with his brothers and cousins. Sarah Hrdy's analysis of human motherhood—which, you may recall, does not regard it as entirely unconditional—reaches similar conclusions about maternal self-sacrifice:

At issue is not whether some mothers value the survival of one of their offspring more than their own lives. The question is whether such mothers evolve as species-typical universals of the female sex. The answer is yes, but under narrowly defined circumstances. Typically, self-sacrificing mothers are found in highly inbred groups, or when mothers are near the end of their reproductive careers. The forty-one-year-old mother who gives her life for her only child is not the same individual who decades earlier might well have aborted her first.[65]

Like Haldane's flippant remark, this argument supposes that there is a deeper logic at work in our response to such difficult dilemmas, and that this logic can ultimately be understood in terms of inclusive fitness.

These are thought-provoking perspectives on parental self-sacrifice, but it would be unwise to transpose them directly onto Shakespeare's play. The most obvious problem is that they are predictions about tendencies across populations, and not about individual behavior. If we cannot suppose that they will work on a real-life individual, then we cannot expect them to explain a literary character either. More important, the theory of inclusive fitness is silent on the manifold cultural meanings and beliefs—a developed, impersonal sense of justice, the idea of an afterlife with attendant rewards, and so forth—that can inspire human self-sacrifice, irrespective of biological kinship or close social affiliation.[66]

In the two Roman tragedies I have explored, Shakespeare suggests how powerful and dangerous this human capacity to structure natural needs into norms can be, since it even comes close to extinguishing such a central aspect of human nature as parental love. The complexity of the Shakespearean parental instinct—pushed to the brink of extinction by extreme circumstances, but also strong enough to reassert itself in the most unlikely places—bears out the Baconian insistence with which I began this chapter: that "Nature is Often Hidden; Sometimes Overcome; Seldome Extinguished."

3

Filial Love in King Lear

Virtually every biological system featuring important contact between close genetic relatives surely contains a shifting equilibrium between the incentives for selfishness and those for altruism. As ecological and social conditions change over time, the balance point—or balance zone, in fact, since it will usually span a range of values—moves toward greater or lesser co-operation among kin.

Douglas Mock and Geoffrey Parker, *The Evolution of Sibling Rivalry*, 411

In act 4, scene 2 of *King Lear*, Albany turns to his wife Goneril and attributes her evil actions to a particular form of denial:

> QI fear your disposition;
> That nature which contemns its origin
> Cannot be bordered certain in itself.
> She that herself will sliver and disbranch
> From her material sap perforce must wither,
> And come to deadly use. (4.2.32–37)[1]

What Albany expresses here has always been an important principle in human self-knowledge, from traditional myths of creation to modern historical scholarship. Knowing where we come from can tell us important things about who we are, and ignorance or disdain for our origins can even be dangerous. Today, some four hundred years after Shakespeare wrote these lines, we can add what neither Albany nor his famous author could possibly have known: that the tree of life from which Goneril seeks to extricate herself is the result of a natural process of selection that has been at work for billions of years. From the majestic perspective of evolutionary time, mankind is not even a branch on this single tree, but a newly sprouted twig that may one day give rise to new and unanticipated life forms. And while contemporary disdain may not come to "deadly use," as Albany puts it, this book rests on the conviction that students of human nature who "contemn their origin" come perilously close to willful blindness.

88

Of course, what Albany criticizes in Shakespeare's play is something more specific than a general denial of our origins. He is expressing outrage at Goneril's heartless treatment of her father, the old king, who has been stripped of his followers and sent packing into the storm after providing her with half of his kingdom. How, Albany wonders in chorus with the other elderly in this play, can a child be so monstrous that she denies the natural bond between parent and child? Is such love nothing else than a shallow convention that is thrown off as soon as it is deemed expedient? Or are Goneril and Regan freaks of nature, the unfortunate exceptions to a natural law that prescribes love and respect for one's parents? As their father puts it in one of his darkest moments: "Is there any cause in nature that make these hard hearts?" (3.6.75-76).

This chapter will approach Shakespeare's most magnificent tragedy with the guiding assumption that filial love is neither natural nor conventional, as long as these terms are seen as mutually exclusive. Human beings are naturally disposed to love others, but we also have to learn to love, and in the case of filial love this means (among other things) enjoying prolonged contact with at least one loving and nurturing caretaker. Unfortunately, even the most luminous childhood is no guarantee. No matter how much love parents shower on their children, there is also good reason to believe that filial love will always have a somewhat weaker foundation than its parental counterpart. For those parents who are in some way dependent on their grown-up children, this is not exactly good news, and it is not surprising that most cultures have turned filial love into a societal norm (with varying degrees of formality and success).

In *King Lear*, Shakespeare stages an early modern version of this anxiety: an exploration of the complex and conflicted relation between love and duty. My approach to this literary theme will be to disentangle a biocultural nexus of interacting factors such as: (1) the evolutionary phenomena of parent-offspring conflict and sibling rivalry; (2) a series of culturally and historically specific ambiguities concerning the meaning of the word "love" and the nature and extent of children's duties toward their parents; and last, but not least, (3) a collision between the biologically determined reality of a deteriorating regal brain and a sociocultural organization that invests the same brain with absolute power. Like the previous chapter, this one will begin with a theoretical discussion of the overriding topic and set some literary parameters for the ensuing argument.

Filial Love

Is it a coincidence that the Bible contains a commandment to honor thy father and mother, but not a commandment to care for thy offspring? Or did this injunction arise precisely because filial love is a more tenuous affair that sometimes requires active cultural intervention? To some, the question may seem almost rhetorical in nature, while others will be considerably less certain. Since this study assumes that we cannot understand love if we do not understand the nature of the lover, the best way to approach this question is to place ourselves in the position of the child.

In *Culture and Human Nature*, Melford Spiro identifies the following universal properties of childhood:

> Because of prolonged helplessness, requiring dependency on others for the satisfaction of their survival needs, children are everywhere raised in family or family-like groups whose members, to a greater or lesser extent, provide them with nurturance, gratification, and protection. As a result, children everywhere have the following characteristics: the need to receive love from, and the motivation to express love for, the loving and loved objects; feelings of rivalry toward those who seek love from the same (scarce) love objects; hostility toward those who would deprive them of these objects; and so on.[2]

It goes without saying that helplessness in itself cannot generate such a broad and universal emotional repertoire. There has to be something inside the child that regulates its basic needs and allows it to signal them to the caretaker. Consequently, children are not born as the blank slates posited by behaviorism or as the symbiotic mother-appendages of traditional psychoanalytic theory: "Far from being passive recipients, responding only reflexively to stimuli—as was once thought—babies come into the world actively ready to communicate their needs, feelings, and motives to other persons, as well as ready for sympathetic engagement of vocal, facial, and gestural expressions."[3] From the first moments of their lives and for years to come, children's most fundamental objective will be to ensure their own survival and development by attracting parental investment in the form of attention, food, and love. As we saw briefly in the previous chapter, attachment theorists have uncovered important homologies in the behavior of human and other primate infants, for instance in the response to separation from the primary caretaker. In fact, human and chimpanzee infants even share that most formidable of extortionist tools, the temper tantrum.[4]

As everyone knows, having needs and desires is one thing, and gratification is another. There is virtually no end to the nurturing and attention that a child can attempt to elicit, but all parents and other caretakers have limited time, energy, and resources. This leads us directly to the biological phenomenon of "parent-offspring conflict." Parents are torn not only between their own somatic and reproductive efforts (if you give your children all the food you can find, then you will die of starvation and take your children with you) but also between the conflicting desires of individual offspring. This means that parent-offspring conflict finds yet another biological corollary in "sibling rivalry," which denotes "any features of animals or plants that have the effect of promoting individual survival and/or reproduction at the expense of siblings (current and future)."[5]

Some species solve this problem quite callously—if that is the right word for such unthinking behavior—by always feeding the mouth that is closest at hand and letting the brood sort out the rest for themselves, or even by having one sibling push the other from the nest. Humans, with their superior intelligence and complex emotional dispositions, have a much wider range of options and dilemmas. Even a brief look at the history of parental investment uncovers a plethora of reproductive strategies, from discriminatory approaches like sex-based infanticide and primogeniture to principles about uncompromising equity.

The inescapable conflict with parents and siblings over attention and resources is not simply negative from the child's point of view. By negotiating and inevitably frustrating needs that will always exceed what can be reasonably offered, parents help socialize their children. In all likelihood, having to weigh your own interests and needs against those of others at an early age is an important factor in the development of empathy.

Since we are dealing with a universal and biologically rooted dilemma, we can expect historical differences in this area to be no more—and no less—than variations on a larger theme. Even if the majority of Shakespeare's contemporaries took a more positive view of "hierarchy" and "obedience" than most people do today, we saw in chapter 2 that early modern parents were not necessarily despots intent on breaking their children's wills. Literary critics who focus only on, say, domestic manuals written by religious moralists are likely to give a distorted picture of parental attitudes and activities in this period.

In *Some Thoughts Concerning Education* (1693), John Locke observed that the struggle between parents and children is both natural and necessary. Almost as soon as they are born, children want to have their own way and to dominate others, and it is a parent's responsibility to subdue this tendency without damaging the child. For Locke, "the true secret of education" is to maintain a child's free and active spirit while also instilling restraints and a willingness to submit to parental authority. Too much curbing and breaking of children's wills leaves them even worse off than those whose inclinations are not bridled at all, but allowing children "unrestrained self-assertion" is also a big mistake. With some irritation, Locke observes that certain parents (remember, we are talking about late seventeenth-century parents here) seem totally incapable of restraining their children. These brats "must not be crossed, forsooth; they must be permitted to have their Wills in all things; . . . The Fondling must be taught to strike, and call Names; must have what he Cries for, and do what he pleases. Thus Parents, by humoring and cockering them when *little*, corrupt the Principles of Nature in their Children."[6] Caring for your children is thus a natural dilemma that involves striking a subtle balance between their short-term and long-term interests.

Of course, it is not only children who have needs. Since parents all over the world invest so much of themselves and their resources in their offspring it is only natural—even for those who fully embrace the ideal of unconditional love—to worry a little about the returns. In the essay on parental affection that I discussed at the beginning of the previous chapter, Montaigne suggests that the depth of parental love is not matched by children's love for their parents: "It is no wonder if back-againe it is not so great from children unto fathers. This other Aristotelian consideration remembred: That hee who doth benefit another, loveth him better than he is beloved of him againe: And hee to whom a debt is owing, loveth better, than hee that oweth."[7] As Jon Elster has pointed out, the idea that people can even feel hatred for their benefactors is a frequent theme in writers like Montaigne and La Rochefoucauld. He also advances two potential explanations depending on the nature of the relationship: among equals it creates an obligation that constrains the recipient's freedom, and in a hierarchical relationship it increases the inequality between the two.[8]

When it comes to the specifics of the parent-child relation, however, the most natural explanation for such affective asymmetries comes again from evolutionary theory. Since a parent's inclusive fitness is so obviously dependent on the continued well-being of the child, even long after the child has grown up, it is only to be expected that most parents should be disposed to feel stronger love for their children than vice versa once the latter have outgrown their most pressing dependence. When you think about it, parental love, especially in its modern guise, actually has something tragic about it. While the life expectancy of most of our early ancestors probably did not extend far beyond the maturity of their children, modern parents often live on for thirty or forty years after their children have left home (which, in an era of unprecedented geographical mobility, can mean moving to the other side of the planet). Many pick up new hobbies and return to their previous somatic indulgences. But with the insight that you love your children far more than they can ever love you, that you are ultimately dispensable, and that life will inevitably go on without you, comes the first intimation of death. As Cordelia says to Lear: when I take a husband, he will carry away half my love.

In *The Passions of the Mind in General* (1604), Thomas Wright understood his own love for his parents as a strictly natural phenomenon: "I loved my parents as authors of my being and imparters of life, and this without teacher by nature was I instructed."[9] But like any other emotion, a child's love for the parent is naturally inflected by specific circumstances. In many ecological and economic situations, such as subsistence level or politically unstable societies, parents need to bind their children closely to themselves as a means of life insurance, while modern welfare states have disconnected children from some of their responsibilities toward their ageing parents. In all cultures, people also translate or transform fundamental biological problems into normative assumptions about rights, duties, and metaphysical moral distinctions. Early modern England was certainly no exception to this rule, as can be gleaned from these paradoxical lines in Burton's *Anatomy of Melancholy:*

> Nature bindes all creatures to love their young ones; an henne to preserve her brood will runne upon a lion, an hinde will fight with a Bull, a Sowe with a Beare, a silly sheep with a Fox. So the same nature urgeth a man to love his Parents . . . and this love cannot be disolved, as *Tully* holds, *without detestable offence:* but much more God's commandement, which injoynes a filiall love and an obedience in this kinde.[10]

In typical seventeenth-century terms, Burton conjoins a descriptive fact with a normative rule, a feeling with a behavior, and therefore ends up with a love that is both unshakeable and subject to detestable infringements.

As Alan MacFarlane observes in one of the best histories of English family life to date, English thinking about children's duties toward their parents was indeed ambiguous throughout the early modern period:

> Throughout the period from Chaucer to Malthus there was a central ambiguity, a certain anxiety and uneasiness, a lack of a clear and obvious set of duties and responsibilities in relation to the old. Two contrary messages were being transmitted: that the primary responsibility of individuals was to themselves, their wives and children, but at the same time they somehow also had a responsibility toward their parents. This latter duty was ultimately optional: just as parents had the right to disinherit their children, so, reciprocally, children had the right to "disinherit" their parents.[11]

It is not surprising, therefore, that some contemporary writers warned parents who had sufficient funds to make arrangements to avoid ending up at the mercy of their children in old age. In some cases, written contracts were even produced that stipulated the rights of elderly parents with respect to the family hearth, although these were rare in England compared to Scandinavia and other parts of Europe. This situation does not necessarily reflect poorly on filial love itself in this period but rather attests to a conflict between different sets of duties: "It was not merely that the children were undutiful, but—more fundamentally—that their duty was not, ultimately, to their parents. They were to forsake mother and father and cleave to their wives. If they had children their responsibility was more to their children than to their parents."[12] In MacFarlane's view, the gradual transition toward capitalism in English society did have its effects on how the bond between parents and children was conceptualized. Ever since the fourteenth century, the nuclear family had been the central economic as well as reproductive unit in England. Together with a relatively low degree of social mobility, this meant that what we have termed "somatic" and "reproductive" activities were more closely connected. Investing in children was also investing in oneself. As he puts it, "Part of the transformation brought by capitalism is to make children seem a problem, a burden, a cost. As children pick up the message, they reciprocally turn their old people into burdens, problems and costs" (74–75).

For an age that thought so readily in terms of analogies and correspondences, and where the family was typically conceived as a "little commonwealth" upon which all else rested, there were certainly connections to be made between dissolving family ties and feudal ideals, on the one hand, and an increasing individualism and social mobility on the other. As John Donne put it so famously (and conservatively) in *An Anatomy of the World*, "'Tis all in pieces, all coherence gone; / All just supply, and all relation: / Prince, subject; father, son, are things forgot."[13] Closely connected with these anxieties about the rights and duties of children and their parents was what Keith Thomas calls "the gerontocratic ideal." As he puts it, the sixteenth and seventeenth centuries are "conspicuous for a sustained desire to subordinate persons in their teens and twenties and to delay their equal participation in the adult world. . . . [S]uch devices were also a response to the mounting burden of population on an inflexible economy."[14]

Once more the biological concepts of parental investment and parent-offspring conflict allow us to broaden these historical perspectives and to moderate their specificity. First of all, there have been very few parents in human history whose personal interests have always coincided entirely with their children's, and anything a parent does to ensure the survival of offspring always happens at the expense of other options. We may not want to see it that way, but loving and nurturing another person restricts our freedom and incurs considerable costs to the self. What was different prior to the modern age was the degree of concrete *returns* for parental investment.

Similarly, the early modern idea that children's responsibilities toward themselves and their offspring trumped their filial duties was not merely the result of cultural standards or biblical injunctions, but probably mirrored a universal moral dilemma for human beings. As for the gerontological ideal, finally, it is best understood as a response to deeper regularities in human experience that had become exacerbated mainly by contemporary demographics. In all primate species there comes a time when a previously dominant generation must yield to younger strengths, and this rarely happens without conflict. Humans are no different. In periods of intense social change, demographic imbalances, or in deeply individualist societies, we can expect such conflicts to become intensified as an older generation senses the impatient breath of a younger generation on the nape of its neck.

How to Divide a Kingdom

To argue that the domestic anxieties I have discussed are in some way relevant to Shakespeare's *King Lear* should not require special pleading. In the first act Lear announces that his plan for the division of the kingdom is designed to prevent "future strife" (43) among his children and their spouses. This statement is worth mulling over from a biocultural point of view. At the most basic and universal level, Lear is seeking to mitigate the effects of parent-offspring conflict and so prevent an attendant sibling rivalry. But no conflict in the history of mankind has ever been determined by biological dispositions alone; we also need an environment where evolved needs are calibrated by specific ecological conditions, generating particular desires and expectations that are then either gratified or slighted.

The pagan world in *Lear* has one central characteristic in common with Shakespeare's England: it is a society that has passed through the agricultural revolution and developed into a kingdom where wealth is tied to land. This makes it possible for individual families or clans to amass considerable wealth and pass it along as inheritance, thus leading to unprecedented social stratification of the kind that Shakespeare exposes so mercilessly through the voice of his repentant king. *Lear* is a tale about individuals on the top rung of this social ladder, whose parent-offspring conflicts and sibling rivalries take on extraordinary political consequences since so much is at stake. Their battles will be fought, not with kitchen utensils, but with entire armies. The characters move against the backdrop of a universal predicament that has been intensified substantially by a specific sociocultural arrangement.

This is not to say, however, that Shakespeare's play mirrors this larger sociocultural context in a straightforward fashion: as we shall see, it is quite unusual. When Kent and Gloucester discuss Lear's impending abdication in the opening lines of the play, they describe it in the same terms as the king himself. The original plan for the division of the kingdom—whose exact nature is never disclosed—is perceived as an act of prudence where the king has set aside his own nepotistic affections:

> KENT: I thought the King had more affected the Duke of Albany than
>   Cornwall.
> GLOUCESTER: It did always seem so to us: but now, in the division of the
>   kingdom, it appears not which of the dukes he values most. (1.1.1–5)

It is not entirely clear—either in this exchange or in Lear's own statement above—whether the underlying motive is a desire for justice or just political expediency, but the division is still noteworthy on biocultural grounds. As Thomas McFarland

observes, Lear violates "the accumulated wisdom of Elizabethan statecraft"—
whatever you do, don't divide your kingdom!—expressed in such authoritative texts as
Thomas Elyot's *The Governour* and King James's *Basilikon Doron*.[15] More specifically,
he departs from the principle of primogeniture that was standard practice among
the European nobility.

To hand over practically everything to the firstborn son may strike us moderns as a deeply unjust system, but that does not make it arbitrary:

> From a Darwinian point of view, primogeniture (along with sex-based in-
> heritance) is a strategy for long-term lineal success in a saturated agrarian
> habitat. According to the theory of inclusive fitness, wealthy parents ought
> to invest more heavily in their male offspring. There are fewer physiologi-
> cal limitations on a male's capacity to sire offspring, and wealth can mag-
> nify this capacity far beyond that attained by a female. If a wife dies in
> childbirth, a wealthy male is likely to remarry. . . . Whenever wealth is tied
> to land, parents will tend to adopt primogeniture to avoid diminishing the
> family's socioeconomic status.
>
> In non-elite families, sons are at a disadvantage compared with daugh-
> ters. Landless sons cannot compete successfully against wealthy sons, but a
> sister can marry upward in social station. Under these circumstances, par-
> ents ought to invest in daughters, using dowries to improve their daughters
> social status.[16]

What this means is that Lear, who has three daughters and no sons, not only
rejects the cultural principle of primogeniture but also adopts elements of a "non-
elite" inheritance strategy even though he is the supreme ruler of his country.
Although we cannot be sure about the nature of Cordelia's portion—she is, after
all, not mentioned by Kent and Gloucester—the original division of the kingdom
betrays a sense of fairness rather than cultural conformity.

The greatest hermeneutical problem with the first act is that Lear's original
plan and the disastrous love test that follows hard on it cannot be reconciled easily. As many critics have pointed out, it makes little practical sense for Lear to set
up a competition among his daughters when the individual prizes have already
been decided on. This would suggest that the love test either replaces the original
plan (as I shall argue) or is only a ruse or entertainment without practical consequences. But even if we should grant either of these interpretations, the logic
behind the love test—that is, its method and objective—is still diametrically opposed to that of the original plan. Where the original scheme *subordinates love* to
other concerns in an attempt to *prevent rivalry* among the next generation, the love
test does the exact opposite: it turns Lear's children into bitter rivals for their
father's munificence and measures them *only* by their capacity for love.

How do we tackle this curious situation? We can define Lear's behavior as simply contradictory and leave it at that, or we can attempt to reconcile its diametrically opposed perspectives on love and rivalry. To pursue the latter approach, as I will, quite naturally involves a close consideration of Lear's motivation in the first act, and our first step must be to clear away some widespread but unfounded assumptions about the old king.

King Lear has been a frequent target for critical moralism ever since the eighteenth century, when Samuel Johnson complained about its lack of poetic justice. In its most recent guise, the moralistic view hones in on the ideological or political credentials of Shakespeare's play and seeks to assess whether it can be considered "progressive" or "reactionary" by either modern or early modern standards. Such readings are often distinguished by what Graham Bradshaw terms "the fear of being taken in"—that is, the idea that tragic identification, empathy, or involvement can be detrimental to the critic's political agenda.[17]

For instance, when Lear enters with his dead daughter in his arms, Kathleen McLuskie comments that "even the most stony-hearted feminist could not withhold her pity even though it is called forth at the expense of her resistance to the patriarchal relations which it endorses."[18] The underlying assumption seems to be that one would normally be disposed to avoid being moved by Lear's agony since he is a patriarchal figure that deserves no sympathy. As fellow feminist Lynda Boose observes, McLuskie operates with a sharp "linguistic opposition between feminism and pleasure,"[19] but I would add that this is only the extreme version of a more widespread tendency. For most ideological critics who have shelved their "literary" prefix and started reading "texts," it makes little difference if we are reading a newspaper, a political pamphlet, or a Renaissance drama, since all of these are doing some sort of "ideological work" that can be subjected to a moral-political critique.

A more fruitful and instructive alternative, in my view, is to read *King Lear* the way it was intended: as a literary tragedy that invites empathetic identification. Since empathy is a question of intellectual and emotional *understanding* rather than acceptance or justification, it is perfectly possible to feel deeply for someone even though we disapprove of his or her actions. My reading of the play will also support W. F. Blissett's strict Aristotelian definition of Lear's hamartia as an "initial error or erroneous self-commitment" rather than a "'tragic flaw,' with all its penumbra of tedious moralization about how characters in tragedy should have conducted themselves so as, presumably, to have lived harmlessly and forever."[20]

Apart from general indictments on the systemic or thematic level, the critical canon also contains widespread denunciations on the level of character and plot. As a male patriarchal parent, Lear must somehow be to blame not only for his own behavior, but also for that of his callous daughters: "How did [Goneril] get that way?—a question leading directly to Lear. For isn't her defensiveness ultimately the mirror and consequence of his? It must be an index to his *habitual*, not merely his *recent*, behavior, an index to a chronic rather than a critical problem of relationship."[21]

What is at issue here is not whether Lear is flawed—I would agree that he is, like many literary characters and most real human beings—but whether he is also responsible for his children's flaws. In *Coriolanus*, we saw some reason to draw such conclusions since Volumnia more or less catalogues her own contributions to her son's personality. The fact that *Lear*, by contrast, contains almost no references to events prior to the first scene makes such an indictment a case of almost pure theoretical inference—and questionable theory at that. In Shakespeare's time, few people believed that parents were always responsible for the sins of their children, and in the last couple of decades we have also come a long way from the kind of social determinist psychology that, for example, attributed mental disorders like schizophrenia straightforwardly to maternal neglect. If it could be established clearly that the sins of the children are really the sins of the fathers, then our prison facilities would probably look very different than they do today: there would, quite simply, be more parents and grandparents in them.

The second idea that must be questioned here is one of the strangest, and yet most widespread, critical inferences about Shakespeare's play: that Lear entertains some sort of incestuous relationship to one or more of his daughters.[22] This reading has a pedigree that is almost as old as the Freudian tradition, and it also appears to have gained in popularity since the publication of Jane Smiley's *A Thousand Acres* (1992).[23] This novel builds on Shakespeare's story but replaces its pagan king with a Midwestern farmer who abuses two of his daughters sexually.

To argue against the incest reading of *Lear* is not to assume that Shakespeare could not possibly have construed the relationship between Lear and his daughters in such a lurid way. Everyone who has read *Pericles* knows that its plot revolves around an incestuous relationship, and it could even be argued that there are some vaguely incestuous double entendres when Volumnia talks about her son in *Coriolanus* (e.g., 5.3.123–25). By contrast, the free-floating inventiveness with which critics have uncovered supposedly incestuous subtexts in *King Lear* has really been quite remarkable. For instance, there is a memorable moment in the play when Lear wants someone to "anatomize Regan; see what breeds about her heart. Is there any cause in nature that make these hard hearts?" (3.6.74–76). This is how Richard McCabe understands these lines in his study of incest in English Renaissance and Restoration drama: "One way or another he will be intimate with his daughters."[24]

I want to stress that McCabe's book has many merits and that I have learned a great deal from it. But his interpretation of Lear's musings illustrates what is perhaps the greatest problem with incest readings of the play: the vagueness of the central concept, and the resultant tendency to see incest (whatever this means) everywhere. When Diane Dreher argues that "Lear's intense love for Cordelia reflects all the symptoms of pseudo incest"[25] the reader waits in vain for a clarification of what "pseudo incest" is and what its "symptoms" might be. Other writers solve this problem ingeniously by writing, not about incest, but about *latent* incest, which makes the claim entirely unfalsifiable. As an instance of that most pernicious contribution of psychoanalytic theory to literary study—what I call *the argument from absence*, where the absence of something becomes an argument for its presence in repressed form—the claim for "latent incest" cannot be either supported or questioned on the basis of what Shakespeare actually wrote.[26]

Without entering into the contemporary debate about incest, the ruggedness that surrounds this subject in literary studies—and the apparent ease with which it is diagnosed—clearly stems from the Freudian heritage that still looms so large in our discipline. After all, it was Freud who suggested memorably that "anyone who is to be really free and happy in love must have surmounted his respect for women and have come to terms with the idea of incest with his mother or sister."[27] As I suggested in chapter 1, attachment theory and its subsequent developments offer a more useful framework for understanding human relationships because they accept the connection between childhood and adult experience without equating sexuality and attachment.

It is a central contention in this study that we should always be wary of the tendency to subjugate text to theory. Since it is a work of fiction, *King Lear* cannot be expected to comply dutifully with any conception of human nature. But whenever a play has been subjected to systematic theoretical distortions of the kind I have discussed here, a better theory is often needed to put things in perspective. When Cordelia says to her father that her husband "shall carry / Half my love with him" (1.1.101–2), she is not proposing a threesome, nor is she deflecting unwanted stares from her father. *King Lear* is about love, not about incest, and we are now ready to delve deeper into its heart. Our passage must be carved painstakingly through the main protagonist.

The Childish King

Of all the moralistic charges that have been hurled at Shakespeare's main protagonist—that Lear is guilty of incest, misogyny, patriarchal values, and so forth—there is one that probably holds the key to the tragedy he sets in motion. I am thinking of his "childishness," which is a useful term, provided that we soften its derogatory moralism and increase its precision. In the early nineteenth century, A. W. Schlegel pointed to the King's "childish imbecility,"[28] and Diane Dreher summarizes the modern version of this complaint: "Psychologist-critics have noted Lear's infantilism, which leads him to make impossible demands of his daughters. They have pointed out that at 'fourscore and upward' he 'remains a great baby . . . a ranting, towering, very dangerous baby.'" Dreher agrees that Lear is an immature old man who "commits the ultimate folly by making his daughters his mothers."[29] In her discussion of the absent mother, Coppélia Kahn argues that Lear exemplifies "the outlines of a child's pre-oedipal experience of himself and his mother as an undifferentiated dual unity."[30]

These critics have a limited point: there is something childish about Lear's behavior. But the explanation that he is immature or trapped in a developmental phase that he should have shelved at the point of ego-formation seems entirely wrongheaded. We need only turn to Shakespeare's famous description of the seven ages of man in As You Like It to find a more adequate explanation:

> The sixth age shifts
> Into the lean and slipper'd pantaloon,
> With spectacles on nose, and pouch on side,
> His youthful hose well sav'd, a world too wide
> For his shrunk shank, and his big manly voice,
> Turning again toward childish treble, pipes
> And whistles in his sound. Last scene of all,
> That ends this strange eventful history,
> Is second childishness and mere oblivion,
> Sans teeth, sans eyes, sans taste, sans everything. (As You Like It,
> 2.7.157–66)

It seems to me that we cannot even begin to understand the tragedy of love in this play unless we accept the true nature of Lear's childishness. He is not trapped in an early developmental phase but poised precariously between the ultimate and the penultimate "ages" described by Jaques above. He may find himself in a downward slope, but he is not going backward (childish regression) but forward (in that his mind is deteriorating). In spite of what I regard as an unnecessary concession to the modern suspicion of character analysis, John Cunningham puts his finger on the exact nature of Lear's childishness: "While there are dangers in applying the terms of modern psychology too glibly to the work of a writer who probably did not think of 'character' quite as we do, it can be argued that we have here a classic, text-book case of a distressing condition well known in the elderly: senile dementia."[31]

In my view, there are *no* dangers in applying this diagnosis to Lear, either clinical or literary-theoretical. Shakespeare may not have been familiar with terms like "cerebral arteriosclerosis," and it is more than possible that our modern life expectancy or fatty lifestyle has resulted in some differences between our age and his. But as Jaques illustrates in his discussion of the seven ages of man, what we term senility was also a reality for many of Shakespeare's contemporaries who lived long enough. In a society that had not heard of comfy homes for the elderly, someone who was rapidly becoming weaker and whose mind was beginning to slip would quite naturally become worried that his children might not love him enough. He might even turn them into mother figures, as Dreher puts it, but in the special sense of becoming totally dependent on their love and good will. As we have seen, there was a widespread unease in Shakespeare's England about the rights and duties of children toward their parents. It has even been argued plausibly that Shakespeare was inspired by a contemporary case where the daughters of Brian Annesby sought to have him declared unreasonable, and where the third daughter, who refused to take part in this scheme, was called Cordell.

Of course, John Cunningham is not the first critic who has advanced a "senile" reading of Lear's condition. As early as the late 1960s, Stanley Cavell included it among the three "usual interpretations" of Shakespeare's play and then went on to develop his own famous interpretation that was based on a kind of reverse psychology. In Cavell's view, Lear is afraid of love and therefore demands it from his daughters as a means of pushing them away.[32] I find this explanation of the love test contorted and unconvincing, and it makes much more sense to read the test straightforwardly as a misguided plea for love. I also think (and this will be developed in a moment) that Lear's senility is such a central aspect of his motivation, and so carefully established by Shakespeare, that it excludes all readings that regard the love test as a carefully crafted scheme. As long as we are discussing Lear's motivation, the senility reading is not just one reading among others, as Cavell suggests, but a necessary component of any interpretation or dramatic adaptation that wants to stay true to the text—or rather, the *texts*, since the play exists in different versions.[33]

I realize that this may sound offensive to those who take a more relativistic view of literary interpretation than I do. In response, I would say that critical *pluralism* is usually a very good thing because the average literary text confronts us with a complexity that defies simple characterization. But pluralism is necessarily a means to an end, and not an end in itself: *King Lear* does not necessarily become a better or more interesting play just because we have fifty or five hundred different readings of it. What matters is the quality of each reading and that we do not fail to distinguish between what is complementary and what is simply contradictory. Like any other ideal, the "open-endedness" that is celebrated by contemporary critics can become so deeply invested with value that it becomes a prejudice.

With this in mind, let us now examine the love test more closely. There is a fairly widespread critical agreement that something is not quite right about it, but opinions differ as to what the actual problem is. Coleridge, for example, gave up trying to explain it and wrote it off as a "gross improbability."[34] More recently Lawrence Berns has suggested that it cannot be a real test, for if it really were seriously intended then Lear would have waited for all his daughters to speak. It is more likely a "mere formality" that serves no practical or emotional purpose,[35] and hence the opposite of Coleridge's "gross improbability." In Harry Berger's more disturbing view, Lear simply wants to be nasty and bully his children in order to preserve his own power: "His darker purpose seems to be to play on everyone's curiosity and stir up as much envy and contention as he can among the 'younger strengths' with the aim of dominating and dividing them, humbling and punishing them."[36] William Dodd, finally, argues from a historicist perspective that "Lear wishes to sugar the pill of absolutism by mystifying it as a system based on love rather than coercion."[37] Since all these readings are in some way concerned with Lear's intention and motivation, most of them are mutually exclusive.

Another thing that makes the love test enigmatic is that Shakespeare has departed quite tellingly from his source, the anonymous *History of King Leir*. In the earlier play, Leir has originally planned to divide his kingdom equally but then comes up with a "sudden stratagem" because his daughter Cordella refuses to marry the King of Brittany. Leir thinks that if he can get her to profess her love for her father, then he can capitalize on this family bond by asking her a small favor—that is, to marry the King she does not love. In Shakespeare's play, by contrast, the sudden stratagem is never given any explanation: "Shakespeare does not prepare us for Lear's odd behavior, or for Cordelia's. . . . In fact, the first scene's lacunae seem quite deliberate. Shakespeare has thoroughly removed the carefully placed hints about motivation that abound in his primary source."[38]

No one has drawn a better conclusion from this evidence than Geoffrey Bullough: "The love test is less thoroughly explained than in Leir. Apparently it is a mere whim of the old King, who at the moment of abdication wants to be assured that he is much beloved."[39] Everything in the first scene bears out this reading. Since we know from the very first line that the division of the kingdom has already been decided on, Lear's introduction of the love test necessarily contradicts the original plan. It also appears unexpectedly in the middle of a different discussion:

> The ᵠtwo great princes,ᵠ France and Burgundy,
> Great rivals in our youngest daughter's love,
> Long in our court have made their amorous sojourn,
> And are here to be answered.

There is no immediate answer or continuation of this topic. Instead, Lear turns away from the people he is addressing and delivers something of a non sequitur to his daughters:

> Tell me, my daughters—
> ᶠSince now we will divest us both of rule,

Interest of territory, cares of state—[F]
Which of you shall we say doth love us most,
That we our largest bounty may extend
Where nature doth with merit challenge. (1.1.45–53)

The impression that this is a sudden whim is also borne out by Lear's admission that he had originally planned to live out his days with his favorite child, Cordelia (1.1.123). Instead, he must now improvise the arrangement of a monthly commute between the houses of Albany and Cornwall—including, perhaps, the one hundred knights that will soon cause him to fall out with Goneril and Regan. In other words, there is much to be said for Blissett's argument, cited above, that Lear's hamartia is better understood in terms of a disastrous "initial error" than a "tragic flaw." Once the snowball has been set in motion, it cannot be stopped.

Rashness is a relative term, and it is a malaise that afflicts at least three characters in this play: Lear, Gloucester, and Kent. So how can we attribute Lear's rashness to something as specific as senility? The most obvious answer is that Lear's daughters give us very good reasons to do so:

GONERIL: You see how full of changes his age is. The
    observation we have made of it hath ᵠnotᵠ been little.
    He always loved our sister most, and with what poor
    judgement he hath now cast her off appears too grossly.
REGAN: 'Tis the infirmity of his age, yet he hath ever but
    slenderly known himself.
GONERIL: The best and soundest of his time hath been
    but rash; then must we look from his age to receive not
    alone the imperfections of long-engrafted condition,
    but therewithal [F]the[F] unruly waywardness that infirm
    and choleric years bring with them.
REGAN: Such unconstant starts are we like to have from
    him as this of Kent's banishment. (1.1.290–302)

While the sisters also attribute Lear's "changes" to "long-engrafted" aspects of his personality, the emphasis clearly falls on the effects of age. What they discuss are typical symptoms of senile dementia: rapid mood swings, sudden fits of anger, and periods of clarity interspersed with spells of confusion. Two scenes later, Goneril again defines her father in terms of a second childhood that calls for definite restraints: "Now by my life / Old fools are babes again and must be used / With checks as flatteries, when they are seen abused" (1.3.19–21).

In his first real confrontation with Goneril about the behavior of his riotous knights, Lear gives us the first intimations that his sense of identity is failing him. It is difficult to say whether he is only commenting sarcastically on his loss of prestige as king or whether there is also an element of genuine confusion at work here:

> LEAR: Does any here know me? ᵠWhy,ᵠ this is not Lear.
> Does Lear walk thus, speak thus? Where are his eyes?
> Either his notion weakens, ᵠorᵠ his discernings are
> lethargied—Ha! ᵠsleeping orᵠ waking? ᵠSureᵠ'tis not
> so. Who is it that can tell me who I am? (1.4.217–21)

When he turns to his daughter, he does not acknowledge any recognition of her identity either: "Your name, fair gentlewoman?" (226). Goneril certainly seems to interpret this as a deliberate sarcasm, but she also attributes it to his recent change in personality: "This admiration, sir, is much o'the savour / Of other your new pranks" (228–29). Since Lear's mind is a fictional black box that only admits inferences based on external evidence, it is impossible to say whether this is a correct interpretation or not. It may, however, be relevant that a "principal way of diagnosing madness [in Shakespeare's England] was to note that the victim could not recognize members of his or her family, or took no delight in them."[40]

When Lear has left, Goneril advises her husband not to trouble himself with the cause of their argument, and rather let Lear's "disposition have that scope / As dotage gives it" (284–85). The word "dotage" had several meanings in Shakespeare's English, from excessive fondness or general stupidity to senility, and there can be little doubt about what Goneril intends. When, in the second act, she admonishes Lear that "all's not offence that indiscretion finds and dotage terms so" (385–86), it is also useful to bear in mind that the word "discretion" was not only roughly synonymous to "sound judgment" or "discerning." According to English law, the age of fourteen was the "age of discretion" that separated responsible adults from children. This would suggest that Goneril accuses her father of being childish and senile in the very same line.

Like her sister, Regan is perfectly lucid about her father's "second childhood" when she finally confronts him:

> O, Sir, you are old:
> Nature in you stands on the very verge
> Of her confine. You should be ruled and led
> By some discretion that discerns your state
> Better than you yourself. (2.2.338–42)

It could, I suppose, be objected that most of this evidence is not trustworthy because it comes from two sisters who either have a chip on their shoulder or a hidden agenda. But if this is the case, then why doesn't Lear protest his vigor or sanity at least once? Indeed, why does no one else stand up and declare that the king is in his right mind? When Goneril stresses the dangers of letting her senile father retain control of one hundred armed followers—

> Yes, that on every dream,
> Each buzz, each fancy, each complaint, dislike,
> He may enguard his dotage with their powers
> And hold our lives in mercy

—her husband's lame response is that "you may fear too far" (1.4.317–21). This looks like an implicit admission that Lear has not been in his right mind lately.

In one of his lectures on Shakespeare, Northrop Frye also gives us a dramatic reason to take the sisters' analysis of their father's state seriously. "When you start to read or listen to *King Lear*, try to pretend that you've never heard the story before, and forget that you know how bad Goneril and Regan are going to be. That way, you'll see more clearly how Shakespeare is building up our sympathies in the opposite direction."[41] John Danby also suggests that "Goneril and Regan can be assumed to be unbiased" in their diagnosis of the effects of old age.[42]

We can also fall back on Lear's own description of his condition when he is finally reunited with Cordelia toward the end of the play:

> Pray do not mock F me F,
> I am a very foolish, fond old man,
> Fourscore and upward, F not an hour more nor less, F
> And to deal plainly,
> I fear I am not in my perfect mind.
> Methinks I should know you and know this man,
> Yet I am doubtful; for I am mainly ignorant
> What place this is and all the skill I have
> Remembers not these garments; nor I know not
> Where I did lodge last night. Do not laugh at me,
> For, as I am a man, I think this lady
> To be my child Cordelia. (4.7.59–70)

While Lear's condition had obviously been exacerbated when he was thrown out into the wilderness, such memory lapses are classic symptoms of senile dementia.

The final support I want to muster for this reading comes from an argument that is really about madness rather than senility, but since both can involve disorientation and an incomplete sense of self and reality, there is a natural link between them. In his marvelously informative *Medicine and Shakespeare in the English Renaissance* (1992), David Hoeniger seeks to challenge the modern critical view that Lear becomes mad after his encounter with Edgar in act 3, scene 4. Hoeniger objects that many of Shakespeare's contemporaries would have "thought of Lear as mentally unstable (and thus ill) from the start."[43] While I think he is absolutely right in the assertion that Lear is confused already at the beginning of the play, I would question his more specific analysis of Lear's ailment as "acute hypochondriac melancholy developing into mania" (330). On the basis of the very detailed diagnoses offered by Lear's own children it seems more reasonable to suggest that his madness—that is, his accelerating disorientation, violent mood swings, and loss of identity—develops out of his senility.

What are the consequences if we accept Lear's senility as an *inescapable* component of Shakespeare's tragedy? It certainly does not reduce its pathos, but rather adds to it as we helplessly observe the speeding deterioration of Lear's mind:

> O Lear, Lear, Lear!
> [*striking his head*] Beat at this gate that let thy folly in
> And thy dear judgement out. (1.4.262–64)

The deep irony is that Lear's folly cannot be evicted. It is an enemy that is eating him up from the inside and that he can escape no more than he can escape his enemies in the outside world.

To assert that Lear's tragedy is in part biologically determined—a question of decaying brain tissue—does not sit particularly well with the current orthodoxy in the humanities. Surely locating the root of the tragedy inside the king's crumbling gray matter is a biological-determinist argument that seeks to elide the political dimensions of the play by letting the private displace the political? I would like to suggest in all modesty that historical materialists, like post-structuralists, have long been guilty of an opposite distortion of Shakespeare's works by eliding the personal and overemphasizing the systemic.

In a recent article that seeks to address this problem, William Dodd argues that there is "no reason why late twentieth-century problematizing of the subject should discourage us from investigating the way characters in plays are—often, if by no means always—presented as interacting persons, provided that we do not make the mistake of totalizing the personal and eliding the systemic."[44] This is a laudable attempt to balance the critical debate a little, but Dodd's rather abstruse explanation of Cordelia's devotion for her father suggests that he has only traveled the road to recovery halfway: "My guess is that it voices post-Reformation social aspirations that have not yet been channeled into the values of middle-class capitalism and which Lutheranism ultimately sanctions rather than inhibits— aspirations for a consensual, disarmed image of political authority" (501).

What is missing here is the distinctly "personal" possibility that Cordelia simply loves her father. If such a reading sounds unsophisticated or trite it is mainly because too many literary critics assume that the most convoluted, abstract, or "structural" interpretation is also the best or most sophisticated one. As is well known in other fields, the simplest or most parsimonious solution to a problem is often the most rewarding.

Of course, this is not to say that Lear's senility in any way precludes a political reading of the love test. Generally speaking, I side with Alvin Kernan's assertion that Shakespeare played a very duplicitous game with the absolutist ideals espoused by his royal patron. Kernan argues that the play flatters James by portraying a king whose power requires no worldly sanctions, and yet the moral emptiness of the heath actively challenges the idea that such assertions have an orderly metaphysical ground.[45] What I would add is that the very idea of a *senile absolutist king* must have been very scary to some of Shakespeare's contemporaries, who might even have identified with Goneril's and Regan's point of view in the first acts. What if *our* king—whose political philosophy is clearly absolutist—should suddenly "enguard his dotage" and decide to "hold our lives in mercy"?

Another effect of Lear's senility is to remove even more ground from the moralistic readings I discussed earlier in this chapter. Since it is difficult to give moral advice to someone who is not in his right mind—or at least to expect compliance—the play becomes even less of a cautionary tale, even less didactic, than it has been seen over the last decades. It becomes almost intolerably bleak. But the most important consequence by far of this reading is that it brings into focus—and, in the current literary-critical climate, *restores*— the fundamental human vulnerability, lovesickness, and neediness that lies at the heart of Shakespeare's play.

Lear may well have been an irascible tyrant in some respects, pompous and selfish, but the love test he invents is not the diabolical invention of a pathological narcissist. It is the confused and desperate whim of a senile old man who has only just begun to realize the full extent of his imminent powerlessness and dependency. The only problem is that this love-hungry old codger is in the midst of his last exercise of royal power when he dreams up his impossible test, and so he turns what should have been a plea for love into a formal public ceremony.

Love and Duty

As numerous critics have argued, it is a central issue in Shakespeare's tragedy that Lear fails to separate his public role as king from his private role as father. Thomas McFarland thinks the "tension between Lear's two roles in life, one as king with its patina of symbolic paternalism, the other as father of a specific family, generates the tragic situation that arises in the play,"[46] and Lawrence Berns takes a similar view: "Private and public interfere with each other for Lear: The very proposing of a love test evidences a certain confusion about the properly public and the properly private. . . . Lear seems to have tried, as it were, to absorb the private into the public, to have confused what can be demanded and enforced by right and law and majesty with what can only arise naturally, what is beyond all external command or control."[47] In *Law and Love: The Trials of King Lear* (2000), finally, Paul Kahn argues for an almost identical reading of Lear: "Is he a loving father or a ruling king? He wants to be both at once, but instead he quickly ends up a king in name but without rule, and a father in name but without love. . . . Lear's tragedy, then, is rooted in his effort to align his private selves, his identity as loving father and royal sovereign."[48] As we have seen, this role confusion is also present in the original division of the kingdom, since Lear seems to replace the royal practice of sex-based primogeniture with a paternal scheme of fair distribution.

Since Kahn's excellent study is the most extended discussion of love in *Lear* to date, it warrants some special attention. As professor of law and the humanities, Kahn takes a natural interest in legal questions, and what he finds in Lear is a fundamental conflict between law and love: "The destruction of love by law and of law by love is a central theme of *King Lear*" (xi). One theoretical and methodological difference between Kahn and myself is that he chooses not to define what is actually meant by love: "A central claim of this work is that love is not a particular emotional experience but a form of experience from within which we can view the entire social and political world. A cultural form—for example, religion, art, science—cannot be defined; rather, it must be explored through a phenomenological inquiry" (xvi). Our second point of divergence concerns the centrality of law in Shakespeare's play. While Kahn's analysis works beautifully as a meditation on law and the passions with reference to Shakespeare, I want to question whether his antithesis between love and law is really the most apposite way of conceptualizing either the love test or Shakespeare's play in general. In contrast to Kahn, I consider a theme of love and *duty* to be more historically adequate as well as more faithful to Shakespeare's play.

At first sight, duty may seem very similar to law, and thus very different from love, but this shift in perspective has clear interpretive consequences. Like law, duty certainly brings to mind impersonal standards of conduct and expectations that are inevitably social in nature, but we must not forget that love also carries with it a sense of obligation. As we saw in the discussion of Sternberg's love triangle (which provides the form of theoretical grounding that Kahn deems unnecessary), companionate love typically involves a desire to promote the welfare of another person as well as some measure of commitment, and the same goes for romantic love. To care for another person is to assume responsibility for that person, which means that it has an intrinsic moral component that is not reducible to societal standards. As readers of *Romeo and Juliet* are well aware, love can even involve a commitment to another person that is totally at odds with social norms.

Duty, therefore, cannot be understood in terms of a dichotomy between law and love, or between private and public, because it can involve them both.[49]

The relation between love and duty becomes even more complex when we add two early modern factors that have been discussed previously in this book. First, there is the semantic flexibility of the word "love" in Shakespeare's English, where a profession of "love" could mean anything from the acceptance of social allegiance to an expression of emotional involvement. In *King Lear*, Kent uses the word in the former sense when he meets Edmund for the first time: "I must love you, and sue to know you better" (1.1.29). "Love" could thus be almost synonymous with duty (in the most formal sense of the word) or regarded as a distinct or even antithetical phenomenon (for instance, as an emotion that had nothing to do with social expectations). In the years before the English civil war, Henry Oxinden wrote to his brother that "they are men of a senseles disposition that thinke [that] is done toward them out of love is done out of duty."[50]

Second, we must also take into account the specific ambiguity and uncertainty that surrounded children's duties toward their parents in the early modern period. Was it a duty for children to love their parents? If so, what was meant by love: to pay one's socially sanctioned respects, or to feel deeply for them, or both? No one could say for sure, though many tried. As we saw earlier, there was not even a consensus that children were obliged to *care* for their parents when they grew old, let alone love them. If parents could disinherit their children, then it seemed reasonable to suggest that children could also disinherit their parents.

If this discussion has served its purpose, the reader will now be struggling to come to terms with the considerable complexity that emerges when we combine these words—love and duty—and explore some of their historical resonance against the backdrop of a universal human predicament. It is this undigested and deeply ambiguous mess that Lear heaps onto his daughters in the love test. When Goneril and Regan respond that they love their father beyond all conceivable measure, there are at least two reasons why their answers cannot be written off as pure flattery. First of all, such hyperbolic rhetoric is perfectly attuned to a formal ceremony where "love" does not necessarily have anything to do with genuine feelings or emotions. We can rest assured that someone who declares herself enemy to all joys except her father's love is not expecting to be believed. Secondly, the sisters are probably just as taken aback as everyone else, and they cannot be sure whether their senile father is in earnest or not. Is this whim an empty game or a grotesque competition that really puts their inheritance on the line? Faced with such uncertainties, even the most devoted truth sayer might consider embellishing her account considerably.

It seems fairly clear, however, that what Lear seeks to elicit from his daughters—or at least from Cordelia—is some sort of emotional response rather than empty verbiage or a formal vow of allegiance. When Cordelia's answers disappoint him, his desire to gauge the depths of her heart becomes explicit: "But goes thy heart with this?" (105). In the language of Antonio Damasio's emotion theory, we can say that Lear has failed to relate his daughter's words to her *emotions* (aspects of which can be observed from outside) and now asks her about the one thing he can never have direct access to: her *feelings* (her subjective experience). His interest is all too human, since emotions have other functions than serving as internal regulators of organismic states. They are also social signals, directed toward other people, that originate from a limbic area in the brain that is not under voluntary control. When we are deeply smitten with love for someone, for example, our emotions communicate that we are bound to that person by something that is potentially stronger than our conscious will. Anyone with a moderately gifted tongue can tell a pretty tale, but only the best of actors can instruct themselves to feel the right thing wherever it is appropriate.

As we all know, Cordelia's first defiant response to the love test is to shock her father and the audience by offering "Nothing." When the befuddled Lear urges her to speak again, she immediately draws a firm distinction between her feelings and her language: "Unhappy that I am, I cannot heave / My heart into my mouth" (91). There are at least two ways of reading this line. If Cordelia is simply pointing to the incapacity of her language to convey her feelings *fully*, then the word "love" remains deeply ambiguous in the lines that follow, and Lear has every reason to be worried about what he hears. Is this all the love she feels for me? If, on the other hand, Cordelia intends a sharper distinction between her language and her feelings—that she absolutely *cannot* or *will not* speak her heart—then she is suggesting that whatever she says in this ceremony will have nothing to do with her feelings. I suspect that Lear chooses the former interpretation while Cordelia intends the latter and that she gives him strong cues to this effect in the lines that follow:

> I love your majesty
>   According to my bond, no more nor less.
> LEAR: How, how, ᶠCordelia?ᶠ Mend your speech a little,
>   Lest you may mar your fortunes.
> CORDELIA: Good my lord,
>   You have begot me, bred me, loved me. I
>   Return those duties back as are right fit,
>   Obey you, love you and most honour you. (92–98)

Much hinges on how we read the word "bond" here. Words like "bond," "bind," and "bound" are used frequently by Shakespeare as metaphors of an individual's commitment to something outside himself. Sometimes this "something" is an impersonal force, principle, or value, such as honor, revenge, or nature. The bond may also have distinctly legal overtones—including those of natural law—as when the lusty goddess in *Venus and Adonis* tells the recalcitrant youth that "by law of nature art thou bound to breed" (*Venus*, stanza 27). In most cases, however, the "bond" characterizes a distinctly interpersonal relationship, the most typical example being the acknowledgment of a debt of gratitude or a social obligation ("I am bound to you").

In the preface to *The Rape of Lucrece,* Shakespeare even defines his own relationship to the Earl of Southampton in such vaguely feudal terms: "Were my worth greater, my duty would show greater; meantime, as it is, it is bound to your Lordship." A more caustic and explicit version of the same relationship can be found in Sonnet 58, where the speaker describes himself as "your vassall, bound to stay your leisure." But what binds the poet so painfully to his noble youth in the *Sonnets* is not only the patronage relation from which he seems to earn his living, but also a strong emotional attachment, and such relationships are also described by Shakespeare in terms of bonds and binding. In *Titus Andronicus,* for example, we are clearly dealing with "service" of a less formal nature when Queen Tamora is described as "faster bound to Aaron's charming eyes / Than is Prometheus tied to Caucasus" (*Titus* 1.1.515–16). The guiding idea is, of course, the proverbial one: that our passions can become so strong that they overrule the decrees of the intellect and make us prisoners.

What this means is that a Shakespearean "bond" can be anything from a lawful and formal obligation to an intense emotional attachment, or any mixture of the two. In the more specific context of parent-child relations, the bond can be virtually synonymous with parental authority, as in the Gardener's advice to the king in *Richard II:* "Go, bind up yon dangling apricocks, / Which like unruly children make their sire / Stoop with oppression of their prodigal weight" (3.4.29–31). But there are also cases where this parental authority cannot be separated from emotional involvement, as when Volumnia says of Coriolanus that there is "no man in the world / More bound to his mother" (5.3.160–61). In other words, a brief survey of Shakespearean bonds will underscore, rather than resolve, the ambiguity that surrounds Cordelia's reply to her father.

On the other hand, it is significant that Cordelia first addresses Lear as *king* rather than *father,* thus defining the "bond" between them as a kind of feudal arrangement where the king gets his expected dues. When she next addresses him as father, she again couches their relationship in terms of quid pro quo by speaking of his love as something that has generated proper returns. This impression is reinforced yet again when she compares herself to her sisters:

Why have my sisters husbands, if they say
They love you all? Haply when I shall wed,
That lord whose hand must take my plight shall carry

Half my love with him, half my care and duty.
Sure I shall never marry like my sisters
ᵠTo love my father all.ᵠ (99–104)

The idea that love can be portioned out in this way makes it a zero-sum game where one person's benefit must be another's loss. It is interesting, therefore, that Cordelia immediately shies away from such implications by specifying exactly what is meant by love: she means "care and duty." Since these are things that have no necessary connection with one's feelings—it is even possible to care dutifully for a hated person—Cordelia appears to be drawing the "sharp" distinction between language and feeling I discussed above. The "love" she speaks of to her father—that is, love conceived as an *action* rather than an *emotion*—has nothing to do with what she feels in her heart. Toward the end of scene 1, when Cordelia is about to leave with the King of France, we find yet another example of a love that is practically synonymous with social or domestic obligations. When Cordelia urges her sisters to "Love well our father" (273), Regan's retort is telling: "Prescribe not us our duty" (278).

In other words, I think it can be argued that Cordelia responds to her impossible situation by distinguishing between two early modern meanings of the word love: a formal obligation that involves just deserts, returns, and social duties, and an emotional involvement or affection that cannot be reduced to such a logic. But this attempt to separate the mouth from the heart is disastrously counterproductive because the heart remains silent and inscrutable, and the rhetorical effect is a crass depiction of "love" as a mere exchange of favors. Like most humans, Lear wants his daughter's love to be *unreasonable*, to be impervious to the kind of cost-benefit analyses that she now throws in his face. As Shakespeare puts it so beautifully in *Antony and Cleopatra*, "There's beggary in the love that can be reckoned" (1.1.15). Part of the problem is that so much of Cordelia's resentment and criticism is directed toward the smarmy performances of her sisters who have already defined love as that which exceeds all possible definitions and boundaries and similes. Ironically, Goneril and Regan have given Lear precisely what he wants (albeit in a debased and useless form), while Cordelia gives him the very thing he dreads.

In the love test, the lovesick and senile king thus places an unreasonable demand on his daughters for an inherently unreasonable emotion. Love, conceived as "bestowal" in Irving Singer's terms, reaches out and makes another person beautiful and valuable. In its purest form it is the Christian ideal of *agape*, a love that is fundamentally unconditional and knows no cause. But even sublunar love cannot be reduced to a zero-sum game or a system of expenditure and returns, and Lear's expectation of what cannot be expected costs him his youngest child and alienates the other two even further. He must therefore settle for the second best alternative: what can a parent *reasonably* expect from his children? The love he hopes for has now become reduced to pure "appraisal" where proper dues and rewards can be calculated. It is interesting to note that after the love test, Lear no longer speaks of love, as if to avoid any confusion between duty and a freely given affection. His language shifts from "love" to "gratitude" and "kindness."

Already in scene 5, Lear describes himself in distinctly self-pitying terms: "I will forget my nature: so kind a father!" (1.5.31). In act 2 he implores Regan to be kinder than her sister has been:

> Thou better knowst
> The offices of nature, bond of childhood,
> Effects of courtesy, dues of gratitude.
> Thy half o'the kingdom hast thou not forgot,
> Wherein I thee endowed (2.2.369–73)

In the storm scene he turns his face to the angry skies and howls: "I tax not you, you elements, with unkindness. I never gave you kingdom, called you children; you owe me no subscription" (3.2.16–18). Two scenes later, all he can think of is "filial ingratitude": "O, Regan, Goneril, / Your old, kind father, whose frank heart gave you all" (3.4.14, 19–20).

The problem is that when Lear gives up on love (conceived as bestowal) and settles for gratitude based on kindness, he is still asking for more than can be expected—or at least exacted—from his callous daughters. To my knowledge, no one has discussed this issue with more clarity than Lawrence Berns: "Gratitude might be thought of as being between justice and love. Like commutative justice . . . gratitude involves an element of calculation. Gratitude should be proportionate to benefits or favors bestowed. But unlike the demands of commutative justice, these obligations are unenforceable, at least by any human court."[51] On the face of it, one would think that a third of a kingdom would be an ample reason for gratitude. But like the emotion of love, gratitude involves a state of mind and feeling that cannot be commanded or even expected. As Regan points out to her frustrated father, there is no reason to feel gratitude for that which is only to be expected:

> LEAR: I gave you all—
> REGAN: And in good time you gave it. (2.2.442–43)

If we go back to the very first lines of *King Lear*, we realize that Regan actually has a good point. The opening exchange between Kent and Gloucester suggests that the division of the kingdom has been a matter of prudence rather than affection.

If this analysis is right, then Regan really has very little to be grateful for. Her original third of the kingdom was hardly given out of love, not even love for her husband. On the political level, we can read it as an attempt to avoid civil war, and this attempt ultimately boils down to an attempt by Lear to mitigate parent-offspring conflict and prevent sibling rivalry. When Regan and her husband are then given half of the kingdom, this unexpected addition is best described as the scraps from Cordelia's table. What Lear ends up with at the hands of Goneril and Regan is the deplorable situation that Montaigne describes in the *Essays:* "That father may truly be said miserable, that holdeth the affection of his children tied unto him by no other meanes than by the need they have of his helpe, or want of his assistance, if that may be termed affection."[52]

Before we turn to the Gloucester family, it will be useful to explore how Shakespeare deepens his theme of love and duty by embodying it in other characters. Oswald, first of all, is a character who has received his fair share of bad press in Shakespeare criticism. Some of it may be deserved, but much of the critical displeasure fails to appreciate the ingenuity with which Shakespeare has crafted him. Paul Kahn, for example, sees him as representative of Plato's drones in the *Republic:* people who "do not attend the powerful because of a concern for the public order, but as a means of private gain" and who "will follow the course of power, subordinating loyalty to advantage."[53] I think this is a misreading and that Oswald is a far more interesting character who provides another important piece of the puzzle regarding love and duty.

Oswald certainly is a scary figure, but not because he is a timeserver. On the contrary, he appears to be unconditionally loyal toward his superiors. When Regan tries to enlist his services at the expense of his mistress Goneril, Oswald replies that "I may not, madam; / My lady charged my duty in this business" (4.5.19–20). Regan's promise to "love thee much" (23) in exchange for a peek at her sister's secret letter does not help. Oswald only promises to do that which will not interfere with his allegiance to Goneril: namely, to murder Gloucester if he should come across him. In the next scene, the dying Oswald—whose moonlighting has cost him his life—asks his bane Edgar to deliver the letters he is carrying to Edmund in the English camp. The fact that Oswald is loyal to his superiors even in death does not escape Edgar, who defines him as a "serviceable villain, / As duteous to the vices of thy mistress / As badness would desire" (4.6.247–49). At this point Kahn seems about to revise his earlier perception of Oswald and admits that it is hypothetically possible to "see him as a person who acts the role he has been dealt with loyalty and even integrity. Yet, I do not think we see him in this way."[54]

Since Kahn rejects this reading of Oswald, I think he also misses his thematic function in the play, which is to provide a complementary perspective on the relation between love and duty. Loyalty is valorized by many characters in *King Lear,* including the sadistic Duke of Cornwall, and what Oswald illustrates is the incomplete match between loyalty and morality. He is a man of principles, and very little else than principles, since he renounces his individual morality and replaces it with blind, passionless obedience. This makes him the exact obverse of Kent, an emotional being who is full of love for Lear—"Whom I have ever honoured as my king, / Loved as my father" (1.1.141–42)—but who is also far from unconditional in his obedience.

When the enraged Lear threatens him, Kent's reply crystallizes the difference between duty and obedience: "What wouldst thou do, old man? / Think'st thou that duty shall have dread to speak, / When power to flattery bows?" (147–49). Unlike Oswald, Kent has an individual point of view, a sense of duty that is rooted in his emotions. The same goes for the Third Knight, who approaches Lear in the first act: "I beseech you pardon me, my lord, if I be / mistaken, for my duty cannot be silent when I think / your highness wronged" (1.4.62–64). When Gloucester seeks out Lear on the heath, finally, we get another example: "My duty cannot suffer / T'obey in all your daughters' hard commands" (3.4.144–45). Technically, Gloucester may owe his allegiance to his new masters, but his moral and emotional duty lies elsewhere.

What this suggests is that duty, which was severed so brutally from affection early in the play, can be reunited with emotional experience only once it has been demoted from the sphere of formal, contractual bonds. The public sphere, with its demands on social decorum, drains relationships of their emotional content, and any duty that is worth its salt must be rooted in emotion, not just abstract principles. It follows directly from this that duty cannot be robotic and unconditional, as Cordelia demonstrates so tellingly in the love test. There is an important connection here with the play's complex imagery of feeling and seeing, especially in the indictment of those who "do not see because they do not feel." This reading is also compatible with Kahn's analysis of the conflict between love and law in Shakespeare's play, but with the important addition that it softens his dichotomy considerably. Strictly speaking, love cannot ever be freely given or "unlawful" in any absolute sense, because it imposes its own demands and duties on the self.

Is There Any Cause in Nature?

For someone like Edmund, on the other hand, "duty" is no more than a word that has useful effects when used judiciously in particular contexts. It is a sign of Shakespeare's genius that he could create a literary character that invites so many conflicting responses, including pathos, abhorrence, and iconoclastic glee. At the beginning of the second act, Edmund manages to turn his father against his legitimate half-brother Edgar by convincing him that the latter has sought his life. In a stroke of diabolical genius he casts himself—the most unlikely candidate on earth—as a champion of the natural bond between parents and children, and claims to have reminded his parricidal brother "with how manifold and strong a bond / The child was bound to the father" (2.1.47–48). The plan works perfectly since the gullible Gloucester immediately promises Edmund, who is now his "Loyal and natural boy" (84), the land that was originally intended for Edgar. The Duke of Cornwall also expresses his admiration and receives a telling answer:

> Edmund, I hear that you have shown your father
> A child-like office.
> EDMUND: It was my duty, sir. (2.1.105–6)

In her study of bastards in Elizabethan drama, Alison Findlay reads this passage somewhat differently than I do. Approaching the matter from what appears to be a Lacanian perspective, she regards Edmund as "torn between the contradictory ideologies of the goddess Nature—where all are equal socially—and the stratified legitimate hierarchy. In terms of value systems he is schizophrenic" (126). I think this is a mistaken attribution of mental conflict, based on a mistaken theory.[55] Edmund is not "torn" at all; he is simply regurgitating some cultural flotsam in the hope of manipulating his superiors. In his famous soliloquy on legitimacy and bastardy he has already defined himself as Nature's child, as opposed to the child of custom:

> EDMUND: Thou, Nature, art my goddess; to thy law
> My services are bound. Wherefore should I
> Stand in the plague of custom, and permit
> The curiousity of nations to deprive me?
> For that I am some twelve or fourteen moonshines
> Lag of a brother? Why bastard? Wherefore base? (1.2.1–6)

In Melford Spiro's terms, introduced in chapter 1, we can say that Edmund has learned the rules and values of his culture but has also refused to become enculturated by them. This affords a cool detachment that enables him to step back and employ these rules and values as manipulative fictions rather than genuinely held beliefs. Edmund's dishonest defense of the parent-child bond is therefore directly analogous to his satirical endorsement of astrology a little later in the same scene. After hearing his father lament the disastrous results of recent eclipses in the sky (1.2.103–12), Edmund first delivers a scathing critique of astrology, but then he recycles his father's worries to Edgar as if they were his own (140–49). When Edgar wonders, "How long have you been a sectary astronomical?" (150), Edmund changes the subject, but it is easy for the audience to fill in the correct answer: ever since it became convenient for me.

His nasty personality notwithstanding, Edmund is best described as an illegitimate child with a number of legitimate complaints. One of these hinges on the relation between nature and custom. There is no room here for a more detailed discussion of the manifold and complex meanings of "nature" in Shakespeare's play,[56] but it is clear that Edmund sees a fundamental opposition between the dictates of nature and those of culture. On the one hand, there is very little difference between the nasty doctrine he espouses—"the younger rises when the old doth fall" (3.3.25)—and the social Darwinist assumption that the survival of the fittest (which for Herbert Spencer meant the strongest individual) is a natural norm. All humans need to do is look to nature, follow its example, and let each individual fend for himself. Such a natural world, driven by competition and conflict, has no room for love, and when parents become old and weak they must be discarded. On the other hand, Edmund also distinguishes sharply between nature and culture and regards the systems of primogeniture and legitimate birth as essentially arbitrary inventions: "Why should I / Stand in the plague of custom, and permit / The curiosity of nations to deprive me?" (1.2.2–5).

These seemingly opposed positions are compatible for Edmund because he locates all normative authority and all genuine values in nature, leaving human culture no genuine role to play other than that of a distorting mirror. He is, in other words, heir to a primitivistic tendency in Western thought where "Nature and Art are paired antithetically, with Art as the pejorative term."[57] In Edmund's view, that which is not dictated by nature is necessarily unreal and arbitrary—including love, which becomes just as much a social fabrication as astrology or the filial duties he derides.

Edmund is, of course, a parent's ultimate nightmare: a child who is not only loveless but who actively seeks your death. As such, he raises some difficult questions. Should we think of him as a conventional Vice figure, whose evils need no explaining and are not amenable to psychological analysis? Is he an abused child who wreaks excessive revenge on a neglectful parent? Or is he—to venture a mixed metaphor—simply a rotten egg that bites the hand that feeds it?

To ask such questions about Edmund's nature and motivation is not, as some would have it, to engage in anachronistic psychologism of a kind that Shakespeare himself would have balked at. Edmund's behavior more or less cries out for some sort of explanation, whether you are an Elizabethan theatergoer, a modern literary critic, or perhaps just a regular *Homo sapiens*. As we have seen, a similar question is raised within the play by Lear with respect to his fiendish daughters: "Is there any cause in nature that make these hard hearts?" (3.6.75–76).

Whether we can *answer* such questions satisfactorily is a different, and more pertinent, issue. The question why Edmund turned out the way he did is, I think, ultimately unanswerable, but it will still be worth asking here for two related reasons. First, we must not forget that *negative* evidence can be just as important as *positive* evidence, since it enables us to exclude what is improbable or simply false. Second, an examination of Edmund's motivation will provide a necessary backdrop for my central, and perhaps surprising, claim about Edmund: that his subsequent (if partial) rehabilitation runs directly parallel to Lear's concerns in the love test.

At first sight, the social injustice that Edmund exposes so clear-sightedly might seem like a natural explanation for his heartless treatment of Gloucester. According to this reading, Edmund is a social outcast who takes revenge on the people who have treated him so unfairly. The main problem with this reading is that Edmund sees himself precisely as a victim of cultural strictures rather than of parental neglect; his complaint is with society and not with his father. Not once does he give any suggestion that his father has acted out of order. He is simply not an angry child but a cold fish: totally indifferent, as if Gloucester and the other people around him were actors in some bad comedy and he had been given the onerous task of making it more tragic.

A second mode of explanation might latch on to this remarkable detachment and define it as symptomatic of paternal neglect. For what can a child hope for from a parent? Resources, yes, but also love, and we saw in the discussion of the Roman plays how devastating the effects of insufficient attachment can be even on our fellow primates. Has Edmund become loveless because Gloucester has not loved him sufficiently?

Such a reading of Edmund finds more support from the play, particularly from the first lines when Gloucester procures Kent's patronage for his bastard son. Much depends on how this scene is staged, for if Edmund stands next to the old men and hears their conversation before he is addressed, then Gloucester is being quite thoughtless and cruel in spite of the jocular tone.

> KENT: Is not this your son, my lord?
> GLOUCESTER: His breeding, sir, hath been at my charge. (1.1.7–8)

This response conjures up many different scenarios, not least because several meanings of the early modern word "charge" could be relevant. Apart from the sexual sense of "breeding," Gloucester could be saying that he has shouldered the *task, duty* or *responsibility*;[58] the figurative *burden, load,* or *weight*;[59] or the *pecuniary burden* or *cost*[60] for Edmund's upbringing. Considered in isolation, Gloucester's "charge" could therefore involve anything from actually raising his bastard son to covering the economic expenses engendered by his sexual transgression. It seems fairly clear, however, that Shakespeare intended the latter, pecuniary sense (which is also the one chosen by the latest Arden editor, R. A. Foakes). A brief comparison with other plays reveals that when Shakespeare uses the construction "at X's charge," money is usually concerned.[61]

Provided that we are prepared to deduce Shakespeare's putative intention from his general word usage, Gloucester's response appears to replace fatherhood with economic responsibility. Is this reference to money intended to exclude all other aspects of fatherhood, such as love, or is he simply loath to use the word "son" for a bastard? It is impossible to say at this point. Gloucester continues· "I have so often blushed to acknowledge him that now / I'm brazed to't" (9–10). This admission is more straightforward, but it does not give us any definite clues about their relationship, since public embarrassment does not equal private contempt.

When Gloucester introduces Edgar into the picture, his formulation certainly sounds like a major clarification, even a declaration of love: "I have a son, sir, by order of law, some year elder than this, who yet is no dearer in my account" (18–20). But as Harry Berger points out, even these words do not necessarily say anything at all about Gloucester's feelings for either son: "This seems to mean that he likes Edmund as much as Edgar, but the phrase points with equal force in the other direction: he likes Edgar as little as Edmund."[62]

When Gloucester returns to the subject of Edmund in the first scene, it can perhaps be argued that he is more interested in joking about his private sin than explaining his relationship to his bastard son:

Though this knave came something saucily
to the world before he was sent for, yet was his mother
fair, there was good sport at his making, and the
whoreson must be acknowledged. (20–23)

It is, however, possible to draw a pretty grim conclusion from Edmund's perspective: that Gloucester thinks he has enjoyed great sex with a beautiful woman and must now own up to what he has done. This makes Edmund the awkward price that must be paid for sexual pleasure. Significantly, the word "must"   which suggests duty rather than willingness—is echoed almost immediately in Kent's formal promise that he "must love" Gloucester's bastard son (29). The final glimpse we get of Gloucester's and Edmund's relationship in this scene is Gloucester's rather offhand assertion that his bastard son has been away from home "nine years, and away he shall again" (31–32).

But once again a seemingly plausible interpretation—and one that Shakespeare almost seems to have encouraged deliberately—turns out to be mistaken. Gloucester's declaration of love for his sons may be ambiguous on the sentence level, as Harry Berger points out. But we are also informed at other points in the play that Gloucester has "loved" Edgar (and, by extension, Edmund), "no father his son dearer" (2.4.164–65). Edmund, for one, does not seem to find his father's words ambiguous at all. He regards them as sufficient confirmation that he can now safely overthrow his brother: "Our father's love is to the bastard Edmund / As to the legitimate" (1.2.17–18). One would not expect such confidence from someone who has just been told that he is loved as *little* as his brother.

This means that the sentimental reading of Edmund—that he has not been loved, and so cannot love—fails, or at least fails to procure sufficient evidence in its favor. The picture that emerges is of someone who has been loved, who probably knows in theory what it is to love, but who seems strangely impervious to the emotion himself. When he discusses Gloucester's love for his children, Edmund speaks of himself and his brother in the third person as if they were both counters in some abstract strategy game. The same strategic attitude is at work further on in the play, when Edmund considers Goneril's and Regan's advances: "Which of them shall I take? / Both? One? Or neither? Neither can be enjoyed / If both remain alive" (5.1.58–60). Like Iago, Edmund has considerable empathy in the restricted sense that he understands other people's emotions and how to manipulate them, but that is also all he knows. Or so it would seem, at least, until well into the fifth act.

In the section on *Titus Andronicus* we saw how Shakespeare vindicates parental love with particular force by attributing it to the unlikeliest candidate on offer: Aaron the Moor. Something of a similar nature happens in the last act of *King Lear*, when the dying Edmund hears Edgar's account of his father's death and is quite unexpectedly "moved" to compassion (5.3.198–200). As with parental love in the Roman plays, Edmund's volte-face seems to suggest that filial love cannot ultimately be easily repressed. What is perhaps even more noteworthy about this scene, however, and which appears to have escaped the previous commentary on Shakespeare's play, is how another famous utterance by Edmund also brings us "full circle" in the play's treatment of love.

When it is discovered that Goneril and Regan have destroyed each other, Edmund clings to their ménage à trois as evidence of love: "Yet Edmund was beloved: / The one the other poisoned for my sake, / And after slew herself" (5.3.238–40). It is important for our overall interpretation of the play to realize how closely this statement parallels Lear's attitude in the love test. In both cases, rivalry is conceived as a central token of love, and the disastrous consequence of this conception is not lost on the audience. In both cases, we are at least temporarily unsure about how to grasp Lear's and Edmund's words: is this merely an expression of vanity, or does it answer to a deeper need? For both Lear and Edmund, most importantly, *the thought of their own death*—Edmund knows that he is dying, and Lear formulates his love test right after his declaration that he will now "unburdened crawl toward death" (1.1.40)—immediately *provokes thoughts about having been loved*. There could, I think, be no deeper testament to the fundamental centrality of love to human existence.

Shakespeare's primary commitment when writing his plays must always have been dramatic rather than philosophical or existential. But it does not seem unduly speculative to conclude from this striking reversal and others we have studied so far—Aaron, Titus, and Coriolanus—that he had a profound but also nuanced belief in the depth of filial as well as parental instincts; that he fully granted love's vulnerability to interference but also thought that it could only be suppressed and never fully extinguished.

Edgar is the one character in *King Lear* who embodies filial love in its most unconditional form; where Cordelia loves but also knows how to set limits, Edgar never speaks up at all. In fact, his love for his father is so unconditional that it has made some critics a little queasy. When Gloucester rashly denounces him as an attempted parricide and seeks his life, Edgar reacts almost psychotically in the adoption of his Poor Tom identity, but he never seems to express any anger or confront his father. Not surprisingly, some critics have attributed a measure of ill-repressed vindictiveness or even perversion to him in the Dover Cliffs episode, where he pretends to lead his father to the top of a cliff and then lets him commit a mock suicide. It seems immoral to play with another human being in this way, let alone one's own father, and the scheme also bears an unpleasant resemblance to the mock executions that belong to the torturer's standard repertoire.

In fact, it seems likely that Shakespeare realized that this was a potential spectatorial response and then sought to prevent it. After all, he gives Edgar this rather clumsy aside as Gloucester gets ready to jump to his "death": "Why I do trifle thus with his despair / Is done to cure it" (4.6.33–34). Since Edgar's shock therapy is quite successful and replaces Gloucester's despair with stoic acceptance, we have no reason to doubt his stated intention. As far as I can tell, there is no other evidence for a more sinister motivation in the play. The fact that Edgar never confronts his father is also easily explicable with reference to his own words: "When we our betters see bearing our woes, / We scarcely think our miseries our foes" (3.6.100–1). Edgar's own pain at having been betrayed by his father is simply eclipsed when he beholds the latter's bleeding eyes

Edgar, then, does not present us with a difficult psychological puzzle, nor can we reduce his love for Gloucester to either self-interest or ecological pressures. It is, quite simply, irreducible, and this leads me to my final destination in this chapter: the moving reunion and restoration of love between Lear and Cordelia in the French camp and the question of love's potential transcendence.

As in *Coriolanus*, the relation between parent and child is reversed symbolically as Lear attempts to kneel before his daughter, shedding the paternal and royal authority whose abuse has caused so much trouble. In other words, we witness yet another Shakespearean scene where an individual's deep emotional experience is at odds with his cultural role and the latter is therefore discarded. Since Lear has now reached "second childhood" his posture is not unlike that of the prodigal son as he admits to his disastrous error of judgment:

LEAR: Be your tears wet? Yes, faith; I pray weep not.
    If you have poison for me, I will drink it.
    I know you do not love me, for your sisters
    Have, as I do remember, done me wrong.
    You have some cause, they have not.
CORDELIA: No cause, no cause. (4.7.71–74)

This is how Northrop Frye understands this passage and its function in the wider context of the play: "What is the cause of love, friendship, good faith, loyalty or any of the essential human virtues? Nothing. There is no 'why' about them: they just are. . . . Cordelia's answer, 'No cause, no cause,' is one of the supreme moments of all drama. And yet when Cordelia says that, she is saying precisely what she said at the beginning of the play: she will have nothing to do with these silly conditional games."[63] Strictly speaking, Cordelia is not really talking about love here; she is saying that she has no axe to grind, no cause to hurt her father. But there is still much to be said for Frye's observation that love has no cause, provided that we understand it in strictly phenomenological terms. It is impossible to find the cause of the love we feel since this emotion involves a myriad of strong impulses that are not accessible to the conscious self. This was just as true in the early modern period as it is today: "If a man urge me to tell wherefore I loved him, I feele it cannot be expressed, but by answering; Because it was he, because it was my selfe. There is beyond all discourse, and besides what I can particularly report of it, I know not what inexplicable and fatall power, a meane and Mediatrix of this indissoluble union."[64] But as Montaigne's formulation suggests, it is one thing to say that we are unable to *grasp* the cause of love, but quite another to say that it *has* no cause in a philosophical sense. As Lear says in Aristotelian and proverbial terms, nothing will come of nothing.

To think of love as having no cause may still be a tempting perspective for a culture like ours, where love has so often been understood in terms of a spiritual transcendentalism. An "uncaused" phenomenon, after all, would be one that floated above the material world of cause and effect. But there are several reasons why this is a questionable interpretation—not only of love itself, but also of Cordelia's actions.

First of all, there is no real evidence that Shakespeare conceives of love in religious terms in *King Lear*, except perhaps in the most general sense of Christian grace and forgiveness.[65] While the dramatist probably shared many of the most central ideals of his culture and was reasonably well versed in theological matters, critical attempts to turn Cordelia into a Christ figure tend to overlook a basic fact: that forgiveness is part of the universal human repertoire of conflict resolution. Christians may well be unique in their willingness to turn the other cheek, but they are not the only ones who do so. And as William Elton demonstrated so thoroughly and convincingly in 1966, *King Lear* need not be understood in specifically Christian terms but is better described as a "syncretically pagan tragedy."[66] Just as Shakespeare pictured a distinctly Roman world in his Roman plays, so he imagines a world in *Lear* that is prior to revelation and that therefore holds no providence. The characters certainly invoke their gods, but they do so in vain: "As flies to wanton boys are we to the gods, / They kill us for their sport" (4.1.38–39).

This leaves the possibility of a more secular love that is still conceived in terms of *agape*, or pure *bestowal* in Irving Singer's terminology: that is, a love that is by nature indifferent to the nature of its object and therefore spreads itself indiscriminately. The view taken by the philosopher Ilham Dilman, for example, is that true love must be "gratuitous."[67] For Erich Fromm, similarly, love is an unconditional faculty of the soul that has nothing to do with its object: "If I love my brother, I love all my brothers; if I love my child, I love all my children; no, beyond that, I love all children, all that are in need of help."[68]

The question is, however, whether this perspective really does justice to the scene before us. Would it really inspire such strong feelings if Cordelia responded to her father as the proverbial man in the street, as someone who must be loved like all other men? If you had to choose, what would it mean for you to be loved deeply and truly by another person: to be loved gratuitously and universally, as these philosophers would have it, or to be loved as the unique and special individual that you are? What Montaigne describes in the passage above is the very opposite of such beautiful abstractions: *because it was he, because it was myself.*

My purpose here is not to question the existence of admirable humans who have attained Fromm's universal love of mankind, in spite of the considerable natural constraints one might expect on such emotional profusion. What I do mean to suggest is that the scene of forgiveness between Lear and Cordelia is intensely beautiful and moving, not because Cordelia's love for her father is unconditional, transcendental, causeless, or an instance of *imitatio Christi*, but because it is *irreducible*. An irreducible love, unlike its transcendental counterpart, has any number of causes and is far from gratuitous. We can surmise that Cordelia loves Lear because he is her father, because he has suffered immensely, because he is senile and weak, because he is begging for forgiveness, because it is a child's duty, and so forth. But if we were to combine all these causes they would still not allow us to calculate the grand sum of her love.

Given its roots in evolved attachment structures, love is not something we can portion out according to individual desert, poetic justice, or our personal convenience. It is a powerful force that arises from the depths of our psyche, binding us fast to the ones we love. This is why Shakespeare's Cleopatra declares that "there is beggary in the love that can be reckoned." Lear knows very well that he can *expect* nothing from his daughter after what he has done, and yet he receives everything. This is the ideal aspect of love, the element of limbic bestowal that gilds the object of our affections, much like the magical eyebeam celebrated by Renaissance poets. Like most ideals, the element of bestowal also has its troubling undercurrents. While it is true that *King Lear* treats us to an intensely beautiful reconciliation between parent and child, we must not forget that it also tells the story of two abused children who cannot help loving their thoughtless tormentors.

I do not mean to suggest, of course, that love in *Lear* is a matter of pure bestowal. As we have seen throughout this chapter, the tense and continuously shifting relationship between love and duty in *King Lear* (sometimes antithetical, sometimes almost synonymous, sometimes subsuming one another) renders the situation far more ambiguous and uncertain. If we go back one last time to the first scene of the play, France's response to Cordelia's social disgrace shows how bestowal is ultimately intertwined with appraisal:

> Gods, gods! 'Tis strange that from their cold'st neglect
> My love should kindle to inflamed respect.
> Thy dowerless daughter, King, thrown to my chance,
> Is queen of us, of ours and our fair France. (1.1.256–59)

We admire France for his moral stature and compassion. But he also recognizes that his love for Cordelia cannot be pure or transcendental because it is at least partly shaped by other people's actions and impressions. He seems to fall in love with Cordelia's suffering just as much as he falls in love with her as a person, which seems to undermine his earlier contention that "love's not love / When it is mingled with regards that stands / Aloof from th'entire point" (240–42). In the next chapter, where we turn to romantic love in *Troilus and Cressida* and *All's Well That Ends Well*, we will look more closely at this tension between amorous appraisal and bestowal.

4

Romantic Love in Two Problem Plays

The stage is more beholding to Love, than the Life of Man. For as to the stage,
Love is ever matter of Comedies, and now and then of Tragedies: But in Life it doth
much mischiefe. Sometimes like a Syren, Sometimes like a Fury.

Francis Bacon, "Of Love." *Essayes*, 31

The first significant unifying feature of these plays is that we are left pondering the
questions raised by the action rather than contemplating the sense of loss charac-
teristic of tragedy or feeling the release or joy inherent in Shakespeare's romantic
comedies.

Vivian Thomas, *The Moral Universe of Shakespeare's Problem Plays*, 14.

In the first chapter of this study I suggested that romantic love is not an arbitrary invention, ideological fabrication, or social construction specific to Western culture. It is the realization of a universal human potential. All over the world, and for thousands of years, people have been seized with an intense desire for lasting physical and emotional union with someone they deem unique and special. They have found, sometimes to their consternation, dismay, or even desperation, that other vital concerns have suddenly become fleeting and unimportant; that they cannot stop thinking about this wonderful person; and that it may even be difficult to imagine a life without him or her.

Even though this experience probably goes to the roots of an evolved human nature, we have seen that its universality does not preclude variation in both form and expression. Love's paradox of sameness and difference is prepared for already on the level of the genome, since our genes code for membership in *Homo sapiens* as well as for individual uniqueness. What is more, no individual life trajectory will ever be the same. The paradox is further intensified by the impact of human culture, which regulates individual behavior and structures the world materially and conceptually. One particular culture may seek to suppress, fail to recognize, or perhaps subordinate romantic love to other concerns, while another may elevate it as the supreme ideal in human existence. To the extent that it is successful, a cultural norm or social environment can do more than regulate antecedent desires; it can also have a decisive impact on how love itself will be experienced. We need only compare the ravenous hunger of a gourmand who sifts through the menu with that of a desperate famine victim to remind ourselves that the same basic desire can be experienced very differently depending on its potential for realization.

If romantic love is indeed universal, then we have little reason to suppose that Shakespeare's contemporaries were radically different from modern Westerners in this respect. Four hundred years is a very short time in the history of the species, and most of the cultural heritage is shared. Pining lovers were certainly to be found outside the narrow elite circles that sighed as they read their Petrarch or contemplated the prospects of an arranged marriage:

> Cases in the church courts reveal that passionate attachment was a common experience further down the social scale and suggest that the ideal of romantic love was deeply rooted in popular culture. . . . We read of men and women of the fifteenth and sixteenth centuries who fell ill and almost died of love or threatened suicide. People were often described as saying that there was only one person they could possibly marry as long as their lives lasted.[1]

The plight of these early modern lovers illustrates the need to distinguish carefully between romantic love (a relatively unchanging emotion) and marriage (a social institution that can have different functions and definitions depending on the culture, epoch, social class, and so forth).[2] While the early modern marital union certainly could be a vehicle for love, or even its deepest expression, there has never been any necessary dependence between the two in any culture.

In late fifteenth-century France, Montaigne even drew a firm line between love and marriage, defining the latter as a "covenant which hath nothing free but the entrance." In his aristocratic experience, married life certainly had its "plaine, and more generall delight," but passionate love marriages were usually the fickle creations of ardent youths. "I see no marriages faile sooner, or more troubled, then such as are concluded for beauties sake, and huddled up for amorous desires. There are required more solide foundations, and more constant grounds, and a more warie marching to it: this earnest youthly heate serveth no purpose."[3] Whether or not we share this view, Montaigne reminds us that humans do not necessarily love the one they marry, and they do not always marry the one they love.[4]

To distinguish between marriage and romantic love is also, by extension, to distinguish between two kinds of *choice* (that may or may not coincide). First, there is the choice of a marriage partner. This was such a momentous and irrevocable decision in early modern England, given its Christian system of lifelong monogamy without escape clauses, that mutual attraction or passion was usually deemed an insufficient criterion. Moreover, there were often several parties who had an interest in the match. For those who did not have substantial property, marriage was often a matter of free choice and parental consent a formality, while others were far more constrained. As John Gillis points out, the criteria for marriage typically included "the advancement of the individual or the family, the ideal of parity, the character of the proposed partner, and personal affection or love."[5]

In comparison to the choice of partner, the second kind of choice—that of romantic love object—is far more nebulous and mysterious. Why does Jack choose to love Jill, of all people on earth? At first sight, the word "choice" may seem slightly out of order here, since Jack may well have fallen for Jill in direct defiance of his own conscious intentions or expectations. But this only forces us to restate the question on the level of the unconscious mind, for somewhere deep down a choice has been made by something that is just as much "Jack" as the conscious self he identifies with. Can we say anything meaningful about such a choice, or is it truly inscrutable in an absolute sense?

In the two Shakespearean problem plays under consideration here, *Troilus and Cressida* (c. 1602) and *All's Well That Ends Well* (c. 1603), romantic love is nothing if not a problem. This is partly because it is an ambivalent source of delight and anxiety, and partly because Shakespeare turns its nature into a philosophical problem. More specifically, he appears to hone in quite systematically on the element of *choice* in love as well as marriage, with a particular eye to the subtle valuations and evaluations that underpin the choices we make.

Even at a cursory glance, the thematic symmetry between these plays (which may have been written in sequence) is striking. In both plays we find extensive debates about the value of a woman called Helen or Helena, and the plays approach this issue from opposed and complementary directions. In *Troilus and Cressida* it is the risk of *overvaluation* that is at stake, as the Trojans argue whether the beautiful Helen has really been worth seven years of abortive bloodshed. In *All's Well*, the young nobleman Bertram comes under considerable social pressure to acknowledge that he has *underestimated* the socially inferior but highly accomplished Helena. My overriding objective here will be to show how systematically these plays approach the question of love: if *Troilus* is the thesis, then *All's Well* is the antithesis that followed hard upon.

The intimate connection between love and value had its own linguistic resonance in the early modern age, as Terence Hawkes pointed out in 1959 after consulting the *Oxford English Dictionary*. He observed that the word "love" had "two different, almost opposite meanings" in Shakespeare's time, since it could mean either personal affection or the estimation of value.[6] As we have just seen, these senses may not have been so opposed after all, since any kind of love (including the ideal of unconditional *agape*) is dependent on some form of valorization. What this brief exercise in historical semantics really demonstrates, in my view, is that the early modern word was sufficiently flexible to incorporate two impulses that are always at work in love.

On the one hand, we are fundamentally social animals who attune our desires to those of others and who can even desire something or someone just because other people do so. The logical consequence of this tendency, if it is left unchecked by other emotional impulses or cultural strictures, is the proverbial "meat market" where individuals size each other up, compare the other person to what else is on offer, and then deliver themselves to the highest bidder. In *Troilus and Cressida*, Shakespeare paints a very dismal picture of the tendency of individual desire to collapse into social appraisal, so that love becomes a fleeting assessment of a person's relative value in the sexual marketplace. Such love has an identifiable shelf life; it lasts until someone more interesting becomes available.

Some would perhaps take the cynical view that this is the whole spine-chilling truth about the human affections, at least if they are left unchecked. But even though our basic emotional systems are hypersensitive to social cues, it would be a mistake to regard them as straightforward effects of our proximal social relations. What the cynical-relational view forgets, first of all, is that humans are not simply rational agents involved in some sort of abstract strategy game. We are concrete, messy creatures of flesh and blood who are strongly predisposed by an evolutionary process to attach and commit ourselves to other humans; we are, in Irving Singer's terms, designed not only to appraise value but also to bestow it actively in the form of love. Second, the human paradox of sameness and difference ensures that this active bestowal will rarely be exactly identical to that of another person. In *All's Well That Ends Well*, Shakespeare explores the *limitations* of the social appraisal that predominates in *Troilus* by highlighting the inescapable *incongruity* between individual desire and the social consensus. Given this tension between individual desire and social expectations, the play also returns us to a central issue in *King Lear*—the relation between love and duty—by raising the question of whether love can be expected or deserved.

Troilus and Cressida

A good way to approach the nature of romantic and marital choice in these Shakespearean problem plays is to make a brief detour to the romantic comedies. Numerous critics have remarked over the years that the young women in these plays seem to enjoy a good deal of self-confidence and power, while the men often look like blundering amateurs who are typically one step behind in the amorous repartee. Most recently, Maurice Charney has observed that "in the comedies, the women lead the love game. They are strikingly intelligent and witty and enjoy role-playing, especially when they are disguised as boys."[7] How can we explain this considerable latitude and self-confidence of women in the comedies, who stand out so markedly against the demure, self-effacing virgins and destructive mothers that stalk the tragedies?

There is more than one way to answer this question. First, it is in the nature of a romantic comedy to lick the icing off the cake, so to speak. The social pressures that confront the lovers are there mainly to create the dramatic tension required for comic release, and we know more or less from the start that any hindrances will eventually be overcome. Even more crucially, a romantic comedy deals with the most emotionally intense phase of a relationship—that of courtship or mate choice—and then discreetly closes the curtain before we have time to worry about things like spousal compatibility, marital boredom, or potential infidelities. (This is a simplification on my part: the endings of Shakespeare's comedies are not always free of doubts about future happiness, and one critic even goes so far as to declare that "the makings of marriage in Shakespearean comedy are not promising ones.")[8] In such a dramatic world, where the stress lies on human inventiveness, the power of love, and our triumph over adversity, it is not unreasonable to expect that women will be depicted as more resourceful and in control of their destinies than in, say, the tragedies.

Of course, this still fails to explain why Shakespeare's comic heroines seem *more* resourceful than the *men*. There must be a more specific connection between gender identity and genre. Maurice Charney does not seek to answer this difficult question, but he does embrace the currently orthodox view among literature professors that "the characteristics of gender are constructed socially and historically rather than physiologically. . . . What it means to be a man or a woman is a social and historical construction rather than an innate set of masculine or feminine traits" (6, 133).

I have already raised substantial objections to such dichotomies—where nature is first opposed to culture and then neatly removed from the equation, leaving only culture—and will return to this issue again in chapter 5. For now it is sufficient to note that the constructivist approach will typically define literary characters in relation to oppressive cultural stereotypes. From such a perspective, Shakespeare's comic heroines will be understood as carnivalesque role reversals, as subversive inversions of everything that women were expected to be in a patriarchal culture. Charney writes: "What is interesting in Shakespeare is how male and female characters seem to play against conventional expectations. It is as if Shakespeare is determined to set up a counterpoint between what is expected and what actually occurs, so that characters have latitude to move in and out of preconceived stereotypes" (150).

The inversion of expectations that Charney touches on here is indeed a frequent dramatic strategy in Shakespeare, but his comic heroines are probably more than just reversals of cultural stereotypes. In contrast to the broad constructivist perspective, I would like to suggest that the relative freedom of these literary characters may reflect the interaction of broader tendencies in human nature with Shakespeare's specific historical environment. In chapter 1 we looked briefly at the theory of parental investment, which predicts successfully that sex differences in parental investment will have consequences for the reproductive strategies of either sex. Given the relative differences in reproductive conditions for men and women, it seems likely that the traditional stereotype of ardent males and choosy females did not simply fall out of the sky. At least until the modern age of contraception, women have always had more to gain from carefully scrutinizing the commitment and quality of a sexual partner, while men have not had a comparable evolutionary incentive for discrimination.

As we saw in chapter 1, there is nothing ideologically suspect or misogynistic about this idea as long as we avoid confusing it with normative assumptions that *all* men or women either *are* or *should* be this or that—coy, sexually passive, and so forth. What is more, we saw that being choosy is not the same thing as being coy, and it is quite possible to be a choosy sexual predator. There is no reason to confuse this account with a reductive picture of men as desiring "subjects" and women as passive "objects." Female choice and female objecthood are not easily compatible since an object has no agency and so is inherently incapable of choice. Finally, it must be remembered that the patterns predicted by parental investment can result not only from subconscious predispositions but also from conscious deliberation: "Even if women enjoy sexual variety as much or more than men, for thousands of years they have not needed to be rocket scientists to understand that they make a greater potential commitment per copulation than do men."[9]

For young women in Shakespeare's England the tendency toward female choice was often curtailed, or at least partially circumscribed, because the patriarchal society they lived in defined them either as dutiful daughters, dutiful servants, or dutiful wives. But there were at least two phases in women's lives when they could enjoy an unparalleled degree of freedom and power. One was widowhood, which meant that a woman might finally be in legal control of her own property, and the other was the period of courtship and betrothal:

> Betrothal could obliterate differences in rank and alter the relationship between the sexes. It gave females a measure of choice and a degree of power more equal to that of men. For a brief moment they were the center of attention. Having been courted and fought over, they were in a position to make demands that were not possible for mere spinsters or wives. Betrothal was for them a magic moment, when they were the object of their lover's most ardent affections, their parent's sentimentality, and their rivals' envy.[10]

As long as the betrothal had not been consummated sexually, it could be broken off if conditions were not satisfactory. We have also seen that even if some parents expressed strong views on the choice of partner, marriage was always legally a matter of individual consent. It is not unreasonable to suggest, therefore, that Shakespeare's comic heroines "lead the love game" because the dramatist understood the uniqueness of this phase in the life of the average English woman. In this significant phase between the cultural roles of obedient daughter and obedient wife, many women were able to embrace more fully the ecological niche carved out by sexual selection. What Shakespeare's romantic comedies stage is not an inversion of patriarchy but an affirmation of natural female choice.

It is a defining trait of Shakespeare's problem plays (or problem comedies, as they are sometimes called) that they present their audience with an essentially comic plot but hold back the expected comic release. In this way, they breed ambivalence and doubt rather than just a pleasurable sense of resolution and wish fulfillment.[11] While the comic element is more subdued in *Troilus and Cressida* than in the other problem plays, its female protagonist can be described as a disillusioned cousin of the comic heroines.

When we first encounter Cressida in act 1, scene 2, she displays a razor-sharp wit, cool mastery of the situation, and a marked predilection for bawdy jokes as she banters with her uncle Pandarus. A little further on in the same scene, however, she reveals a darker side as she explains her reluctance to admit her love for Troilus:

> Women are angels, wooing:
> Things won are done; joy's soul lies in the doing.
> That she belov'd knows naught that knows not this:
> Men prize the thing ungain'd more than it is. (1.2.286–89)

This passage has attracted much critical attention. As Lu Emily Pearson points out, Shakespeare takes over the idea that "love too easily attained is not prized" from Chaucer's version of the story.[12] Charles Lyons reads the passage with a slightly different emphasis, as a comment on love's finitude in which Cressida is "acutely aware of the disintegration of love in the flux of Time."[13] This is an apt formulation, but we must not forget that Cressida defines the problem explicitly in gender terms: it is *women* who are temporary angels and *men* who do the prizing. This is clearly how she construes her own situation, for compared to Troilus she "displays a good deal more apprehension over the dangers of romantic idealization; she speaks in a vocabulary of fear and Troilus in a vocabulary of hope."[14] Carol Thomas Neely, finally, sees *Troilus and Cressida* as an instance of a common tendency in several Shakespearean plays where the men "idealize their beloveds, and the women deny, mock, and qualify their lovers' protestations of commonplaces." According to Neely, the women attain "verbal superiority" and "seize control of courtship" before they pay the price of subordination within marriage.[15]

True to the recent ideological fashion that has privileged abstract, systemic explanations over individual or psychological explanations, many critics actively deny that this tension can have anything to do with Troilus and Cressida as individuals. It must be a stereotype produced by their oppressive patriarchal culture.[16] As I intimated above, such an approach will find it difficult to explain how Cressida and her comic colleagues manage to "lead the love game" (Charney) or "seize control of courtship" (Neely) when their culture is meant to push them in the opposite direction. At first sight, it may seem like a solution to argue that they take control by *reversing* or *subverting* the dominant assumptions of their culture, but that would contradict the original idea that individual agency is irrelevant. In this way, the systemic reading becomes caught in a double bind of its own making.

A better approach is to acknowledge that this tension between male idealization and female choice has deeper roots than arbitrary cultural strictures. From the perspective of parental investment theory, it is only to be expected that the average man will be slightly more prone to "idealize" a prospective sexual partner, at least in the sexual short term, while the average woman will have a greater incentive to prolong the courtship (which means more time for assessment and choice). No wonder, then, if women are "angels, wooing" and the average man proves a little more trigger-happy.[17] When Shakespeare browsed through book 3 of Ovid's *The Art of Love,* he could even find detailed instructions for women on how to capitalize on this difference by keeping men on their toes: "Neither promise yourself too easily to him who entreats you, nor yet deny what he asks too stubbornly. Cause him to hope and fear together."[18]

This is, of course, exactly what Cressida does, like many other Shakespearean women. In act 2, when she has finally revealed her love, she repeats her earlier fear that this admission will alter the balance of power between them:

> TROILUS: Why was my Cressid then so hard to win?
> CRESSIDA: Hard to seem won; but I was won, my lord,
>   With the first glance that ever—Pardon me:
>   If I confess much you will play the tyrant. (3.2.114–17)

Her fear that Troilus may become a "tyrant" can be read on several complementary levels. As we all know, strong emotions of this kind can be difficult to express because they acknowledge our dependence on another person, which leaves us vulnerable and weak. For Cressida, allowing herself to be "won" also means relinquishing the more specific power afforded her by female choice. But Shakespeare was too aware of the shaping force of human culture to depict human relationships as purely "natural" in the sense of direct expressions of innate mechanisms or universal needs. A little further on, Cressida laments her position in a society that reserves the romantic initiative for men: "And yet, good faith, I wish'd myself a man, / Or that we women had men's privilege / Of speaking first" (125–27). This complaint may in fact be slightly beside the point, since taking the first step would not have insured her against the brevity of male idealization, but her words are still a lucid example of how culture can pick up on a widespread tendency in human nature and turn it into an oppressive normative rule.

When Cressida observes dejectedly that "men prize the thing ungain'd more than it is" (1.2.286–89), her words underscore the connection we have traced between love and value. Seen from this perspective, idealization is an overvaluation of the love object, and more than one philosopher has even gone so far as to contend that love itself is a form of idealization. The idea certainly did not originate with Freud, as the following lines from Francis Bacon make clear: "It is a strange thing, to note the Excess of this Passion; And how it braves, the Nature, and value of things, by this that the Speaking in a perpetuall *Hyper-bole*, is comely in nothing, but in Love."[19] When Cressida associates men with overvaluation, however, her underlying wish seems to be that our love could somehow go beyond subjective attributions to assess a person's value more accurately. What seems to prevent love from becoming rational—that is, a balanced mediation of passion and judgment — is mainly its subservience to time. Given enough time, one might hope to assess the other person more accurately.

It is possible to piece together a broad critical consensus that this relation between value and time is an important and multifaceted theme in *Troilus and Cressida*. Frank Kermode provides the first building block with his observation that "the language of the play is almost everywhere concerned with questions relating to value—to puzzles arising from the difficulty that value is differently conceived by different people. A broad distinction exists between the view that value can be intrinsic, or that it depends on some transcendental criterion, and the sceptical view that it depends wholly upon attribution, that the value of anything is the value one places upon it."[20]

Someone who takes the more skeptical approach can hardly avoid the nagging suspicion that even our sense of who we are is highly dependent on what people think of us. On the one hand, there are several attempts in the play to dissociate a person's social value from his personal identity, as in Thersites' "A plague of opinion! A man may wear it on both sides, like a / leather jerkin" (3.3.261–63). On the other hand, even more attention is paid to the dependence of personal identity on a person's social value and the ultimate dependence of value on time.[21] As Lyons puts it, "The ambiguous exploration of value conducted by the characters in *Troilus and Cressida* seems to be an attempt to determine their personal identities."[22] The first scenes of the play contain a veritable orgy of comparisons between different characters: Is Troilus a better man than Hector? Who is the greatest warrior in the Trojan camp? Is Helen really better looking than Cressida?[23]

We need only consider a few more interpretations to realize that few of Shakespeare's plays can boast such carefully crafted and interconnected systems of theme and supportive imagery. Indeed, the recent critical history of *Troilus* is a wonderful example of how a cumulative and pluralistic research tradition can expand and enrich our experience of a literary work. In one of the best readings to date, Vivian Thomas notes that the interrogation of value, identity, and time is also at work in the use of mercantile images: "Imagery of trade and commerce is used frequently and to great effect in bringing down all ostensible values to market prices."[24] Another strand of imagery that concretizes these abstract questions about value and time is that of food, appetite, and satiety. As Nicholas Grene puts it, "*Troilus and Cressida* is a play to put you off your food. The eating images that are everywhere in the play combine ideas of rampant, predatory appetite, with the sordid association of satiety. Ravenous hunger and the sick after-effects of overeating coalesce."[25] This graphic imagery becomes a metaphor for all forms of human desire, where nothing seems exempt from the endless circle of desire, consummation, satiety, and renewed desire. A third and more historically specific imagery is that of religious idolatry, which constitutes yet another overvaluation of its object: "Despite the obvious differences between the idealistic Trojans and the rational Greeks, both are variously engaged in making the service greater than the god, in performing parodies of true worship."[26]

The gist of this sophisticated Shakespearean inquiry is condensed into the following passage, which reads almost like a thesis statement on the inevitable transience of our most cherished values (and hence of our social status and identity):

> O let not virtue seek
> Remuneration for the thing it was;
> For beauty, wit,
> High birth, vigour of bone, desert in service,
> Love, friendship, charity, are subjects all
> To envious and calumniating Time. (3.3.169–74)

It is against this bleak background that Shakespeare explores the nature of romantic and marital choice. A pivotal moment is act 2, scene 2, when the Trojans debate whether Paris's abduction of the beautiful Helen has really been worth the loss of so many lives during the seven-year siege. Hector's position is that Helen has been substantially *overvalued*:

> If we have lost so many tenths of ours
> To guard a thing not ours nor worth to us

(Had it our name) the value of one ten,
What merit's in that reason which denies
The yielding of her up?
. . .
She is not worth what she doth cost the keeping. (2.2.21–24, 52)

Curiously, Hector's idealistic brother Troilus does not counter with the courtly swagger or verbose rhetoric we might expect from him. Instead he delivers a deeply skeptical retort that forces Hector to clarify his position:

TROILUS: What's aught but as 'tis valued?
HECTOR: But value dwells not in particular will;
    It holds his estimate and dignity
    As well wherein 'tis precious of itself
    As in the prizer. 'Tis mad idolatry
    To make the service greater than the god;
    And the will dotes that is attributive
    To what infectiously itself affects,
    Without some image of th'affected merit. (53–61)

This passage has been instrumental in prompting critics to draw the distinction between "intrinsic" and "extrinsic" conceptions of value that Kermode embraces above. Strictly speaking, however, we are rather dealing with an extrinsic perspective, offered by Troilus, and an attempt by Hector to reconcile the intrinsic with the extrinsic. If anything, Hector's solution brings to mind the Platonic concept of *anamnesis*, that we cannot recognize the good unless we already have an idea of the good lodged inside us.[27] What is more, it is questionable whether the otherwise idealistic Troilus can really be regarded as a spokesman for skepticism or relativism on the basis of a single line. The rest of the debate shows that he is more concerned with honor and constancy than he is with questions about value.[28]

The critic who has pushed hardest for a strictly "extrinsic" or relational conception of love and desire in *Troilus and Cressida* is René Girard.[29] According to his triangular theory of mimetic desire, desire does not originate in the *subject* or the *object* but models itself on a third party who is either a rival or a mediator.[30] Desire, in other words, is "mimetic" in that it imitates the desire of another person, which makes it unpleasantly akin to envy. There is something to be said for this perspective, since we all know that it is possible to desire something or someone because other people do so. Nor is there any doubt that desire can be enhanced by the presence of rivals, as Ovid observed some two thousand years ago: "Some women there are whom timid indulgence serves without reward, and, when no rival exists, their passion wanes."[31] But the problem with Girard's theory, like so much recent theory, is that it makes room only for social relationships and forgets that they are always forged by individual organisms. If we argue that A loves B because C loves B, then we still have not explained why C loves B in the first place.

Girard's analysis of mimetic desire in *Troilus and Cressida* is accompanied by a clear division of moral sympathies. Troilus is accused of "disgraceful behavior" (128) because he leaves Cressida after their first night of lovemaking even though she pleads with him to stay. On this "fateful morning," Girard suggests, Troilus's desire is "completely dead" (128) because there can no longer be any rivals for Cressida's attentions. She is finally his, and this is the natural end of a mimetic desire. So when it is decreed that Cressida will pass over to the Greeks in exchange for Antenor, this forced separation fits Troilus hand in glove because it enables him to continue desiring her and seeking her out. From now on, their clandestine meetings will happen only on *his* terms, and he will have new mimetic rivals among the Greek lords—most notably her custodian, Diomedes—to rekindle his desire. For Troilus, Cressida's departure is as much a gain as it is a loss.

Is this a convincing claim about Shakespeare's male protagonist? I think not. Part of the problem is that Girard's theory places such an exclusive emphasis on the "relational" aspect. Another weakness is that he frequently overstates his case in his attempts to squeeze the play into his triangular a priori conception of desire. In an earlier published version of this reading, he even argues that Troilus "has pushed Cressida into the arms of Diomed,"[32] and he was wise to retract this opinion since Troilus clearly has nothing to do with the exchange. What is more, we can certainly debate the nature of Pandarus's motivation in acting as go-between, but it is probably not "completely obvious" to all readers that he is secretly in love with his own niece.[33]

Fortunately, it is always possible to tone down assertions of this kind and turn them into more productive questions. The gist of Girard's reading is that Cressida's worst fears have come true; that she has been an "angel, wooing" who must sooner or later be cast aside (however politely, with references to ribald crows and so forth) when she has yielded to her lover's advances. Has Troilus's love for her waned already after their first night together? Is his desire yet another example of the evanescent and undependable appraisals that dominate this play? To answer these questions, we must first consider what the play (and Troilus in particular) has to say about marriage and commitment.

Let us return to the central debate over Helen in act 2, scene 2, where Troilus puts forward a lengthy argument in favor of keeping her. Immediately after his brother has contended that "value dwells not in particular will," Troilus draws a parallel between the theft of Helen and the nature of the marriage vow:

> how may I avoid,
> Although my will distaste what it elected,

> The wife I choose? There can be no evasion
> To blench from this and to stand firm by honour.
> We turn not back the silks upon the merchant
> When we have soil'd them, nor the remainder viands
> We do not throw in unrespective sieve
> Because we now are full. (2.2.66–73)

Troilus is a passionate young man and clearly something of an idealist, but he does not idealize passion. On the contrary, he appears to view marriage much like many of Shakespeare's contemporaries would have viewed it, as a careful mediation between feelings and pragmatic considerations. But Troilus also adheres strongly to the ideals of honor and constancy— or more specifically, to the honor that derives from constancy, which in matters of love translates into a belief in binding commitment. At this point in the play, when he is still waiting anxiously—indeed, at times almost deliriously—to consummate his love for Cressida, he can also stand back and meditate almost naturalistically on the war between commitment and desire. The two analogies he employs toward the end of the passage (one mercantile, and the other connected with appetite and satiety) reinforce our impression of a universal transience that can be dealt with but never defeated.

It is only our sense of honor and constancy that can oppose this natural course, as Troilus suggests again in a passage that focuses explicitly on the issue of valuation:

> If you'll confess [Paris] brought home worthy prize—
> As you must needs, for you all clapp'd your hands
> And cried "Inestimable!": why do you now
> The issue of your proper wisdoms rate,
> And do a deed that never Fortune did—
> Beggar the estimation which you priz'd
> Richer than sea and land? (87–93)

Troilus may be young and idealistic, but he is neither stupid nor naive. As we have seen, he is aware that even our most cherished values (including love) are subject to time and may one day turn into indifference or even hatred. His ideal of constancy, therefore, is neither a childish fantasy nor a metaphysical ideal, but the product of a painful realism that has first been accepted as true and then deemed intolerable. He seems to have concluded that we cannot win the war against time, but that it may at least be possible to win a few battles by refusing to accept the natural deflation of love's value.

It is, of course, more than a tad ironic that Troilus should defend the abduction of Helen from her husband Menelaus by invoking the unshakeable marriage vow. Paris, who can hardly be immune to such contradictions, soon proposes to amend his theft of Helen "in honourable keeping her" (150). But Hector isolates the blind spot in all this talk of constancy and honor; what is at stake is not whether it is right to *keep* Helen, but whether it was right to *take* her in the first place. He then proceeds to naturalize marriage as an unalienable right to property:

> Nature craves
> All dues be render'd to their owners: now
> What nearer debt in all humanity
> Than wife is to the husband? If this law
> Of nature be corrupted through affection,
> And that great minds, of partial indulgence
> To their benumbed wills, resist the same,
> There is a law in each well-order'd nation
> To curb those raging appetites that are
> Most disobedient and refractory. (174–83)

Does this description of the marital union sound distasteful to a modern sensibility? If so, this is probably because the Elizabethans were less embarrassed than we are to acknowledge that marriage is not only a formal correlate of powerful feelings. It is also a question of contractual ownership, where I am yours and you are mine, and where we surrender some of our individual rights to each other. Hector's speech is unsettling because he strips marriage of all *other* motives that might soften this proprietary dimension. According to Christian liturgy, marriage was (and still is) a sacred union that had three basic justifications—procreation, avoidance of fornication, and mutual comfort and support[34]—and many of Shakespeare's contemporaries also had the expectation that it should be a loving union. But in Hector's account, it is only the threat of fornication and adultery—the "raging appetites"—that looms large.

Troilus and Hector are on opposite sides in the debate over Helen, and yet they invoke a remarkably similar conception of marriage. They confront us with an almost Manichean conflict between commitment and lust, where marriage constitutes a desperate attempt to impose some fixity and order on the wavering passions. This ties in with Irving Singer's contention that marriage "appears in Shakespeare as the domestication of nature, a human control upon the primitive instincts that are needed for survival."[35] Whether Shakespeare also "idealizes marriage because it satisfies social as well as biological need" is a more difficult question, not least because it depends on what genre and play we are discussing. In the comedies, marriage is very much a matter of plot resolution, and the ideal of happily-ever-after is never really put to the test because the curtain has gone down. In *Lear*, Edmund derides the life-denying "dull stale tired bed" of marriage

(1.2.13), which shows that the dramatist was at least capable of more disillusioned thoughts. In *Troilus and Cressida*, finally, the "idealization" of marriage is far from synonymous with satisfaction, but rather stems from a disillusioned recognition that human desire is insatiable:

> This is the monstruosity in love,
> lady: that the will is infinite, and the execution
> confined: that the desire is boundless, and the act a
> slave to limit. (3.2.78–81)

The marital union in Shakespeare's play is best described as an attempt to circumscribe *choice* and thus to remove the amorous sphere from the endlessly shifting appraisals and comparisons that flesh is heir to: *Is Cressida as beautiful as Helen? Is Hector a worthier man than his brother Troilus? Is Hector as worthy today as he was yesterday?* Choice presupposes comparison, comparison directs desire, desire is a form of valuation, and value is a slave to time.

Given Troilus's strong views on marriage and commitment, would we not have expected him to marry the woman he loves? According to Nicholas Grene, there is "a simple explanation as to why marriage is excluded as a possibility" between Troilus and Cressida: "Shakespeare has inherited the story . . . from the medieval courtly love tradition in which the central passion was virtually always extramarital."[36] This may well be so, but it is still notable that Shakespeare comes close to actually describing a formal union between his lovers in act 3, scene 2. Their long oaths of eternal love and commitment are surrounded by contractual (3.2.55–56) as well as sanctifying language (202–4), and Pandarus even defines himself as a "witness" (168).

In her eminent study of Shakespearean courtship, Ann Jennalie Cook notices the close connections between this scene and English marriage customs. She defines the scene as a "butchered form of both the betrothal and the wedding ceremonies," a "deformation of solemn rites" which "leads not to the altar but to bed."[37] The question is, however, whether this debased view is really shared by the main protagonists, in spite of the bantering that surrounds their union. When Troilus later discovers that Cressida has betrayed him, his reaction gives us some idea of how he, at least, has understood the nature of their union: "Instance, O instance! strong as Pluto's gates: / Cressid is mine, tied with the bonds of heaven" (5.2.151–52). He regards his union with Cressida as a binding contract that has been sanctified before the gods.

Why does Shakespeare approximate an English marriage so closely in the portrayal of a pagan liaison? We can, of course, only speculate about his intentions, but one important effect is that he endows Troilus and Cressida's relationship with all the expectations, claims, and demands of a real marriage, while also denying them the legal capacity to enforce them.

We can now return better armed to the suspicion raised by René Girard, that Troilus loses interest in Cressida because he has attained undisturbed possession of her. Has Cressida been proven right in her fear that women are "angels, wooing"? Shakespeare leaves us no doubt that Cressida betrays Troilus by giving herself to Diomedes, but has Troilus already betrayed *her* at that point by falling very quickly out of love? As we have seen, there is no reason to share Girard's moral denunciation of Troilus, since the latter is nothing if not moral and idealistic. We have also seen that Troilus cannot have attained "undisturbed possession" of Cressida since the two are not married. But is there perhaps some telltale quality to Troilus's love that might point us in Girard's direction?

It has sometimes been argued that the "sensuousness" of Troilus's dialogues betrays his lack of genuine love for Cressida as a person.[38] Of course, there is always a point where our interpretations attach themselves to fine textual nuances and endow these with subjective significance; a passage may have a "feel" to it that we cannot quite capture, or justify, in analytical language. But if we restrict ourselves to those aspects that are open to intersubjective assessment, then Troilus shows every sign of being romantically involved in the first acts. Most obviously, he exhibits a strong desire for emotional and physical union, and it is not strange if his rapture should grow a little "sensuous" given the immediate context; he is, after all, waiting to make love to the woman he loves for the first time. He also thinks intrusively about her (1.1.33), feels emptiness and despair in her absence (36–42), idealizes her (49–64), is possessive of her, and reorders his life priorities by promising to love her forever. So while Shakespeare did not have recourse to a modern definition of romantic love, he still includes most aspects in his portrayal of Troilus.[39]

Since we have no reason to assume that Troilus's romantic feelings are not genuine, the question is rather if his feelings, however real, prove so evanescent— and so in keeping with the larger themes of the play—that they vanish after only one night? This leads us to a delicate evolutionary complication in the relationship between the sexes. When Balthasar in *Much Ado* observes that "men were deceivers ever," most people read this line in the straightforward sense that Shakespeare probably intended: men *consciously deceive women*. But since the identity of the deceived is not stated, the passage can also be taken to mean that men *deceive themselves unconsciously* about the implications of their own feelings. In fact, it can even be in their genetic interest to do so, for as evolutionary theorists have long recognized,[40] self-deception is sometimes beneficial for the human organism. If we accept the basic tendencies predicted by parental investment theory—that the average woman will be more selective and more disposed than the average man to look for signs of lasting commitment, while the average male has a stronger evolutionary incentive to seek out short-term encounters with numerous women—then it follows that a man will sometimes do well to subconsciously confuse his testosterone-driven short-term interest with long-term commitment. Why is this self-delusion a functional evolutionary strategy? Because the most convincing liar is the one who believes every word he says.

The *locus classicus* in this area is the morning-after scene (act 4, scene 2), where Cressida pleads with Troilus to stay with her after their night of lovemaking. When Troilus excuses himself and urges her to go back to sleep, Cressida first questions his feelings for her—"Are you aweary of me?" (6)—and then seems to conclude that her worst fears have been confirmed:

> Prithee, tarry.
> You men will never tarry.
> O foolish Cressid, I might have still held off,
> And then you would have tarried. (4.2.15–18)

As in the wooing scene, Cressida sees her own experience as representative of what normally happens between men and women. As Janet Adelman points out, the event is not exactly unique in the Shakespeare canon:

> This scene is in the normal pattern of Shakespeare's morning after scenes in which the woman typically wishes to hold the man with her, while the man asserts the necessities of the outside world. But both Romeo and Antony have more pressing reasons for leaving than Troilus; and neither Juliet nor Cleopatra responds to the parting with the sense of betrayal, and with the analysis of betrayal, that Cressida expresses here. Immediately after the consummation, that is, the lovers seem already separate, as Cressida had feared.[41]

The question is, however, whether this morning-after scene really tells us anything about Troilus's feelings for Cressida, or vice versa. For example, if Shakespeare consistently regarded women as somewhat cuddlier than men, then he would not be the first exponent of this view in human history. From the perspective of parental investment theory, one might certainly expect a greater average female desire for prolonged intimacy that would corroborate such folk-psychological assumptions. The contemporary division of labor in Shakespeare's England might also have contributed to this Shakespearean pattern, since early modern women were tied more closely than men to the domestic sphere.

Such theorizing may help explain why the average Troilus gets out of bed more quickly than the average Cressida, but it does not explain why this particular Troilus wants his wife to stay in bed when he leaves. We can deduce from his first line—"Dear, trouble not yourself, the morn is cold" (1)—that Cressida has offered to follow him to the gates of the house and that he seems more intent on sneaking out on his own. That Cressida actually shares this concern for secrecy is confirmed a little further on, when Aeneas and his followers knock frantically on the door: "I would not for half Troy have you seen here" (42). The most likely reason for these worries is embarrassment, since the young lovers have enjoyed their first night together.

When Troilus realizes that his whereabouts are fully known to the other Trojans, he reveals himself, and Aeneas explains that Cressida must promptly be exchanged for Antenor. Troilus's brief response has led many critics to attribute indifference to him:

> TROILUS: Is it so concluded?
> AENEAS: By Priam and the general state of Troy.
>   They are at hand, and ready to effect it.
> TROILUS: How my achievements mock me!
>   I will go meet them; and, my Lord Aeneas,
>   We met by chance: you did not find me here. (68–73)

After these words Troilus leaves without even saying goodbye to Cressida. According to R. A. Yoder, he seems to accept her sudden departure from Troy not only with composure but even with relief: "There is, in this central incident of the play and moment of high passion, an obvious flattening of the character supposedly most susceptible to feeling. It is not an undramatic step. . . . Troilus is calmed, even relieved in returning to his public role—he belongs to 'the general state of Troy.'"[42] Troilus's use of the word "achievements" is also a bit lurid, since it brings to mind a sexual conquest or trophy, rather than the consummation of a strong emotional bond.

It is true that compared to Cressida—who disowns her blood ties and refuses to be turned over to the Greeks—Troilus does not give us much of a verbal reaction here. This is a notable difference from Chaucer's version, where Troilus becomes hysterical, runs around, dashes his head against the wall, and concludes that he must kill himself.[43] But Shakespeare has also been unfaithful to his source in another telling way. In Chaucer, Troilus is present at the meeting where the exchange of Cressida for Antenor is decided on, but he raises no objections even though he has the chance to speak (which at least suggests silent compliance). In Shakespeare's version, the decision has been made when Troilus is not present, which means that Shakespeare exonerates him—consciously or not—from any collusion in it.[44]

In my view, the most plausible explanation is that Shakespeare wanted to avoid giving Troilus two melodramatic speeches and therefore saved his fuel for act 5, scene 2, when Troilus reacts to Cressida's betrayal. Too much hysterical inveighing against fate and misfortune would have become tedious. Nor is it strange that Troilus should leave immediately, since Aeneas has made it clear that there is no time for long-winded reactions and long adieus: "My lord, I scarce have leisure to salute you, / My matter is so rash" (61–62). Cressida must be handed over to the Greeks within one hour, and it is not surprising if Troilus wants to spend that hour assessing and ascertaining the unexpected situation. When he returns in scenes 3 and 4, at any rate, he has accepted the decision and urges Cressida to do the same.

In other words, Troilus's main feelings for Cressida remain inscrutable and can only be resolved in performance (if this should be the director's desire). As Vivian Thomas suggests, "It would appear that the character in Chaucer's poem and Shakespeare's play remains an enigma, inviting interpretation but unwilling to yield a simple solution."[45] Cressida is even harder to understand, since her "famous inconstancy is accompanied by a radical inconsistency of characterization" and Shakespeare gives us "no place to ground our speculation" about her motivation after the departure from Troy in act 4, scene 4.[46] What is particularly difficult to grasp is how she can react with such passion and desperation to her separation from Troilus—

> I will not, uncle. I have forgot my father;
> I know no touch of consanguinity,
> No kin, no love, no blood, no soul so near me
> As the sweet Troilus! O you gods divine,
> Make Cressid's name the very crown of falsehood
> If ever she leave Troilus! (4.2.98–103)

—and then yield so easily to Diomedes' advances. In Chaucer no less than three years pass before Criseyde's departure from Troy, and it takes another ten days before she gives her love to the Greek lord. By contrast, "Shakespeare's lovers have only one night before Cressida is whisked off to the Grecians" and into the arms of Diomedes.[47] It could be that her desperation involves some acknowledgment of her own susceptibility and that the word "leave" above refers ambiguously to physical separation and sexual infidelity. But once again, I think the most convincing interpretation is dramatic rather than psychological. When Shakespeare turned to the story of Troilus and Cressida, he picked up one of the most worn-out story lines in English literature,[48] and the most significant effect of Cressida's inconsistency and obscure motivation is to make her betrayal shocking even to an audience that knows what is going to happen. Shakespeare may have deliberately sacrificed her credibility as a character in order to achieve this effect.

The curious thing about Cressida's betrayal of Troilus is that it happens so quickly, which violates our intuitive expectation that deep love should involve commitment. As we have seen, this time compression seems to be characteristic of her entire relationship with Troilus, at least as it is presented on stage. Cressida, who has actually tried her best to buy time, ends up consummating her love for Troilus directly after revealing it to him; Shakespeare waits no more than eighteen lines of text before the exchange with Antenor is proposed; Cressida must depart from Troy the very next morning; on that morning she is given less than one hour's notice before Diomedes arrives to take her away; and it does not take long before she says goodbye to Troilus and gives her sleeve to the Grecian. Earlier in the play, her attempts to buy time and prolong the courtship have also been eroded by the intensity of her own passion.

To use a modern analogy, it is as if Shakespeare has taken the taped version of an ordinary broken marriage—where passion flares up, there is some hesitation, love is consummated, cools down, and gives way to disillusionment and divorce—and then fast-forwarded it at a tremendous pace. This structural speeding up of time, supported by carefully planted figurative language, not only serves the dramatic purpose of condensation but also reinforces the play's thematic concern with the passing of time and the transience of all things human. If even our personal identities are shifting and unpredictable, then love and desire must obviously be even more so.

When this heightened sense of time is fused with the potential endlessness of human desire and fleeting evaluations, the result is a dramatic world of pure "appraisal," where everyone seems expendable and the characters must constantly look over their shoulders. I may be deeply and mutually in love with another person, but love is here today and gone tomorrow, and neither of us can know what will whet our appetites tomorrow. In such a world, the emotion of romantic love certainly exists and attempts to assert itself, but it lacks the element of commitment (which can only unfold in time) and is quickly pared down to a flickering sexual passion. As the caustic fool Thersites puts it so memorably, what we are left with is "Lechery, lechery, still wars and lechery! Nothing else / holds fashion" (5.2.192–93). Even Paris, who has brought war and destruction on his people by abducting the beautiful Helen, subscribes to such a view of what it means to love:

> He eats nothing but doves, love, and that breeds
> hot blood, and hot blood begets hot thoughts, and
> hot thoughts beget hot deeds, and hot deeds is love. (3.1.124–27)

If love is nothing else than a rapid succession of hot deeds, then there is no sense of the creative aspect—the element of bestowal—that might counter the mechanisms of the human meat market. Such love is not a matter of giving, but merely a rapid and revocable act of assessment.

In *Troilus and Cressida*, all attempts to defend love against the onslaught of time thus prove ineffectual. Marriage is the last, desperate safeguard against the rapidly shifting passions, and it founders because it can regulate only one form of choice (that of partner) but is helpless to legislate another (that of love object). The second alternative offered in this play, which proves even more helpless, is Troilus's escape into oblivion when he comes face to face with cuckoldry:

> TROILUS: Let it not be believed for womanhood.
>   Think, we had mothers; do not give advantage
>   To stubborn critics, apt, without a theme
>   For depravation, to square the general sex
>   By Cressid's rule: rather, think this not Cressid.
> ULYSSES: What hath she done, prince, that can soil our
>   mothers? (5.2.127–32)

The sly fox from Ithaca is right, of course. Any reasonably logical person will see that this is an absurd reaction since the behavior of a single woman can tell us nothing about womanhood in general. But there is also considerable psychological and emotional insight in Shakespeare's portrayal of this folly, for how many lovers have not been betrayed and lost their faith, not just in the loved one, but in love itself? According to Allan Bloom, "Love insists on the universality of its object, and to the extent that its object is another human being, love is therefore either an illusion or a disappointment. True logic leads to human isolation."[49] With respect to *Troilus and Cressida*, he concludes that Shakespeare's pessimistic message "seems to be that heroes are not heroes, because they are either fools or knaves, and that love is a sham and deception" (79).

As I hope to have shown, however, the problem with love in Shakespeare's play can be defined with much more precision. *Troilus and Cressida* confronts its audience with a world of endless comparisons and revised opinions, where *esse* is truly *percipi*. While previous critics have detected that the play is deeply concerned with value, they have failed to clarify that the consistent concern is with *overvaluation*. When Shakespeare also unleashes "envious and calumniating Time" on his over-estimated characters (by structural, thematic, and figurative means), making the assessment of other people even more fleeting and fetishistic, they are reduced to ghostly shadows or empty husks.

Against the backdrop of this rapidly eroding landscape, the characters Troilus and Cressida at first seem worlds apart. Unlike just about everyone else in the play—the self-obsessed Ajax and Achilles, the vulgar Pandarus, the cynical

Thersites, the cool, politic Ulysses, the inept Agamemnon, the vulgar and reductive Paris, to mention only a few—they are capable of deep, authentic feeling and have enormous faith in their own capacity for commitment. They have grave doubts about love, to be sure, but these invariably concern the other person's sincerity and not their own. This positive impression is, of course, constantly undercut by attitudinal and situational irony (for an audience that knows the outlines of the Troilus and Criseyde story) and by our all-to-human suspicions about male idealization of women. Does Troilus delude Cressida, and perhaps even delude himself, about the real nature of his feelings for her? Nevertheless, our inevitable disillusionment does not stem so much from the revelation of character (say, a deceitful, double-dealing Cressida, or a bored, sexually satisfied Troilus) as from our disorientation when we cannot reconcile their professed feelings with their ensuing actions. Like the lovers themselves, who never really have the time to get to know each other properly, we never develop the analytical intimacy that might bridge this gap.

But as Charles Lyons observes thoughtfully, the Cressida who loves Troilus is not less real than the Cressida who betrays him.[50] Their love is not a lie, but a painfully ephemeral truth. We are confused and disheartened because the dramatist first portrays a universal passion with great beauty and sympathy, and then violates it by severing the natural bond between emotion and behavior. It may be in the nature of people to love and to lose each other, to turn future hopes into present vows and then watch them collapse over time, but we would never expect it to happen so *quickly*.

All's Well That Ends Well

In all likelihood, Shakespeare composed All's Well That Ends Well a few years into the seventeenth century, soon after his searching excursion into Troy. According to David Hoeniger, "The story of Troilus and Cressida was obviously on Shakespeare's mind while he was composing All's Well."[51] There are several points of tangency between the two plays, including two references in All's Well to characters used in Troilus. When Lafew leaves Helena alone with the King, he refers to himself as "Cressid's uncle / That dare leave two together" (2.1.96–97). More significantly, it does not seem to have escaped Shakespeare's highly associative mind that he was now writing a second play involving a woman called Helen:

> COUNTESS: Sirrah, tell my gentlewoman I would speak
> with her—Helen I mean.
> CLOWN: Was this fair face the cause, quoth she,
> Why the Grecians sacked Troy?

> Fond done, done fond,
> Was this King Priam's joy? (1.3.67–72)

In *All's Well*, Shakespeare set out to retell a very different story, a folkloric piece derived from William Painter's English translation of Boccaccio. In Shakespeare's version, the young Helena heals the French King's fistula in exchange for the right to choose any husband she wants. When she chooses the unwilling Bertram, the latter refuses to consummate the marriage and escapes to the Florentine wars, whereon Helena follows him and ingeniously gets him between the sheets (and thus into the marital fold). But while the plot similarities between *Troilus* and *All's Well* are not very striking, the Clown's song returns us to the problem of value— and more specifically, the risk of overvaluation—that seems to have preoccupied Shakespeare in the earlier play. How could the Trojans and the Greeks have deemed this woman so important that they embraced this horribly protracted bloodshed for her sake?[52]

What the story of Helena and Bertram enables Shakespeare to explore, among other things, is the other side of this coin: the problem of underestimation. Almost all the characters in *All's Well* are convinced that Bertram has seriously underrated the beautiful, intelligent, and virtuous Helena, and this opens up a thought-provoking tension between social consensus and individual point of view. As a consequence, *All's Well* approaches the relation between value and choice from a new (and fully complementary) direction, compared to *Troilus*. In his Trojan play, Shakespeare emphasizes the relational aspect of desire and anatomizes the dependence of individual appraisal on social appraisal, with all the endless comparisons and reappraisals that this gives rise to. In *All's Well* it is instead the limits of the relational aspect and the ultimate incongruity between individual desire and social appraisal that come into focus. In *Troilus*, fifty thousand flies can't be wrong; in *All's Well*, one of the flies simply won't hear reason.

Let us turn to act 3, scene 5, where Shakespeare revisits the question of love's choice. At this point in the play Bertram has left both court and wife behind and woos a chaste Florentine woman by the appropriate name of Diana. His insistent and unsuccessful advances are related by different characters to a recognizable pattern where men promise women everything between heaven and earth in order to procure casual sex from them, and women try their best to extract signals of genuine commitment from their suitors:

> Beware of them, Diana: their promises,
> enticements, oaths, tokens, and all these engines of
> lust, are not the things they go under; many a maid
> hath been seduced by them; and the misery is,
> example, that so terrible shows in the wrack of

maidenhood, cannot for all that dissuade succession,
but that they are limed with the twigs that threatens
them. (3.5.18–25)

Like Cressida in Troy, this Florentine woman also confronts her impatient suitor
with the undependable and fleeting nature of men's desires:

> DIANA: Ay, so you serve us
>   Till we serve you; but when you have our roses,
>   You barely leave our thorns to prick ourselves,
>   And mock us with our bareness. (4.2.17–20)

Although Diana is young and inexperienced in the ways of the world, she can
safely fall back on her mother's advice since men are predictable beings: "My
mother told me just how he would woo / As if she sat in's heart. She says all men /
Have the like oaths" (4.2.69–71). When Helena later learns of Bertram's attempts
to get Diana into bed, she completes the picture by describing men as alien creatures who will happily jump into bed with women they do not even *like*, with no
thoughts about prior commitments:

> But O, strange men!
>   That can such sweet use make of what they hate,
>   When saucy trusting of the cozen'd thoughts
>   Defiles the pitchy night; so lust doth play
>   With what it loathes for that which is away. (4.4.21–25)

Shakespeare is repeating the pattern from *Troilus and Cressida*, where an ardent male,
beside himself with sexual desire, is held at bay by a woman who seeks to assess
his real intentions because she suspects that his oaths may not be entirely ague-
proof. Readers and audiences of all conflicting creeds and convictions—from neo-
Victorians to literary queer theorists—will agree about one thing: this is an instantly recognizable stereotype about male sexual behavior (and, by extension,
differences between men and women).

What kind of substance we attribute to the stereotype is a different matter.
As we have seen, the ground rules are laid out by the average psychological differences predicted by parental investment theory, endowing men with a stronger
evolutionary incentive to think in the sexual short term (and perhaps even to delude themselves actively by confusing short-term interest with long-term commitment). But when Diana's mother warns her about the "wrack of maidenhood,"
it is obvious that her fears are largely inspired by cultural norms that have only an
indirect relationship to such evolved dispositions. (I will return to some of these,

including the sexual double standard, in chapter 5.) In other words, the insights offered by parental investment theory may be essential for a fuller understanding of this passage, and the cultural assumptions it expresses, but they are hardly sufficient in themselves.

An interesting similarity between *All's Well* and *Troilus* is that both plays make much of the bioculturally grounded stereotype yet work against it in their main plots. In *Troilus*, the young woman who worries so much about being betrayed by her lover soon betrays him instead, and in *All's Well* we find a female protagonist in dogged sexual pursuit of a highly reluctant male.[53] Not surprisingly, Helena's conquest of Bertram in *All's Well* has attracted a good deal of commentary from feminist critics, who typically regard her as a heroine because she refuses to bow down to the expectations of her patriarchal society. According to many of these readings, anyone who takes objection to Helena's methods in procuring her husband must either be vaguely sexist or at least anxious about women holding power.[54]

According to Diane Dreher, for example, Helena is "Shakespeare's most problematic woman hero. While she is admired for her virtue, her actions make many people uncomfortable." The typical critical objections to Helena's actions, one might add here, have been that she demands Bertram for her husband in payment for health services rendered to the King and that she tricks him into bed by pretending to be Diana. But in Dreher's view, the real reason why people object to Helena's behavior is that she is of the female persuasion: "If we admire the heroes of romance for their courage and determination, do we find Helena any less admirable because she is a woman?"[55] Kay Stanton argues similarly that the real reason why some critics find the play disturbing is that the women win.[56]

Since many feminist critics canonize Helena it is only to be expected that they will also give the recalcitrant Bertram the short end of the stick. To be sure, there are few critics of any school who would regard this character as a moral beacon, for reasons that will become clear a little later in this text. But the feminists in question take this widespread critical reserve toward Bertram more than one step further in their attempts to turn his unwillingness to marry Helena into a feminist issue. According to Carol Thomas Neely's verdict, Bertram is guilty of a wide range of flaws and misdemeanors: misogyny, self-love, revulsion from Helena's sexuality, and fears about his own sexual inadequacy.[57]

Along similar lines, Alison Findlay declares that the King's notorious fistula is "symbolic of the disease which affects the French court and Bertram in particular: an obsessive form of homosocial bonding based on fear of female passion."[58] She even contends that "refusing Helen[a]'s love is a rejection of female desire within romance" (97). This is nothing less than a direct equation of the general with the specific: if Bertram dislikes Helena, then he dislikes a woman, which means that he dislikes women. If we applied the same logic to real human beings, then any man who turned down a marriage proposal or sexual invitation from a woman would be a misogynist.

I have perused the text several times in search of anything that might back up these assertions, but my attempts have so far been unsuccessful. I can find no evidence whatsoever that the French court is subject to an obsessive fear of anything, including female sexuality, or that Bertram either hates women, is overly in love with himself, or has fears about his own potency. I also find it difficult to understand why the King's fistula—wherever it may be located[59]—should be a symbol of such fears. Since these critics have not provided me with any evidence to this effect, my provisional conclusion must be that they have responded to Shakespeare's rejection of *one* sexual stereotype in the main plot (that all men are ardent stags and all women are coy) by imposing *another* stereotyped assumption of their own making.

I would also like to question Diane Dreher's contention that Shakespeare tests his audience's gender assumptions by "reversing the roles of men and women in romance."[60] While Shakespeare clearly *rejects* the sexual stereotype in this play, he does not *reverse* it, for then we would expect Bertram to exercise female choice and Helena to court him vigorously. As I have suggested repeatedly, the crude feminist account of male "subjects" and female "objects" forgets that a choosy person is every inch as much a "subject" as a less discriminating one. What Shakespeare gives us in *All's Well* is rather *female choice with a vengeance*, since Helena assumes the roles of both chooser and wooer, and Bertram has no say in the matter at all. He is, to use common feminist parlance, reduced to an object. It is quite possible, as Dreher suggests, that some people would have responded differently—at least in Shakespeare's time—if Bertram had received Helena from the King rather than the other way around, but even a feminist analysis cannot waive the moral problem that Helena's actions accentuate. Is it right to turn another human being into chattel, to be bartered and sold in this way?

This is not to say that Shakespeare gives us a negative portrait of Helena. On the contrary, the play reminds us repeatedly about her beauty, intelligence, resourcefulness, and moral fiber. There is also considerable pathos in her tortured recognition of the social barriers that stand in the way of her love:

> I am undone; there is no living, none,
> If Bertram be away; 'twere all one
> That I should love a bright particular star
> And think to wed it, he is so above me.
> In his bright radiance and collateral light
> Must I be comforted, not in his sphere.
> Th'ambition in my love thus plagues itself:

The hind that would be mated by the lion
Must die for love. (1.1.85–93)

It is possible that Helena thinks of Bertram as "above" her in more ways than one, but the main reason she defines her love as "ambitious" is that it refuses to respect the class differences that separate them. This conflict between individual merit and class privilege is an obvious theme in *All's Well*, and a particularly cynical historical materialist might even suspect that Helena is really more in love with Bertram's class than with him as a person. I think Shakespeare convinces us of the depth of Helena's passion for Bertram as a person by complementing the abstract astral imagery above with the kind of concrete details that lovers delight in:

> 'Twas pretty, though a plague,
> To see him every hour; to sit and draw
> His arched brows, his hawking eye, his curls,
> In our heart's table—heart too capable
> Of every line and trick of his sweet favour.
> But now he's gone, and my idolatrous fancy
> Must sanctify his relics. (93–99)

We can ask ourselves, however, whether there is not a sense in which Helena loves Bertram too much. It is a curious and ironic aspect of strong emotion that it often stands in direct opposition to empathy.[61] The underlying mechanism is not difficult to understand, once we bear in mind that our emotions form part of a motivational system whose purpose is to direct our attention toward or away from a given object (either real or imagined). The more emotionally involved we get, the more riveted and unilateral our focus becomes, as our strong emotions make us less sensitive to conflicting information from the environment. Empathy is, of course, all about such sensitivity to external cues, and it presupposes a measure of disengagement from one's own experience and interests in order to be possible at all. As Vivian Thomas puts it beautifully, with respect to *Troilus and Cressida*, "Detachment does not cancel feeling but provides for cool analysis of the situation and feelings of the characters, heightening both insight and understanding and deepening sympathy."[62]

Concerning romantic love, such an interpretation finds intriguing support from the neuroscientific experiments discussed in chapter 1. According to Andreas Bartels and Semir Zeki, romantic love not only *activates* certain brain areas but also *deactivates* "regions associated with negative emotions, social judgment and 'mentalizing,' that is, the assessment of other people's intentions and emotions." In fact, these deactivated areas have also been associated with "moral judgment" and "attention to one's own emotions."[63] If Bartels and Zeki are right, then their research promises a neuroscientific foundation for two proverbial ideas: that love is blind and that all is fair in love and war.

What I want to suggest is that Helena's romantic passion for Bertram is so strong that it simply blocks her empathy for him. It makes her incapable of assessing either Bertram's point of view or the moral implications of her own actions. It is noteworthy that she never stops to ask whether her love is requited or not before she demands him for her husband; instead, her full attention lies on the question of her own desert and whether it may be possible to transcend the class barriers that separate them. When the Countess coaxes her into revealing her love, she declares, "Nor would I have him till I do deserve him; / Yet never know how that desert should be" (1.3.196–97). Whether Bertram is interested in the match or not does not seem to be an issue. When the wedding ceremony has taken place, she promises to "eke out that / Wherein toward me my homely stars have fail'd / To equal my great fortune" (2.5.73–76). Discussing her fate with the women in Florence, she once again returns to the question of her own "deserving" (3.5.61). But what exactly would it mean to *deserve* the love of another human being? Is there not beggary in the love that can be reckoned?

The idea that Helena loves Bertram excessively—so much that she practically loses sight of his point of view—also receives support from the Countess's reaction when Helena's passion is disclosed. The Countess has allowed Helena to live in the same household as her son. She makes it clear that both children are equally dear to her—"Which of them both / Is dearest to me I have no skill in sense / To make distinction" (3.4.38–40)—and she is clearly delighted at Helena's romantic interest in Bertram. But her wish to honor Helena's feelings and even aid her in her marriage plans does not rule out a measure of reserve regarding the element of passion:

> COUNTESS: Even so it was with me when I was young;
>   If ever we are nature's, these are ours; this thorn
>   Doth to our rose of youth rightly belong;
>   Our blood to us, this to our blood is born;
>   It is the show and seal of nature's truth,
>   Where love's strong passion is impress'd in youth.
>   By our remembrances of days foregone,
>   *Such were our faults,* or then we thought them none. (1.3.125–32: italics
>   mine)

The Countess regards Helena's passion as a "natural" phenomenon in the most primal sense of the word, and yet it is ultimately a "fault." She does not explain exactly where the fault lies, but it seems likely that it has to do with the inordinate and unrealistic intensity of youthful passion. Such a view is in keeping with most Renaissance thinkers on the subject, who neither idealized nor debunked our natural propensity for love but stressed that the heat of passion must be domesticated by mature, cool reason. As we have seen, the most widespread assumption in England was that passion was an insufficient criterion for marriage, and among the nobility this idea was more or less taken for granted.

At the risk of oversimplification, the four-hundred-year difference between Shakespeare's treatment of romantic love in *All's Well* and the most widespread modern view can be summarized as follows. When we retrace our steps back to the early seventeenth century, we discover essentially the same universal emotion. The factor that separates the majority of modern men and women from Shakespeare's contemporaries is the transition from absolute to serial monogamy: unlike them, we can afford to idealize romantic passion because our vows of eternal love are never binding. This development is, in turn, part and parcel of an increasingly individualistic culture in which emotional experience has more and more become an end in itself; only when we feel strongly do we realize our potential as human beings. For most of Shakespeare's contemporaries, such a single-minded perspective would have been unthinkable.

Helena's early modern "fault" is thus that she loves Bertram too passionately, at the expense of other concerns. From the perspective of Sternberg's love triangle, we can say that her passion (defined as a strong desire for union with Bertram) has eclipsed the element of intimacy (more specifically, the desire to promote his well-being). Interestingly, it is only when the outraged Bertram attempts to reject Helena's demand that she begins to see his side of the picture and even urges the King to retract the promise of Bertram's hand in marriage: "That you are well restor'd, my lord, I'm glad. / Let the rest go" (2.3.148–49). But this insight comes far too late, since Bertram has already offended the King by rejecting his designated bride, and the latter quickly enforces the marriage in order to save face: "My honour's at the stake, which to defeat, / I must produce my power" (2.3.150–51). In the next act, Helena becomes more attuned to the fact that Bertram has feelings too, and her concern for him has now grown so strong that she even embraces exile for his sake (3.2.99–129). Readers and audiences may have different views about this self-abnegation, but it must certainly inspire pathos, and it also seems clear that she has now lost some of her passionate tunnel vision.

As for Bertram, the sympathy that he inspires derives less from his own actions than from his impossible situation at the hands of Helena and the King. As early as in the fourth line of the play, Bertram acknowledges his impending lack of freedom as a legal minor at the King's disposal: "I must attend his majesty's command, to whom I am now in ward, evermore in subjection" (1.1.4–5). In the following act, Shakespeare also gives us the first hint of a conflict between youthful desires and courtly servitude. While other "young lords" are given permission to take part in the Italian wars, Bertram reflects gloomily that "I am commanded here, and kept a coil with / 'Too young,' and 'The next year' and "Tis too early'" (2.1.26–28).

This scene is psychologically, thematically, and structurally significant because it establishes Bertram as a frustrated adolescent even before he is confronted with the marriage offer he cannot refuse. Historically speaking, we also need to bear in mind that early modern men usually did not marry as early as Shakespeare himself did, at the age of seventeen. They typically waited until the age of twenty-five or thirty, and "even the privileged did not rush to the altar as adolescents."[64] No wonder, then, if Bertram feels that he is being robbed of his youth without even receiving the expected recompense of a wife from the nobility or acknowledgment of his maturity. He is considered too young to go to war but old enough to marry, while from his perspective it is the other way around.

It is also highly telling that Helena does not reveal her choice of Bertram immediately but first inspects *"three or four* Lords" that the King presents her with. This is one of Shakespeare's additions to his source material, and we can therefore surmise that he intended the scene to have some sort of dramatic function. The King is clear about one thing: "Thy frank election make; / Thou hast power to choose, and they none to forsake" (2.3.56–57). But to be on the safe side and ensure total compliance from the four lords, he makes no bones about the costs they will incur if they attempt to refuse Helena's suit: "Make choice, and see, / Who shuns thy love shuns all his love in me" (2.3.73–74).

As we saw in the discussion of *King Lear*, the word "love" was often used in Shakespeare's England as a kind of euphemism for social allegiance rather than emotion, which means that the King is voicing a considerable threat. Not surprisingly, all four lords respond politely and affirmatively to Helena's brief interview, but it is also clear from Lafew's scornful comments on these young whippersnappers that they are only paying lip service to the King's demand. They may say the right thing because they have to, but their tone and body language communicate a hostility that is meant to discourage Helena from choosing them: "Do they all deny her? . . . These boys are boys of ice; they'll have none of her" (2.3.87, 94–95).

This brief exchange has at least three important consequences for how we understand the events that follow. First, it gives us an early reminder that the King is capable of enforcing obedience in action, but that he cannot enjoin others to feel what he expects them to. In other words, the scene portrays the same split between action and emotion, love and duty, that we came across in *King Lear*.

Second, the negative reactions of no less than four young noblemen give us some basis for a contextual evaluation of Bertram's refusal of Helena. When Bertram does not want to marry a "poor physician's daughter," we have already been instructed by Shakespeare that his distaste for social disparagement is representative of what a young man in his position can be expected to feel. Lafew may be there to heap scorn on the four lords because they reject Helena, but if Bertram is at fault, then he is at least in good company.

Third, the duplicitous politeness of the other young lords is actually bound to highlight Bertram's courage and integrity—or, from a less admiring perspective, his rash insubordination—when he first refuses to accept the King's decision and even talks back to him. Again, a comparison with *King Lear* suggests that Shakespeare may have intended the former, since Bertram's refusal to equate love and obedience reminds us of the Earl of Kent.

When Bertram expresses his reluctance to pay the King's debt of gratitude for him, the King responds with an elaborate argument that focuses on the nature of honor and, more specifically, its relation to virtue. Some things that we honor are innate (such as beauty, intelligence, and youth) while others (such as wealth and social status) are acquired, and if Bertram is content to choose Helena on the basis of the former, then the King promises to provide the latter. But Bertram remains intractable: "I cannot love her nor will strive to do't" (145–46). This response harbors an interesting ambiguity since Bertram does not explicitly refuse to *marry* Helena, but rather signals his own incapacity and unwillingness to *love* her. This is especially interesting since the King's speech has consistently focused on the question of *likes* and *dislikes*, as in his concluding offer: "If thou canst *like* this creature as a maid, / I can create the rest" (143–44). Is he simply expecting Bertram to accept Helena for his wife, or does he even expect him to *feel* for her?

There is no way of knowing how the King interprets Bertram's withholding of love, except that he regards it as a blatant act of insubordination that necessitates a face-saving exercise of royal power. Returning ominously to his own distinction between innate and acquired honor, he reminds Bertram that it is "in us to plant thine honour where / We please to have it grow" (157–58), and he ends by escalating this threat into a promise of sheer "revenge and hate" (165). Faced with such a staggering display of brute power by his sovereign, Bertram quickly backs down and delivers the lie that is expected of him:

> BERTRAM: Pardon, my gracious lord; for I submit
> My fancy to your eyes. When I consider
> What great creation and what dole of honour
> Flies where you bid it, I find that she, which late
> Was in my nobler thoughts most base, is now
> The praised of the king; who, so ennobled,
> Is as 'twere born so. (168–74)

This passage, which holds dramatic center stage in Shakespeare's play, is best read as an ironic comment on the endless comparisons and evaluations that dominated in *Troilus and Cressida*. While Shakespeare's earlier play stresses social contingency and personal interdependence, *All's Well* turns the tables on this idea and brings home the fundamental absurdity of a purely relational concept of desire. Lacanians and Girardians, take note! Bertram may well submit to his king in all sorts of ways, and he certainly has a very strong incentive to do so in the case of Helena, but how could he possibly submit his fancy, his liking, his love, to another person's will? The absurdity of expecting love from an arranged marriage is also highlighted satirically in Thomas Middleton's *Women Beware Women*, when Hippolito allows Isabella a quick peek at her future husband: "See what you mean to like; nay, and I charge you, / Like what you see" (1.2.76–77).[65] There may well be a measure of sarcasm in Bertram's recognition that the King has now persuaded him to renounce his "nobler thoughts."

What is more, this is not the first time in Shakespeare's play that a member of the older generation uses threats to extract a profession of love. Earlier in the play, Helena has also received a dose of emotional blackmail when the Countess forces her to confess her love for Bertram:

> Therefore tell me true;
> But tell me then, 'tis so . . . I charge thee,
> As heaven shall work in me for thine avail,
> To tell me truly. (1.3.172–73, 180–82)

Since the Countess is so convinced that she has gauged Helena's true feelings for her son, she will only accept an affirmative answer, and there is a disturbing lack of clarity about the nature of the "avail" that will either be given or withdrawn. As a dependent in her household, Helena has every reason to be nervous about the Countess's intentions, and Shakespeare makes it clear to us that she fears the consequences if the Countess should take objection to her love.

So far, we have seen that *All's Well* dramatizes the problem of love's choice in two ways. The play highlights the incongruity between individual desires, and it explores how this absence of consensus can easily degenerate into a savage but ultimately ineffectual exercise of power. While Bertram's marriage requires individual consent in order to be legal, the King makes it painfully clear to his young ward that consent can always be enforced through the use of power. But the King himself confronts a major stumbling block, since although he can enforce marriages as well as professions of love, he cannot enjoin his individual subjects to feel the appropriate thing: "Bertram can be compelled to marry but he cannot be compelled to love."[66] Helena's plight, finally, is that her love for Bertram is so strong that she cannot but force it on him, and it is not strange that she receives only resentment in return. When they part at the end of act 3, scene 2, and Helena unsuccessfully solicits a kiss from her unconsummated husband,[67] the pathos generated by both characters is almost intolerable. For Bertram, the path to lawful and earnest passion has been closed down by a shotgun wedding, and all that remains to him in the way of love and passion is the dishonest seduction of other women. Helena, who cannot help her feelings for Bertram, does not even receive a farewell, but only cold contempt.

Since Shakespeare has clearly sought to balance our judgment of the main characters in the first acts of the play, it is all the more remarkable that the sympathy they attract from other characters should be so very lopsided. One of Shakespeare's most striking modifications to his source in Painter is the addition of an older generation that frequently passes judgment on the younger characters. R. L. Smallwood argues convincingly that these "new and sympathetic characters" have been invented mainly for the purpose of supporting Helena and directing the audience's response in favor of her actions: "In her search for Bertram's love she has the support and sympathy of everyone in the play except Parolles—and even he betrays some little affection for her in his words of parting in the first scene."[68]

At the same time, this older generation is deeply critical of Bertram's disobedience and his failure to appreciate Helena. The little sympathy that Bertram musters—except from the notoriously undependable Parolles—comes from two lords who do not vindicate his actions so much as mitigate them with reference to universal ills: "As we are ourselves, what things we are!" (4.3.18–19). "Is it not damnable in us to be trumpeters / of our unlawful intents?" (25–26). "How mightily sometimes we make us comforts / of our losses!" (62–63). The referent for the pronoun "we" is not entirely clear throughout this inventory of Bertram's escapades, but the lords seem to move seamlessly from the specifically male view of corrupting young ladies to a broader concern with the human condition: "The web of our life is of a mingled yarn, good / and ill together" (4.3.68–69). Like the four lords that Shakespeare has inserted just before Helena pounces on Bertram, these characters seem to have been added in order to communicate a distinct message to us: Bertram may be a bad boy, but in that case he is in very good company.

So while Helena receives unfailing moral and practical support from a wide range of characters—the King, Lafew, the Countess, Diana, and her mother—there are practically no expressions of sympathy for Bertram. That Bertram has chosen Parolles—who turns out to be highly undependable—for his friend and ally may also reflect poorly on his judgment of character in the case of Helena. In the final act, this moral division becomes even more salient when Bertram, who now finds himself unfairly suspected of conjugal murder as well as fornication, tries to save his own hide by slandering Diana most foully. Why does Shakespeare first emphasize the brutality of the initial marriage deal and then withdraw all sympathy from Bertram while showering Helena with praise and support? This is a problem that any reading of this play must confront.

According to Ann Jennalie Cook, we may be dealing with a case of dramatic expediency here: "All interpreters of this play have trouble with Bertram's behavior.

What they fail to see, perhaps, is the difficulty of dealing effectively with a union that would, in fact, have represented a disparagement in rank. . . . Shakespeare's contemporaries may have required clear proof of a nobleman's ignobility in order to accept his marriage to a heroine of common birth when the union is presented in a sober courtly context."[69] There is probably a good deal of truth to this analysis. As a popular dramatist whose principal project was to please, Shakespeare was constantly performing something of a balancing act before his heterogeneous audiences, some of whom would probably have responded in the manner of the four lords to Helena's marriage proposal. The limitation of Cook's argument, however, is that it does not take into account the possibility that Shakespeare was not just responding to sociological pressures but also had something to say. In all likelihood, he was seeking not only to delight, but also to instruct. To make more sense of Shakespeare's probable intentions, we must return to the difficult questions about value and desert, love and duty, that inform such diverse plays as *Lear* and *Troilus* but have so far only been touched on tangentially in this discussion of *All's Well*. Is it possible for Helena to deserve Bertram's love? Is love itself something that can be deserved?

When the last scene of *All's Well* begins, the King, the Countess, and Lafew appear once more to deliver their verdict on Bertram's actions. Interestingly enough, the King seems less concerned with Bertram's insubordination than with his failure to appreciate Helena's true worth:

> KING: We lost a jewel of her, and our esteem
> Was made much poorer by it; but your son,
> As mad in folly, lack'd the sense to know
> Her estimation home. (5.3.1–4)

As in her earlier discussion of Helena's "fault," the Countess turns to youthful passion for explanation as well as amelioration of her son's actions, calling them "natural rebellion done i'th' blade of youth" (6). Lafew, finally, suggests that Bertram may have offended everyone, but he has done the worst damage to himself by losing

> a wife
> Whose beauty did astonish the survey
> Of richest eyes; whose words all ears took captive;
> Whose dear perfection hearts that scorn'd to serve
> Humbly call'd mistress. (15–19)

The gist of Lafew's words is that Bertram is to blame for not having perceived what was evident to everyone around him: that Helena was the most wonderful wife he could possibly have asked for. In spite of this transgression, it is agreed that the youth must be forgiven, and arrangements are made for his marriage to Lafew's daughter Maudlin.

When Bertram enters, he not only accepts the new marriage offer but delivers a beautifully crafted speech on how his secret love for Maudlin had warped his mind so much that he did not see Helena for what she was:

> Thence it came
> That she whom all men prais'd, and whom myself
> Since I have lost, have lov'd, was in mine eye
> The dust that did offend it. (52–55)

Strictly speaking, it is impossible to say whether Bertram is telling the truth or not, but most critics have been entirely unconvinced and regarded this as a convenient lie. Bertram is offering the King the very thing he had denied him earlier in the play: a profession of love for the woman he was expected to marry. (In fact, he even makes up for his earlier indiscretion by making not one, but two, professions of love.) It is also noteworthy that he now accepts the same logic employed by the older generation: he really should have loved Helena because everyone else did.

Of course, if Bertram is dishonest about his love for Lafew's daughter, then he may well be lying about his belated love for Helena too. Nor do we have any reason to believe that he has really embraced the consensus principle that Helena is wonderful because everyone else thinks so. But the King's power is now as absolute as it can get, and he readily accepts Bertram's apology with another reference to the eternal human condition: "Our rash faults / Make trivial price of serious things we have, / Not knowing them until we know their grave" (60–62). Yet again the problem turns out to be *underestimation*: Bertram has not managed to assess Helena's value correctly.

For many critics, this is simply the gist of *All's Well That Ends Well*. Noting that Shakespeare spends the early scenes "establishing Helena's true worth," A. G. Harmon endorses the same consensus principle as the older generation: the fact that Bertram and Parolles fail to see what is apparent to everyone else "reveals something about their own worth."[70] According to Charles Lyons, the only ethical problem in the play concerns the use of deceit to achieve love and marriage, and "Bertram's primary sin—from which all his other sins derive—is his inability to see the inherent value of Helena, 'this good gift.'"[71] Along similar lines, Carl Dennis suggests that Bertram "must choose either to affirm or deny the intrinsic excellence of Helena, and he proves too superficial to choose rightly."[72]

Here we can see clearly the advantage of reading *All's Well* alongside its sister play. A reader who comes directly from *Troilus and Cressida* will be naturally suspicious of such invocations of "intrinsic" or "inherent" value or worth, especially since any "intrinsic" quality must ultimately be established relationally through comparison. There are also problems with equating the play's overriding message with the perspective of the older generation, as if Shakespeare's other critiques of forced marriages counted for nothing. In *The Merry Wives of Windsor*, for example, Fenton convinces Anne Page's father that their clandestine love marriage has saved his daughter from "a thousand irreligious cursed hours / Which forced marriage would have brought upon her" (5.5.225–26). Page does not object.

The King in *All's Well* is at least being rigorously consistent with his quasi-Aristotelian distinction between innate or essential qualities (such as beauty and intelligence) and acquired accidentals (such as class or wealth). He has located the true mettle of mankind in the former category and then embraced a consensus principle where everyone—except Bertram, of course—agrees that Helena is the most wonderful person one could ask for. But as we have seen, this consistency is also matched by a consistent error in the King's reasoning—or more specifically, a profound incapacity to recognize the limits of his own jurisdiction. For what he demands from Bertram is not a cool assessment of Helena's intrinsic merits but a profession of love that inevitably mobilizes the same kind of ambiguities that we found in *King Lear*. Is he seeking to extract *feelings* from Bertram, or just acceptance of his forced marriage?

In act 5, it becomes clear that the King has all along expected Bertram to assess Helena's value correctly and then *feel* what is expected of him: "That thou didst love her, strikes some scores away / From the great compt" (56–57). But while this attempt to forcibly collapse Bertram's individual desire into social appraisal results in the latter's outward compliance, it seems just as abortive as Helena's desire to impose her love on him. As David Scott Kastan puts it, she is "forced to admit . . . that her notion of love as something that can be earned—either by healing the King or by satisfying the conditions—is inadequate. Love must be freely given, not compelled."[73]

Shakespeare certainly paints an eerie picture of the King's attempt to compel love, and we have also seen that a similar violence is at work in Helena's vehement passion for Bertram. This aspect of *All's Well* is directly congruent with the love test in *King Lear*, where love is simultaneously a source of violence toward its object (Lear's love for Cordelia) and something that cannot be compelled from outside (Cordelia's love for Lear). But Kastan seems to gloss over a central problematic in *All's Well* by reading together the logically distinct issues of compulsion and individual desert. Love is certainly described as an unenforceable emotion in this play, but this does not mean that it cannot be earned or deserved. While Shakespeare frequently satirized the apparent irrationality of love's choice, he was also sufficiently familiar with the ideas of Aristotle and Lucretius to know that, in the final analysis, nothing will come from nothing. In a world of cause and effect there must be something that makes us love another person, even if it is something as seemingly trivial as the "arched brow" or "hawking eye" that Helena relishes in Bertram. Love cannot be "freely given" in the sense of being gratuitous, any more than it can be totally idiosyncratic in its nature. It is just that this elusive something, this potential myriad of interacting somethings, is so incredibly difficult to grasp.

So while it may be unwise to side wholeheartedly with the King's view that Bertram has failed to perceive Helena's intrinsic excellence, a straightforward negation of this idea will not get us much further. The play's treatment of love is better understood as a riposte to the relational meat market in *Troilus and Cressida*, in that the tyranny of social appraisal is now undercut and called into question by a recalcitrant individual. At least implicitly, it also presents us with a conflict between two conceptions of what love really is. On one side of the barricade stands the lonely Bertram, who regards love as a *feeling* that is not under voluntary control and so cannot be compelled from outside: "I cannot love her nor will strive to do't" (2.3.146). On the other side stands an entire generation of men and women whose life experience has engendered suspicions about youthful passion. They think of love more as a *craft* or an *action*, as something that can be mastered or learned. In their view, Bertram must learn to sort out the wheat from the chaff, structure his feelings, and so become worthy of Helena. "Pure reason alone cannot create values because it cannot create feelings. Reason can, however, elicit, direct, and organize feelings to ensure their fullest satisfaction over a complete life."[74]

The problem is, however, that humans become blinded by their experience and not just by their ignorance. In *All's Well*, neither perspective emerges victorious in spite of Bertram's final capitulation, and the play leaves us in an uncomfortable in-between position. This irresoluble tension between the individual and the collective, between amorous idiosyncrasy and consensus, between what is given in us and what can be changed at will, is adumbrated in the paradox of sameness and difference that I have remarked on earlier in this study:

> Strange it is that our bloods,
> Of colour, weight, and heat, pour'd all together,
> Would quite confound distinction, yet stands off
> In differences so mighty. (2.3.119–22)

Although Shakespeare would not have used these words, this is the human paradox of being a social animal and an individual organism in a nutshell. And a play that fully embraces a paradox of this magnitude cannot be anything else than a problem play. It is therefore highly appropriate that *All's Well* should leave us disconcerted or even mildly queasy, not knowing what to make of the inconclusive reunion between Bertram and Helena. As numerous commentators have observed, it is also quite worrisome to see the King thank Diana for her services by promising her not a box of chocolates, but yet another unspecified young lord in marriage (5.3.325–26). Has this sovereign learned nothing from his most recent experience?

It is, I think, a tribute to the integrity of Shakespeare's popular art that he did not cringe before these tensions but pursued them actively, even at the expense of making his audience uncomfortable. In *Troilus and Cressida,* he collapses individual desire into social appraisal, confronting us with an amorous meat market where love stands helpless before the march of time. In *All's Well,* with its conflict between individual desire and the expectations of the group, he takes us to the final destination in our reasoning about romantic love. Beyond this point lies a complexity so vast, so astounding, that it cannot be comprehended. This is the point where we ask Helena why she fell in love with Bertram, and she first delivers a confusing catalogue of arched brows and hawking eyes. Then she falls silent, throws up her hands, and exclaims with Montaigne: *Because it was he, because it was myself!*

5

Jealousy in Othello

In the third act of *Othello*, Desdemona complains to Emilia that she has given her husband no cause for jealousy. Emilia's response is mysterious:

> But jealous souls will not be answered so:
> They are not ever jealous for the cause,
> But jealous for they're jealous. It is a monster,
> Begot upon itself, born on itself. (3.4.159–62)[1]

As Mark Breitenberg has observed in his study of anxious masculinity in the early modern period,[2] this lack of a viable referent or cause is a typical feature of Shakespeare's jealousy plays. The most horrifying and bewildering aspect of *Othello* is that its main protagonist swerves so very quickly from the role of loving husband and turns into a howling murderer. Similarly, the jealousy that grips Leontes in *The Winter's Tale* has been described by critics as "essentially unexplained,"[3] indeed "almost miraculous."[4]

Although there was no consensus about the exact *causes* of jealousy in Shakespeare's time, most writers on the subject seem to have agreed that it was a very strange and inordinate passion. Robert Burton, for example, was so puzzled by its vehemence that he regarded it as a "[s]pecies apart" from the other passions in his *Anatomy of Melancholy*.[5] According to Edmund Tilney, the author of the domestic manual *The Flower of Friendship*, there was "no greater torment, than the vexation of a jealous minde."[6] On the continent, Montaigne saw this affliction as "the most vaine and turbulent infirmitie that may afflict man's minde."[7]

What is more, Shakespeare and his contemporaries also had strong classical precedents to fall back on for such a view. In Ovid's *The Art of Love*, for example, where the author generally takes a detached and humorous view of sexual matters, the tone changes drastically when we reach the subject of jealousy. While Ovid urges his readers to be reasonable, he also admits to being totally confounded by his own jealous pangs: "In this art, I confess, I am not perfect; what am

I to do? I fall short of my own counsels."[8] So what shall we make of this explosive emotion that flies so completely in the face of common sense?

First we must of course determine more closely what we mean by "jealousy." The following dictionary-style definition will be quite sufficient for my purposes here: that in matters of love or sexuality, to be jealous is to be suspicious or fearful of losing one's love object to a rival. Defined in this way, jealousy is the obverse of envy: it is a defensive and possessive fear of losing the loved one rather than a painful grudge against someone else's good fortune. It has often been pointed out that in Shakespeare's English the word "jealous" could also denote a more general state of watchfulness or fearfulness, but this definition is unnecessarily inclusive when we explore the jealous passions of Leontes and Othello.[9]

We must also accept, with A. P. Rossiter, that what "we say about *Othello* will necessarily depend greatly on our attitudes toward jealousy."[10] Unfortunately, this important point is too often conceived in the relativistic sense that all readers are doomed to colonize the literary texts they read with their own Trojan hobbyhorses. As Brice Wachterhauser has pointed out admirably, such framework relativism rests on the "unjustified prejudice" that "having a historically conditioned point of view implies that one is hermetically sealed in that view."[11] I think Rossiter's words should rather be taken in the basic hermeneutical sense that a certain fore-understanding of the subject matter is required in order for interpretation to be possible at all. It also seems natural to suppose that a deepened theoretical understanding of the subject matter—of the kind I am about to offer—may have beneficial effects on our reading. But what must be resisted, unless we want to fall right back into the trap of unthinking apriorism, is the widespread but incoherent assumption that *Othello* will gladly mirror all our theoretical assumptions back at us. No theory of human nature or historical context, no matter how sophisticated, should ever be more than a dialogical framework or reference point for the analysis of a fictional text.

Anyone who reads up on modern accounts of sexuality or sexual jealousy in English Renaissance literature is soon struck by the predominance of a single mode of explanation, which we have come to know as social constructivism. Most recent books or articles on the subject begin with an assertion that gender and sexuality are "constructions" (as if this were an interpretive axiom) and then spend the rest of the discussion demonstrating the truth of the assertion.

A representative example is Mark Breitenberg's book, where it is assumed that men's anxieties in this period are "historically rather than essentially constructed" (7). Since he has defined early modern men as products of their historical situation, Breitenberg explains their worries as symptoms of "specific social tensions that are endemic to the early modern sex-gender system, the very tensions that produce the masculine subject in the first place" (13). Furthermore, since the act of worrying reproduces the existing sex-gender system, the result is a circular situation where male anxiety is "both cause and effect" (5). Culture generates culture, which generates culture. But what generates that first instance of culture? The answer can only be more culture, since there is no essential self, no human nature, from which it might emerge. Like Emilia's view of jealousy, Breitenberg's patriarchal culture becomes "a monster begot upon itself, born on itself."

As in the preceding chapters, our first step must be to improve on this constructivist framework by combining historical explanation with the fact that humanity is an identifiable species and not just a random assortment of cultural or historical fashions. When we turn to the literary text, it will also be necessary to resist the kind of premature projections and overly reductive explanations discussed above. As I hope to show toward the end of my reading, a combination of the biocultural perspective on human nature with some hermeneutical awareness can serve as a strong corrective to excessive literary reductionism (either biological, cultural, or otherwise). My ulterior purpose will thus be essentially negative: to show that Shakespeare's text is far more enigmatic, mysterious, and interesting than previous critics have claimed.

Throughout, my reading will tackle the central problem raised by Desdemona's and Emilia's remarks on jealousy: the question of its causality. I will also focus specifically on *male* jealousy because we cannot take it for granted that this affliction will be experienced in exactly the same way, or even for the same reasons, by men and women. Modern self-report studies tend to show an equal proclivity to jealousy but also a tendency for men and women—even in countries that are comparatively egalitarian—to respond differently to threats involving sexual and emotional infidelity.[12] Even if we should leave aside compelling evolutionary arguments for such psychosexual dimorphism, we can hypothesize at least small variations wherever social conditions for men and women have differed.

The Nature of Jealousy

Literary constructivist accounts of early modern jealousy typically run into two problems, the first of which is methodological. Since they are looking for a "dominant" discourse that might shape the literary treatment of sexuality, many literary constructivists have (for example) turned to the household manuals that were written by clergymen in the seventeenth century. In one of the best examples to date, Mary Beth Rose uses such material to trace "two dominant forms of sexual discourse" which she applies to literary texts with some interesting results.[13] But as many historians have opined, there are major problems with seeing household manuals as representative of what people actually felt or did in this period.[14] In some cases, even these texts themselves show clear traces of active dissent. William Gouge, the author of a frequently cited collection of sermons called *Of*

Domesticall Duties (1622), was even forced to modify his published text after taking some flak for insisting that women needed their husbands' consent when disposing of family goods: "This just Apology I have been forced to make, that I might not ever be judged (as some have censured me) *an hater of women."* [15] In other words, not everyone seems to have agreed with this patriarchal assumption.

Since it normally fails to heed such warnings, and since it accepts no cause that is not sociocultural, literary constructivism comes perilously close to an inflexible social determinism. While its proponents might defend themselves by defining statements like "the subject is produced by the sex-gender system" in the "weak" sense—that is, that they do not preclude other determinants—the conspicuous *absence* of such determinants in their own analyses is an obvious flaw. As we have seen, it is also methodologically questionable to suppose that literary texts faithfully reproduce social constructions, for at least two reasons. Even if we should accept the constructivist position, it is an obvious truth that literary texts often depend on surprise effects and inversions of audience expectations for their effect, and the element of make-believe always allows for radical departures from reality. Any literary theory that does not concede these points can hardly be convincing.

The second problem with the constructivist account of early modern jealousy is a more serious one: it advances a particularistic explanation of a phenomenon that seems to be universal to human societies. Although the anthropologist Margaret Mead made a famous attempt to uncover an idyllic, jealousy-free culture during her sojourn on Samoa, anthropologists have so far failed to uncover a single culture that is free of this affliction. Jealousy has been recorded in most societies all over the world, from tribes in the Amazon region to the Tiwi islanders of Australia, and it even exists in cultures whose worldviews seem diametrically opposed to the idea of jealousy. [16]

A particularly curious example comes from the Mehinaku tribe of the Brazilian Amazon region, which has become famous among anthropologists for its system of "partible paternity." The tribe believes that a fetus is built up gradually through multiple applications of semen inside the womb and that it is therefore possible for several men to contribute something to the same child. At first sight, this seems like an excellent means of creating strong, extended blood ties within the community while simultaneously eliminating one of the chief sources of male reproductive anxiety. But not only do Mehinaku men become jealous like everyone else; it has been reported that a very large number of the male population experiences "rampant castration anxieties" that involve the potential mangling or amputation of their genitals. [17]

Of course, strong evidence for the universality of sexual jealousy does not automatically demonstrate the need for a biological or evolutionary explanation. As the philosopher Daniel Dennett points out, "Showing that a particular type of human behavior is ubiquitous or nearly ubiquitous in widely separated human cultures goes *no way at all* toward showing that there is a genetic predisposition for that particular behavior."[18] This is a simple and important point, at least if we understand this supposed "predisposition" as a detailed genetic instruction: *when faced with X, do Y.* But Dennett would also be the first to stress that, sooner or later, any social constructivist explanation must come to terms with biology and evolutionary theory for the simple reason that emotions and behaviors are not simply immaterial bundles of free-floating signifiers. They are, to the best of our knowledge, material phenomena that emerge from intricately designed brains and bodies. A theory of emotions that does not acknowledge this fact is like a theory of interior decoration that takes itself for a theory of architecture.

The psychologist Ralph Hupka is one of many social scientists who have realized the necessity of making this move. More specifically, he attempts to grant biology and evolution some explanatory force and yet preserve the social realm as the exclusive constituent of jealousy. In his view, "Our genetic heritage enables us to experience jealousy, but all else is learned," and jealousy is "an inevitable consequence of the solutions to the problems of living in a society."[19] This is clearly a step forward compared to the circular arguments of strong constructivism, since Hupka both accounts for the ubiquity of jealousy and recognizes its biological foundations.

However, since practically all humans are born into some kind of society, we have reason to ask ourselves whether Hupka has really evicted the idea of a biological function or motivation. Living in some sort of society is, in Melford Spiro's formulation, a "biological requirement of the human organism."[20] In other words, Hupka's stance pretty much amounts to saying that the capacity for jealousy is an inevitable consequence of being human. (If he should define "society" more narrowly to exclude smaller units like, say, hunter-gatherer tribes, he would run into trouble since he must explain why these social formations have jealousy too.)

The most obvious biological cause of human jealousy is that we are sexual and affectionate mammals endowed with a capacity for active choice that we usually prefer to exercise if we can. As Geoffrey Miller puts the matter crisply, the "discriminatory nature of sex undermines all egalitarian utopias."[21] When we take a broad sweep of the natural world, it also becomes clear that the males of many different species go to great lengths to prevent their mates from having sex with others. Zoologists call this phenomenon "mate guarding," and it takes a wide variety of shapes in different species. Among mammals, the neuropeptide vasopressin may be a key neurochemical player, since elevated levels of this hormone trigger defensive and aggressive reactions toward potential rivals.[22] Since claustration practices have developed independently among humans on all five continents, and still survive in parts of the Islamic world, it would appear that humans have not been entirely averse to such tactics either. But two other human phenomena—a comparatively high degree of male parental investment and the fact that females have concealed ovulation—provide particularly important clues to the nature of jealousy.

The basic theory of parental investment has been discussed in previous chapters and will not be rehearsed here. A second and more universally familiar issue is that women are automatically assured of their maternity, while men can hardly be equally certain. Like approximately 60 percent of their primate relatives, human females have concealed ovulation and do not advertise their period of estrus openly by means of sexual swellings. As most prospective parents are aware, this makes it hard to time copulation with ovulation, and it also makes mate guarding more difficult. Since female primates have never been troubled by Victorian attitudes to sex—remember, being choosy is not the same thing as being coy—their male counterparts have responded to this problem with two different evolutionary strategies.

On one side of the spectrum, male gorillas have grown large enough to dominate a harem of females, exclude potential rivals, and thus ensure a reasonable chance of paternity. Among the relatively promiscuous chimpanzees, on the other hand, where the average female will mate "138 times with some thirteen males for every infant she gives birth to,"[23] males have instead grown extremely large testes whose copious ejaculations increase their competitive chances inside the female's reproductive tract. The price paid for these strategies, predictably, is that gorillas have ridiculously small testes while the male chimp's body is almost as small as the female's.

And then, placed on his isthmus of a middle state, we find the human male— about 15 percent larger than the female and with a moderate scrotum. We are most likely looking at the result of ancestral mating systems that were fairly competitive but neither characterized by gorilla-style harems nor the intense sperm competition of chimpanzee groups. Even if the *minimum* reproductive contribution of men still remains roughly five minutes, as opposed to the nine months or even several years for women, the average male parental investment has probably been fairly high throughout our history as a species. Compared to close relatives like bonobos and chimps, who could not care less about their individual offspring because they live in promiscuous groups, human males are notable for their high investment in children they cannot safely call their own. By the cold logic of natural selection, which only commemorates genetic fathers and disregards those who actually changed the diapers or brought home the bacon, that spells trouble.

It could, I suppose, be argued that such problems belong to a distant past and that modern women are all paragons of faithfulness. But worldwide studies of blood groups appear to demonstrate that "roughly nine per cent of children have genetic fathers who are different from those who believe they are the father."[24] This is a spectacular figure, given that the vast majority of human cultures are characterized by sexually exclusive monogamy or polygyny. At least when it comes to philandering, we have good reason to embrace Montaigne's suggestion that it is "much more easie to accuse the one sex, then to excuse the other."[25]

Now that we have looked at some of the biological traces of sexual conflict in the biosphere, the question arises whether male jealousy itself can be regarded as an evolved psychological trait. The most daring reply to this question comes from some exponents of evolutionary psychology. According to evolutionary psychologists Margo Wilson and John Daly, the ubiquity of mate guarding, claustration, and legally codified sexual double standards in human civilizations suggests that we may be dealing with an evolved component of the male psyche: "The repeated convergent invention of claustration practices around the world and the confining and controlling behavior of men even where it is frowned upon . . , reflect the workings of a sexually proprietary male psychology."[26]

Another evolutionary psychologist, David Buss, has even gone so far as to contend—in my view, problematically—that jealousy is a necessary component of human psychology whose absence "portends emotional bankruptcy."[27] The main problem with his claim is that even an evolved adaptation would have to be triggered by the perception of a threat (either real or imagined), and this cognitive-environmental aspect precludes a necessary dependence between love and jealousy. It is, for example, perfectly possible to imagine a relationship between two people who have such faith in each other's faithfulness that such worries never arise. In the same work on jealousy, Buss illustrates the treacherous nature of his massive modularity hypothesis—by which he attributes jealousy to a functionally specialized mental module produced by natural selection—in suggesting a novel explanation for spousal homicide. Together with Joshua Duntley, he has proposed that humans come equipped with an evolved "mate-killing module" (121–24); in my view, a grotesque figment of the evolutionary imagination.

As we saw earlier, to demonstrate the universality or ubiquity of a phenomenon is not to demonstrate that it can be attributed to a fixed genetic instruction. It is still possible to object, as Ralph Hupka and many others have done, that this "discriminatory attitude toward women can be accounted for more reasonably by social structures—such as the fact that economic and political power has traditionally been in the hands of men, who then promulgate laws that are consistent with their position of power."[28] One of many problems with *this* assertion, however, is that we still have to account for the existence of male economic and political power, and this new question will sooner or later land us in the realm of biology anyway. In their unified theory of social dominance, which straddles the domains of psychology and sociology and incorporates evolutionary theory, Jim Sidanius and Felicia Pratto argue that "due to the female preference for high-status males, the reproductive interests of dominant males are optimized by the formation of coalitions with other ingroup and dominant males, not only to constrain the economic and political options of females, but also to exploit and debilitate outgroup males."[29]

In all likelihood, human beings do have an innate, general disposition for jealousy, which is all too apparent in very small children. But the view of *sexual* jealousy as a specific psychological adaptation—or more precisely, the algorithmic, modular neural structure posited by many evolutionary psychologists—remains conjectural in spite of a wealth of supporting evidence from the human and animal world. There are too many gaps in the explanation, and the "massive modularity hypothesis" that informs it remains controversial.

It should be stressed, however, that the question of a specific disposition hardly stands or falls with the fortunes of a single research program and its particular theoretical apparatus. Since the mating game is such a central component of evolutionary fitness, and since the problem of ensuring sexual access to the other sex has been a consistent scenario in the history of our species, it is by no means inconceivable that human males (or females for that matter) should gradually have evolved a specific adaptation of this kind. Most likely, the question is not whether sexual jealousy is rooted in human nature but whether it is separable from the attachment drive and involves specialized neural structures. In the light of the functional independence of love and sex, it is at least noteworthy that the same neuropeptide—vasopressin—underpins both *attachment to females* and *aggression toward rivals* in male mammals.[30]

As usual, the suggestion that jealousy is an evolved psychological adaptation should not make us ignore social factors. Parental investment theory predicts that *investment* of any kind (resources, time, etc.) will be a reliable clue to mating patterns in most species, and for humans, to marry and have children is to make a substantial investment that is at once sexual, emotional, and economic. Drawing on this insight, Mildred Dickemann has shown that wherever claustration practices occur they are status-graded: "The higher the socioeconomic status of the family, the greater the intensity of the practice."[31] There is also a correlation between this practice and social stratification, since it receives its most extreme expression in those societies that exhibit the greatest inequalities between the rich and the poor.

Now that we have provided some evolutionary background to the problem of jealousy, we can zoom forward again to the early modern age and enjoy the benefits of a larger perspective. Historians now believe that the monogamous nuclear family had been the typical base of English social structure since at least the fourteenth century.[32] Since the English economy was largely home-based, the family was simultaneously a reproductive and economic unit. Most children left home around the age of fifteen, usually to work in another household, and then spent between ten and fifteen years as singles before they established a new family. Marriage, when it happened, normally took place between the ages of twenty-five and thirty, and men usually married a few years later than women did. But getting married and having children were not things to be taken for granted, since around 10 percent of the population never married[33] and no less than 42 percent of men did not leave surviving children.[34] Although a high mortality rate was obviously partly to blame, some men preferred the freedom of a single life while others lacked the resources to set up a new household.[35]

Marriage was also a fundamental decision in life, since there was practically no turning back once the vows had been made. While a form of separation could be granted in extraordinary circumstances, such as adultery or extreme cruelty,[36] the system of lifelong monogamy—with its rigid codification of sexual proprietary attitudes—may well have added to the intensity of sexual jealousy. Although the sixteenth and seventeenth centuries saw an increasing valorization of sex as a sanctified component within marriage,[37] the Christian stigmatization of lust probably did not help either.

A widespread model for married life in England was, as Susan Amussen puts it, that of "benevolent patriarchy, not authoritarian government." While the division of labor tied English women more closely to the home, they enjoyed much greater freedom than women in southern European countries like Spain and Italy.[38] The majority of women "left home as early as men and experienced an equal if not greater degree of mobility as they moved from household to household,"[39] and England was also notable for its "relaxed attitude toward young men and women spending time together, often in the absence of any chaperone."[40] This is why English plays of the period, like Thomas Middleton's *Women Beware Women* (1622), typically associate claustration of women with (Catholic) southern Europe.

If English women thus enjoyed relative freedom compared to women in other countries, their lives were still circumscribed by a sexual double standard that matched the cross-cultural tendency described by Wilson and Daly. Whenever men broke the marriage vow, the act was defined legally as fornication, while women who did so were guilty of the more serious crime of adultery. This double standard was actively justified with reference to the risk of illegitimacy.[41] The same concern was mirrored in the legal view of sex itself, for whenever sexual misconduct was concerned, officials focused on full intercourse and turned a blind eye on other sexual activities.[42] Of course, this did not prevent either religious moralists like William Gouge or dramatists like Shakespeare—see, for example, Emilia's rejection of the double standard (4.3.85–102)—from criticizing such injustice.

If one should look for the most important social factors that contributed to male jealousy in this period, the best candidates might be a legal and a biological one. The legal candidate can be found in English civil law, which pragmatically defined all children born to a married woman as legitimate, regardless of who had fathered them—indeed, even if "everyone knew that they had been procreated by another father."[43]

> By the Common Law, if the husband be within the foure Seas, that is, within the Jurisdiction of the King of England, if the Wife hath issue, no proofe is to be admitted to prove the Child a bastard (for in that case, Filiato non potest probari) unlesse the Husband hath an apparent impossibilitie of pro-creation . . . if the Issue be borne within a moneth or a day after marriage, between parties of full lawfull age, the childe is legitimate.[44]

This definition has two important consequences for our understanding of male jealousy in this period. First, the typical constructivist argument that jealousy was economically motivated—that it was about property rather than love—becomes dubious since the law actually precluded any practical consequences. For the minority of English men who had substantial property to pass on, and who did not care too deeply whether their children were actually "their own" or not, the rightful succession would still be protected by law. Of course, the law might not protect these men from slander or social shame, which were serious problems in this period, or indeed the more personal chagrin of discovering that someone else had slipped between the marital sheets. The model of benevolent patriarchy probably added insult to injury in this area, and dealt a serious blow to men's sense of manhood, since extramarital liaisons on the part of the wife suggested that the husband could not control her sexuality—or as Othello puts it with respect to Desdemona's supposed unfaithfulness: "O curse of marriage / That we can call these delicate creatures ours / And not their appetites!" (3.3.272–74)

Secondly, and even more important, a law that automatically defined all children born to a married woman as legitimate may have had grave psychological consequences for husbands. Since it probably *did* matter a great deal to most men whether their children were their own or not, this system (which presented them with an impossible burden of proof, and even forced them to acknowledge children that had been fathered by others before the marriage) could well have exacerbated male jealousy considerably. It may well be an important factor, together with the more general importance of honor and reputation in this period, behind the obsession with cuckoldry that characterized early modern England. In the light of this situation, it is possible that the innumerable jokes about cuckoldry in early modern ballads and plays resonate with a historically specific urgency.

The other historical phenomenon that must have contributed dramatically to early modern anxieties about adultery can hardly be written off as some sort of social construction. Instead, it falls squarely under the rubric of biology. I am thinking of syphilis, the gruesome and potentially lethal venereal disease that was almost as frequent a source of black humor as cuckoldry in this period. The two were, of course, deeply intertwined in the popular imagination. Since the first stage of syphilis could go undetected by the afflicted person—especially in women, where the small, painless sore it caused would typically appear inside the reproductive tract—a single act of adultery could have disastrous consequences. Since syphilis did not require actual sexual relations to spread, and sometimes made do with simple physical intimacy, entire families could succumb to the same disease due to one parent's philandering.[45] Even in less extreme circumstances than these, spousal fidelity would have been more than a matter of Christian morality, honor, or even love for the early moderns. As in our AIDS-infested modernity, it could become a matter of life and death, with the subtle difference that Shakespeare would have regarded "safe sex" as an oxymoron.

"One Not Easily Jealous"?

Let us now turn to Shakespeare's *Othello* and consider the problem with which I began my discussion: Emilia's contention that jealousy has no cause. The gist of my argument so far has been that jealousy is not simply a social construction but a universal phenomenon that goes to the heart of human nature. Even if its precise mechanisms still remain unknown and its proximate causes must be both variable and complex, we have at least learned not to focus too exclusively or singlemindedly on Shakespeare's historical context in the interpretation of his play. It is, however, equally important to avoid rushing in and proclaiming aprioristically that Shakespeare vindicates the biocultural perspective on jealousy, since there is no obvious reason to expect him to do so. For all we know, Shakespeare could have been under the impression that jealousy is induced by little miniature devils that are produced in the liver and then released into the brain as soon as people marry.

Anyone who wants to explore the cause (or causes) of Othello's inordinate jealousy must confront an interesting objection raised some years ago by Virginia Mason Vaughan in her excellent contextual study of the play (1996). In essence, Vaughan's argument is that the modern concern with Othello's psychological motivation is really an anachronistic red herring. She supports this contention mainly with references to Thomas Wright's contemporary discourse *The Passions of the Mind*—where psychological motivation is "not an issue," and "it is not necessary to explain sudden changes in behavior"[46]—and Elizabeth Carey's *Tragedy of Mariam*, where Herod's jealousy seems equally unexplained. If Vaughan is right about this, then we have reason to take Emilia's protestation quite literally: we could be looking for something in Shakespeare's play that is not meant to be there. Must our search for the cause(s) of Othello's jealousy be historicized and given up even before it has started?

The thing to remember about such detailed contextual or historical explanations is that they necessarily place selective emphasis on certain texts or historical
records at the expense of others. If we turn instead to Robert Burton's *Anatomy of
Melancholy,* written two decades after Shakespeare's play, we find that the author
lists no less than eight potential causes for sexual jealousy, from melancholy and
impotence to a desire for sexual variety. Nor do we need to dig very deeply into
Shakespeare's own writings to find attempts at causal explanations of emotional
states. In fact, we need go no further than the very remark that prompts Emilia's
rejection of causality—Desdemona's contention that she has given Othello no
cause for jealousy—which obviously presupposes some sort of connection between identifiable grievances and strong feelings. And as we shall see further on
in this chapter, Polixenes in *The Winter's Tale* offers no less than three psychological explanations of the Sicilian king's jealousy.

To those who have traveled some distance from the world of psychoanalytic
theory, this should really come as no surprise. With some hindsight, the most
striking upheaval brought about by Freudianism was not that psychological motivation suddenly became of interest to people but rather that unconscious drives
were brought to light, sexualized, defined as effects of formative childhood experiences, and then emphasized at the expense of all other explanations. Human
beings have always had a strong incentive to interrogate the underlying causes
of each other's emotional responses, especially when these become violent and
aggressive, and Shakespeare certainly expected his audience to do the same with
his main protagonist.

The thing that really clinches the argument, however, is that *Othello* displays
such a pervasive concern with intentions, psychological motivations, and our
fragile attempts to uncover them—both in ourselves and in other people. In one
of the finest book-length studies to date, Jane Adamson finds it "remarkable how
explicitly the play dramatizes and explores the ways and means by which different people 'make sense' of what happens in their lives, including what they merely
imagine to be happening."[47] This preoccupation spreads from the intratextual
level to include the audience's attempts to make sense of what we see before us.
Indeed, the parallel attempts of the characters to decode the meanings of actions
and feelings—either real or imagined—and the audience's attempts to do the
same from an external vantage point constitute an important source of dramatic
identification.

Consider, as a choice example, the famous "motiveless malignancy" that Iago
unleashes on the unsuspecting Othello. As many critics have noted, the problem
is not that Iago gives the audience no psychological motives for his vendetta
against the Moor but rather that he gives us too many:

His reasons reach the audience as merely possible truths or plausible ratio-
nalizations offered in response to some residue of a need in Iago to explain

himself, or to avoid some blunter and more self-wounding explanation. . . .
One gets the strange sense that Iago's own thoughts, for all the energy with
which he addresses himself to them, are composed mainly of uncertain,
half-plausible rumours that circulate in his head and that he repeats to himself and to us.[48]

When we reach the play's denouement, the vanquished Othello desperately seeks
some sort of explanation of the evil that has enveloped him. He first looks down
at Iago's feet to see if they are cloven but immediately rejects this metaphysical
interpretation as a "fable" (5.2.285). Then, presumably still unable to address or
look his foe in the eye, he formulates his overwhelming question explicitly, only
to be frustrated once again:

> Will you, I pray, demand that demi-devil
> Why he hath thus ensnared my soul and body?
> IAGO: Demand me nothing. What you know, you know.
> From this time forth I never will speak word. (300–3)

At this point, the audience *is* Othello. We stand equally dumbfounded and anxious to peer into the black box that is Iago's mind, having lost every fragment of
the superior knowledge that previously separated us from the noble Moor. As a
consequence, we, like Othello, are left with a psychological puzzle that simultaneously demands and denies a reasonable explanation.

A more innocuous (and usually overlooked) example of how the dramatist
complicates the question of psychological motivation can be found right before
Othello's epileptic fit, when the latter exclaims very unexpectedly: "It is not words
that shakes me thus" (4.1.41–42). This is a particularly difficult pill to swallow
since most audiences will be convinced that it is precisely *words*—in the form of
Iago's satanic innuendo—that have inspired Othello's trauma. Can we really have
been wrong about such an obvious aspect of the play?

Throughout *Othello*, Shakespeare plays this Iago-like trick on his audience
by alternatively suggesting and withdrawing evidence about psychological motivation. Since no person on earth has ever had unmediated access to another's
intentions or motivations—let alone those of literary characters—the assessment
of psychological causes must always contain an element of speculation. We must
deal in degrees of probability and ask ourselves, for example, whether it is *reasonable* or *plausible* to suppose that a particular cause has brought about a particular
emotional response or behavior. It is highly relevant in this context that Shakespeare repeats the question "Is't possible?" no less than four times throughout
Othello, which happens nowhere else in his works (2.3.278; 3.3.361; 3.4.70; 4.1.42).
The exact formulation is used by all three main protagonists—Iago, Othello, and
Desdemona—and in three out of four cases it is directly concerned with other

people's intentions and behaviors. It is also difficult not to connect this insistent question with the dramatic parallel that critics have already detected between Othello's hopeless quest for ocular proof and the war council in the Venetian senate. Debating whether or not the apparent impending assault on Rhodes is a tactical ruse, the Duke gradually rifles a "possible" interpretation into something that is held "in all confidence" and finally deemed "certain" (1.3.9, 33, 44); the Turks are indeed heading for Cyprus.

From this discussion we can derive an interpretive lesson that concerns characters, audiences, and literary critics alike. On the intradramatic level, Iago is able to dupe Othello because there will always be a *possibility*, however slight, that Desdemona has actually slept with Cassio (or even with Emilia or Brabantio for that matter). Whether this is a *plausible* proposition is a different question. Like Othello, we too will delude ourselves if we confuse what is merely *possible* with what is *plausible, probable,* or *certain* as we explore the mechanisms that underpin his jealousy. Indeed, the play more or less forces such a dialectical approach on us since the attempts of the characters to make sense of their experience are mirrored by our own endeavor to make sense of the tragedy that unfolds before us. The didactic example of the war council—with its careful movement from *possible* to *certain*—reflects not only on the epistemological failures of the main protagonist, but also on our own attempts to come to terms with them.

It is surprising, therefore, that so many critics have cast themselves so unreservedly into the hermeneutical trap that Shakespeare holds up to view. They have, in short, rehearsed Othello's fatal mistake by jumping to premature conclusions on the basis of flimsy evidence. As is usually the case in the current critical arena, the main instigating factor has been a strong ideological impulse that automatically privileges certain modes of explanation over others, that does not hesitate to skip past strong evidence to the contrary, and that therefore ends up with a distorted account of Shakespeare's play.

An important reason for the drastic upsurge of *Othello* studies in recent years, to the point where this play now eclipses both *Lear* and *Hamlet* in popularity, has been the widespread concern with race, gender, and politics. In such an environment, a play about a black man who kills his wife must clearly be regarded as something of a godsend. But even though it must be hoped that most readers of Shakespeare are against racism and for sexual equality, these political readings must be subjected to the same rigorous examination that one would apply to any others. The alternative—to endorse readings just because they happen to caress our own ideological convictions—would be intellectually dishonest and, ultimately, counterproductive.

Let us start with the widespread contention that Othello's jealousy derives from the color of his skin. In 1977 two articles appeared, written by Ruth Cowhig and Annette Rubinstein, that argued independently for a fairly direct causal relationship between jealousy and racism in Shakespeare's play.[49] More recently, Patrick Hogan (1998) has argued that Othello is subject to "racial despair,"[50] while Karen Newman's influential reading from 1987 proclaims that Othello is subject to a "complicitous self-loathing" because his own blackness is "loathsome" to him.[51] Similar causal explanations can also be found in readings that do not embrace an explicit racial perspective, such as Arthur Kirsch's observation that Othello "fails to love his own body, to love himself, and it is this despairing self-hatred that spawns the enormous savagery, degradation, and destructiveness of his jealousy."[52]

At first sight, the "racial" reading seems to have much to offer. Othello is clearly exposed to racist slander in the first act, and there is also something worrying about his own suggestion later in the play that Desdemona's "name, that was as fresh / As Dian's visage, is now begrimed and black / As mine own face" (3.3.389–91). Not only does Othello seem to recognize that black may not be beautiful, but he even associates the blackness of his skin with the blackness of shame. If we leave the play aside for a moment, it does not seem impossible that a man could be driven half insane by racism and end up murdering his wife. But as we saw above, a *possible* reading is not necessarily a *plausible* or *convincing* reading, and we cannot pass judgment until we have also considered its potential limitations.

For example, when Ruth Cowhig turns racism into something of a prime mover in *Othello*, she skips merrily past material that points us in the opposite direction. When Othello has started to grow jealous, he briefly considers three reasons why Desdemona might lose interest in him: that he is not particularly eloquent, that he is black, and that he is old. For early modern lovers, these were indeed potential risk factors. In *The Art of Love* (the closest thing Shakespeare had to the Kinsey Report), Ovid had stressed that eloquence was a crucial factor for prospective lovers. Household manuals tended to emphasize that too much difference in social rank or age were negative predictors of marital bliss. And there were probably few English people in this period who thought that "black [was] beautiful" compared to rosy English cheeks. But Cowhig ends her citation just before Othello evaluates his improvised explanations of Desdemona's supposed adultery: "Yet that's not much" (3.3.270). Not only are we given no reason to prefer blackness above the other two explanations, but all three explanations are rejected by Othello himself.

We must also remember that the three men that utter some sort of disparaging remarks about Othello's race—Brabantio, Roderigo, and Iago—all have large axes to grind. No other character in Shakespeare's play ever discusses Othello's race or color in derogatory terms.[53] In the case of Brabantio, who vomits forth the most unabashed slurs in the first act, the racism certainly cannot be very deep-seated since we know that he has "loved" and "oft invited" (1.3.129) Othello to his house before the latter betrayed his confidence by stealing his daughter. Nor is it particularly surprising that the three men should focus their vicious comments on the one thing that separates Othello from the other Venetians, since even a nonracist might resort to such cruelties in order to be as hurtful as possible. One surmises that if Othello had worn glasses, they might well have called him "four-eyes" rather than "thick-lips."

As the examples from Hogan and Newman illustrate, it is a necessary component of the racial argument that Othello internalizes the racism that surrounds him; he must feel "racial despair" or "complicitous self-loathing" and then channel it into jealous rage. Such an attempt to explain jealousy by means of social determinism is just as risky *within* literary texts as it is *outside* them. A literary character is not simply an effect of his or her setting, any more than a human being is the straightforward result of social conditioning (which is one reason why classical behaviorism has lost much of its prestige as a psychological theory and why sociologists find it difficult to account for individual agency). To assume that Othello must become jealous because he is black is to deny him a substantial part of what makes him human, namely the capacity to engage self-consciously, critically, and actively with his environment. As we have seen, we do have some reason to suppose that Othello finds his own "begrimed" face aesthetically unpleasing, but this is a far cry from saying that we have uncovered the cause of his murderous jealousy.

However, the most damaging blow to the "racial insecurity reading" does not come from such abstract considerations but from textual evidence that points emphatically in a different direction. For one thing that Shakespeare takes considerable pains to establish in this play is how *loved* and *admired* his main protagonist is. Most characters seem to flush with admiration when they talk about the noble Moor. As they wait for Othello to arrive in Cyprus, Montano expresses his admiration (2.1.34–36). Later in the play, when Lodovico is confronted with Othello's horrendous abuse of Desdemona, he cannot reconcile what he has seen with the person who was everyone's darling in Venice:

> Is this the noble Moor whom our full senate
> Call all in all sufficient? This the nature,
> Whom passion could not shake? whose solid virtue
> The shot of accident nor dart of chance,
> Could neither graze nor pierce? (4.1.264–68)

These are strong words. Othello's reputation has been no less than that of a complete man, one who fully embodies such central Renaissance ideals as virtue, constancy, and martial prowess. That he is capable of genuine love and affection is also suggested elsewhere. Even Iago, his sworn enemy, admits to himself in private that the Moor has a "free and open nature" (1.3.397), indeed, a "constant, loving, noble nature," which suggests that he will prove a "most dear husband" to Desdemona (2.1.286, 288). Of course, since Iago firmly believes that other people's beauties exist only to make him ugly, these noble traits are not to be admired but resented.

It is also clear that Othello is aware of the love and admiration that surrounds him. When he lands on Cyprus he remarks that "I have found great love amongst them" (2.1.204) and that he therefore expects his wife to receive the same good treatment. It is, in fact, the same self-confident awareness of his own worth that has enabled him to steal the daughter of one of the most influential men in Venice—a remarkable social transgression—without any fear of punishment: "Let [Brabantio] do his spite; / My services, which I have done the signiory, / Shall out tongue his complaints" (1.2 17–19). The play gives us no real evidence that Othello is feeling insecure prior to Iago's onslaught on his mind or that he exhibits any signs of either self-loathing or racial despair. It does, however, give us plenty of reasons to think otherwise.

The most recent trend in criticism on Shakespeare's play has been to combine the aforementioned study of race with that of gender. Karen Newman's 1987 article—where it was argued that blackness and femininity are perceived as equally monstrous in *Othello*—was something of a landmark in this area, and later critics have approached the same ideological alloy with similar conclusions. In Ania Loomba's analysis, where "Othello's blackness is central to any understanding of male or female sexuality or power structures in the play," race and sexuality appear to be dialectical counterparts, engendering distinct forms of oppression but also exerting influence on one another.[54] In the same volume of essays, Anthony Gerard Barthelemy puts forward a historical argument wherein sex is rather subsumed by race. At the risk of confusing analytical levels by assigning metadramatic awareness to the main protagonist, he argues that "Othello's sexual anxiety is an intrinsic component of his larger fear of being a stereotypical stage Moor, and his attempt to deny his interest in 'proper satisfaction' is an attempt to deny his kinship to his immediate predecessors Aaron and Eleazar."[55]

Of course, there have also been numerous attempts to explain Othello's jealousy with a more exclusive focus on gender and sexuality—or more precisely, on patriarchal conceptions of male and female—where race becomes a subsidiary phenomenon. In the early eighties, Marilyn French contended that Iago manages to convince Othello so easily because they share a male, patriarchal value structure in which women are either superhuman and divine or subhuman and beastly.[56] According to John Drakakis, it is both ahistorical and ideologically suspect to approach Othello as a character endowed with an individualized psychology since the motive force of his insanity must be located in deeper social and discursive structures (that is, in Patriarchy). The power of these structures is in fact so great that the positive female voices in the play, such as Emilia's, are not really positive at all; according to Drakakis they are merely decoys set up by an omnipotent Patriarchy to give an illusion of dialogue or good will.[57]

A curious point of convergence between these studies and Barthelemy's reading of Othello as Stage Moor is that it becomes very difficult to write an ideologically acceptable depiction of either Woman or Moor: they are either too good or too bad. "By demonstrating virtue, [the] few honest Moors [on the English stage] offer further validation of the more common, harmful, and denigrating representations of black Moors because they prove that it is possible to resist the call of evil, though most unusual."[58] The problem is, of course, that a character painted exclusively in neutral colors seldom becomes interesting from a dramatic perspective.

In an earlier essay that squarely contradicts such double binds while retaining patriarchy as prime mover, Carol Thomas Neely engages in an impressive number of textual omissions and elisions in order to arrive at the following polarization: the men in *Othello* are murderous, foolish, vain, exponents of the whore/Madonna dichotomy, obsessed with reputation and manliness, and habitually blame other people for their own misdeeds. The women, by contrast, are basically good, and the reason why the sexes are not reconciled in *Othello* is that the men "persistently misconstrue the women," while the women "fatally overestimate the men."[59] That is, the men fail to see how good the women really are, while the women fail to see just how much evil resides in the men.

Although there is much to be criticized in these hyper-ideological readings, it would be foolish to deny that there are patriarchal norms and values at work in Shakespeare's play. These norms make their appearance immediately when the enraged Brabantio asserts his power as head of the family, and Desdemona soon affirms them too by professing to exchange one "lord" (her father) for another (her husband). Patriarchal norms are also present, but this time presupposed and rejected, when Emilia delivers her famous critique of the sexual double standard. To this we can add the contextual information that Shakespeare belonged to a culture where, as we saw earlier, ensuring paternity and preventing adultery were particularly grave matters for men due to the nature of common law and other social phenomena.

In fact, Shakespeare may not have had recourse to the jargon of gender studies, but it is quite likely that he consciously depicted a Venetian society that was much *more* patriarchal than his native England, regarding both women's freedom and the intensity of male jealousy. In the *Anatomy of Melancholy*, Robert Burton regarded it as a commonplace that Italians were more jealous and possessive of their wives than were Englishmen: "England is a Paradise for women, an hell for horses; Italy a Paradise of horses, hell for women, as the diverbe goes."[60]

What must be questioned, therefore, is not the existence of patriarchal norms in Shakespeare's play but the idea that these norms are a sufficient cause for Othello's jealous rampage. As Richard Levin points out with respect to his killing of Desdemona, "The characters who comment on it (including Othello himself after he learns the truth) do not view it as one of your everyday patriarchal events; instead, they consider it a horrifying violation of the norms of their world."[61] The function of patriarchal norms or racist vituperation in Shakespeare's play is more likely a matter of dramatic contrast than social determinism. In Hugh Macrae Richmond's view, "The feminist and racial critics have misunderstood and misrepresented a distinctive theatrical experience in Shakespeare: the shock of reverse psychology dependent, for example, on the establishment of a conventionally ideal feminine persona which is then subverted by one significant choice." Richmond links this phenomenon usefully to the Aristotelian concept of reversal, where the shock of the unexpected is an essential part of theatrical effect.[62]

Before we leave the questions of race and gender, let me deal briefly with potential objections to this discussion. First, if both race and gender fail as individual explanatory causes for Othello's jealousy, then it is always possible to argue for an explosive compound of the two (or any number of additional factors). As we saw above, many critics think of Othello's jealousy as inspired by race as well as gender. According to Valerie Traub, "Othello's anxiety is culturally and psychosexually overdetermined by erotic, gender, and racial anxieties, including . . . the fear of chaos he associates with sexual activity."[63] The problem with this line of reasoning, to return to our earlier discussion of probability, is that several merely "possible" causes do not add up to a new cause that is somehow more certain or convincing. It is true that in a court of law, a string of circumstantial evidence might well add to the probability of guilt, but then all the evidence would still point to the same account of what actually happened. In this case, every piece of evidence makes a different case for what has transpired and so cannot support the others.

I argued above that Othello's behavior gives us no reason to suppose that he actually suffers from racist or sexist despair, but it is always possible for psychoanalysts and other negative hermeneuticians to circumvent this problem by arguing that his insecurity or self-loathing is repressed. Othello is simply in denial, and his summary dismissal of age, skin color, and insufficient eloquence is the very opposite of what it appears to be! But like all interpretations that turn the manifest *absence* of something into an argument for its actual *presence*—compare the previous case for "latent incest" in *King Lear*—this reading is no more than a substantial critical inference that rests on two rigid a priori assumptions: a prefabricated notion of what the *real* cause of jealousy is and an assumption that nothing in Shakespeare's text can ever contradict this idea.

Having failed to uncover a sociological cause for Othello's jealousy, we must now consider another explanation of his defeat at the hands of the green-eyed monster: that his love for Desdemona is flawed. Many years ago, F. R. Leavis started something of a critical campaign against Shakespeare's main protagonist wherein he denied that the latter's love for Desdemona was really love at all: "It must be much more a matter of self-centred and self-regarding satisfactions—pride, sensual possessiveness, appetite, love of loving—than he suspects."[64] More recently, James Calderwood has found Othello guilty of self-centered possessiveness toward his wife and defined his love as "flawed from the beginning."[65] As late as 2002, David Bevington suggested that Othello does not really love Desdemona as much as he loves her love for him and that his feeling for her is really a form of self-regard.[66] (To paraphrase Leavis, this would mean that Othello exhibits a "love of being loved" rather than a love of loving.) For both Bevington and Calderwood, it is Othello's deep-seated dependence on other people's praise that makes him vulnerable and ultimately destructive because it twists his love into a conception of Desdemona as an extension of himself.

To argue for a "flawed" love presupposes some sort of normative idea of what a true, healthy love should look like, and we can trace a clear pattern in these critical responses. Othello is to blame because he is in love with love rather than with Desdemona; he is too dependent on the capacity of her love to bolster his own self-image; he is possessive; and he is self-centered or even egotistic. Before we consider more closely what Shakespeare's text has to say on the subject, it will be useful to put some of these claims into theoretical perspective.

As we saw in chapter 1, the emotion of romantic love, with its fusion of passion, intimacy, and commitment, is characterized by—among other things—a desire for exclusivity and emotional dependency on the loved one. Hence we should not be surprised if a romantic lover exhibits at least a mild degree of possessiveness and finds it difficult to imagine a life without the other person. Nor can we expect Othello to love his wife with the kind of selfless *agape* one might expect from a Catholic saint rather than a newlywed husband. It is also difficult to imagine a union between two people that does not somehow turn them into "extensions" of each other. To this we can add that Othello and Desdemona have recently entered into the institution of marriage, which, as we saw in the preceding chapter, is not simply an expression of mutual passion: it is also a proprietary and possessive institution that establishes legal and emotional rights to the other person.

In short, we would have much more reason to be suspicious of Othello's love if he were not in the least possessive or dependent on Desdemona's love (and, say, merely shrugged at the idea of Desdemona and Cassio doing the beast with two backs). Of course, like any aspect of human emotion, this desire for exclusivity and possession can be exaggerated to such an extent that it becomes dysfunctional and potentially dangerous. Is this perhaps what Calderwood and Bevington are arguing for? In that case they must explain why Othello is so relaxed about Desdemona's activities prior to the onset of his jealousy:

> 'Tis not to make me jealous
> To say my wife is fair, feeds well, loves company,
> Is free of speech, sings, plays and dances well:
> Where virtue is, these are more virtuous. (3.3.186–89)

As long as we discard the eternal argument from absence (that Othello is constantly in denial and is therefore always saying the very opposite of what he or his subconscious really means), these are manifestly not the words of an unusually proprietary or zealously mate-guarding man.

There is one more aspect of the "flawed love" argument that we still have not dealt with: the idea that Othello's love is egotistical or self-centered. Bevington's and Calderwood's chief support for their claim comes from Othello's speech at the Senate, when Brabantio has just accused him of having practiced witchcraft on Desdemona. When Calderwood defines the speech as egocentric—it is almost exclusively about Othello himself and says little about Desdemona—he admits that "much of this egocentricity comes with the narrative territory" since the teller of a story is usually endowed with the grammatical "I."[67] But even this disclaimer, which does not seem to affect Calderwood's overriding claim for a self-centered love, overlooks the chief reason why Othello's speech cannot reasonably be described as "egocentric" or "self-centered."

First, it is vital to consider Othello's account of the courtship in its dramatic context. He is, after all, more or less on trial for witchcraft and must be very keen to absolve himself of this charge.[68] He is also in the absurd position of being asked to explain why Desdemona fell in love with him. How could anyone hope to explain such a thing? When Othello retells the story of their courtship and concludes that Desdemona "loved me for the dangers I had passed" (1.3.168), this reads more like a modest attempt to steer the attention away from his own personal characteristics. It is quite simply the best thing available to a man who is forced to answer an impossible question and who has recently indicated that he knows his worth but does not want to brag about it (1.2.19–24). In fact, his account of the courtship also gives us an interesting glimpse into the considerable mutuality and balance of power between himself and Desdemona. Contrary to Harold Bloom's view that Othello is "essentially passive" in the courtship,[69] the passage actually gives us a delicious example of two sensitive lovers who gradually nudge each other toward a mutual confession of love: *This to hear would Desdemona seriously incline . . . I found good means to draw from her a prayer . . . I did consent . . . she wished that heaven had made her such a man. . . . Upon this hint I spake* (1.3.129–70).

If even this should not convince us that Shakespeare's proud warrior houses an affectionate and sensitive soul that is romantically involved with Desdemona, then we can always turn to Iago's aforementioned description of Othello as a kind man who will in all likelihood prove an excellent husband for Desdemona. We can also consider the extraordinary, almost ecstatic delight that Othello gives such beautiful voice to when he is reunited with his wife on Cyprus:

> If it were now to die
> 'Twere now to be most happy, for I fear
> My soul hath her content so absolute
> That not another comfort like to this
> Succeeds in unknown fate. (2.1.187–91)

There may be an ominous sense in which this passage plays on the implications of the age difference between Othello and Desdemona. As Graham Bradshaw remarks, the virginal Desdemona's life "stretches before her, whereas Othello characteristically—and revealingly—thinks of his as a long 'pilgrimage' that has found its goal (1.3.153)."[70] Jane Adamson even suggests that Othello's formulation contains "the clear, troubling signs of a proclivity to fear. His words seem to arise from some wary pessimism, a mistrust of life."[71] But surely the main emphasis falls on the joy that Othello is expressing? While Bradshaw's remark qualifies any simple response to this scene, it does not detract from the impression that Othello is expressing a happiness so intense and overpowering that he associates it with the annihilation of the self.

Like the claim for various sociological causes of Othello's jealousy, the notion that his love for Desdemona is flawed or self-regarding does not hold up well under scrutiny. At best, it remains a weak possibility that is plagued by solid evidence to the contrary. It seems much more convincing to suggest that Shakespeare has deliberately painted Othello's and Desdemona's love in the sunniest colors he could find: a love that is mutual, strong, generous, and calmly defiant of the prejudice and resentment that surrounds the lovers early on. The necessary consequence is that the contrast between the two Othellos—the carefree soul prior to the temptation scene in act 3, and the tortured and doubtful being who finally ends up killing his wife—becomes all the more mysterious and unsettling.

Before we probe deeper into this mystery I must mention another potential explanation of Othello's tragic collapse: that he is literally *moonstruck*. This explanation is seldom (if ever) touched on by literary critics even though it has explicit textual support. When Othello has just smothered Desdemona he is interrupted by Emilia's news that Roderigo has been murdered the same night. He responds: "It is the very error of the moon, / She comes more nearer earth than she was wont / And makes men mad" (5.2.109–11). Since the belief in astrological influence was still widespread in Shakespeare's England, it would be quite ahistorical to dismiss this suggestion out of hand.

This interpretation becomes even more plausible when we consider *The Winter's Tale*, where Hermione attempts to explain her husband's inexplicable jealousy as follows: "There's some ill planet reigns: / I must be patient till the heavens look / With an aspect more favourable" (2.1.105–7). It is true that a quick comparison with other plays (especially Edmund's sarcastic refutation of astrology in *Lear*) will throw a more unfavorable contextual light on Othello's remark, but it does not enable us to refute the more specific claim for astrological agency in *Othello*. The idea of a moonstruck Othello must take its place alongside the other readings that are *merely possible* and therefore *fairly implausible*: racial despair, patriarchal norms, and flawed love.

"The Plague of Great Ones"

By now we are clearly scraping out the last, bitter dregs from our barrel of causal explanation, and this leaves us at something of an analytical impasse. So what could be more refreshing than to leave *Othello* aside for a moment, make a spontaneous leap into the genre of romance, and consider another Shakespeare play that confronts us with a seemingly inexplicable case of jealousy?

The most obvious difference between Othello and his counterpart Leontes in *The Winter's Tale* is that the latter seems to lack any external incentive for his destructive jealousy. Harold Bloom defines him nicely as "an Othello who is his own Iago."[72] When Antenor gets wind of Leontes' jealousy, however, he is convinced that there must be some sort of Iago somewhere in the background, since only the presence of such a malicious figure could explain the king's jealousy: "You are abus'd, and by some putter-on / That will be damn'd for't: would I knew the villain, / I would land-damn him" (2.1.141–43). It seems likely that this explicit reference to the play's own interpretive lacuna—that something vital is missing in the portrayal of Leontes' jealousy—is intended to serve the same paradoxical function as the frustrating concern with psychological motivation in *Othello*. Shakespeare is manipulating his audience by first withdrawing the cause of Leontes' jealousy and then telling us to look for it. If there is no Iago, then what is responsible for this mad outburst?

Another notable difference in *The Winter's Tale* is that the question of paternity looms so large. This difference has a perfectly natural explanation since Leontes and Hermione are parents while Othello and Desdemona are not. Very soon after Leontes experiences the first pangs of jealousy, he begins to examine his son Mamillius closely for those signs of resemblance one might expect in a son, and the result is clearly reassuring (1.2.119–35).

For the sake of honesty, I must add that not all critics would accept this reading, however straightforward and obvious it may seem. (In fact, I just deemed it so obvious that I did not see any reason to cite it in the preceding paragraph.) But according to Stanley Cavell,[73] Leontes is actually seeking to convince himself of the complete opposite: that he is *not* the father of his own son. "We are now so accustomed to understanding insistence or protestation, perhaps in the form of rage, as modes of denial, that we will at least consider that the *negation* of this tale is the object of Leontes' fear, namely the fear that he *is* the father." Although no new evidence is adduced, Cavell's initial suggestion of a mere *possibility* soon grows into a definite claim to have uncovered the roots of Leontes' jealousy, in that "disowning his issue is more fundamental than, or causes, his jealousy of his friend and brother, rather than the other way around" (195). A few pages later we find Cavell expecting "considerable agreement that in Leontes' intrusion we have an Oedipal conflict before us," with the obvious difference that "the conflict seems primarily generated by the father's wish to replace or remove the son" (199).

It seems almost superfluous to point out that we are once again dealing with a formidable argument from absence, where everything is what it is not and an assertion is always already a mode of denial. A reader who remembers Cavell's famous reading of *King Lear*—that Lear demands love because he wants to avoid it—may well piece together the following recipe for an interesting reading: take the most reasonable and logical explanation you can find and then turn it entirely on its head. If somebody objects, just mention Freud and you're in the clear.

I will assume, then, that Leontes is doing precisely what he appears to be doing in this scene: he is examining his son for signs that might allay his fear that he has been cuckolded twice. "No: I'll not rear / Another's issue" (2.3.192–93). There is, of course, a strong evolutionary rationale for such fears that does not contradict but rather underpins the proximal explanation that Leontes loves Mamillius and feels possessive of him. If we want, we can also go on to connect this fear with Shakespeare's historical context, where the problem of paternity was particularly urgent given the nature of common law. If Perdita had been a bastard child born on English soil, she would automatically have been defined as Leontes' legitimate offspring even though he was not the father. We can also add the more specific problems that face any monarch who must ensure the continuation of his lineage, which would make the legitimacy of his firstborn son especially important.

The critic who has argued for the strongest connection between paternity and jealousy in *The Winter's Tale* has done so from a slightly different perspective than mine. In his book-length study of the play, B. J. Sokol contends promisingly that "Shakespeare did not only illustrate but also typically motivated the mental pathologies that he depicted."[74] He also finds *The Winter's Tale* "exceptionally mimetic, especially in its presentation of the progress of Leontes' mental breakdown and subsequent discovery." What is at work in this play, according to Sokol, is the so-called couvade syndrome that is said to afflict expectant fathers with a very broad variety of symptoms (from sympathetic labor pains to downright mental illness).

This is a suggestive idea, but it is not without problems. While the existence of a sympathetic childbirth ritual known as couvade is well accounted for in preindustrial societies, the exact etiology of that unified paternal syndrome that would generate both toothaches and the following paranoid delusions seems more uncertain: "One 'misinterpreted automobile license plate numbers as personal references to important dates in his life'; another 'expressed the delusion that his life was controlled by a computer programme he had created and that his wife was being contacted by "the homosexuals"'; another believed that 'he was being watched by means of electrical apparatus,' and also had 'a dread of everything red'; and couvade-induced animal phobias are also reported."[75] While literary scholars should hesitate to play psychologists or doctors, it seems so much more reasonable to suggest that many expecting fathers experience stress and anxiety, both of which can trigger more serious psychological conditions or even rashes, while certain other fathers may exhibit a different range of psychosomatic responses to their wives' pregnancies (such as sympathetic labor pains). These groups may, of course, overlap, but there is no need for an amorphous couvade syndrome to explain these distinct phenomena, even if all of them arise during pregnancy. This may well explain why the syndrome has not made its way into any medical or psychological dictionaries. What is more, Sokol's early modern examples of couvade are convincing, but he admits that they are only concerned with "psychosomatic manifestations" (42) like toothaches and labor pains (none of which seem to afflict Leontes). There is no mention of anything that might resemble a psychological condition like jealousy or paranoia, which would have been necessary for the historical aspect of Sokol's argument to be more compelling.

When Leontes is urged to see signs of paternity in his newborn daughter Perdita, he refuses to recognize the resemblances that all others find obvious (2.3.95–107). This illustrates another interesting contrast between *Othello* and *The Winter's Tale* regarding the cognitive underpinnings of the jealous mind. In *Othello*, Iago's success derives at least partly from his capacity to maneuver his commander into an intolerable position between hope and despair, so that the latter finally comes to desire the truth—any truth, however painful—more than he desires a faithful Desdemona: "She's gone, I am abused, and my relief / Must be to loathe her" (3.3.271–72). In this way, Iago gradually destroys a faith so firm that it might easily have been deemed unshakeable. In *The Winter's Tale*, by contrast, Shakespeare diagnoses the opposite but equally disastrous tendency of a single error of judgment to poison all other judgments that derive from it. Camillo realizes that his attempts to cure Leontes of his "diseas'd opinion" (1.2.297) are vain because the latter cannot get around the central assumption that constitutes the foundation of his thinking:

> You may as well
> Forbid the sea for to obey the moon,
> As or by oath remove or counsel shake
> The fabric of his folly, whose foundation
> Is pil'd upon his faith, and will continue
> The standing of his body. (1.2.426–31)

The realm of "faith" that Camillo points to is concerned with those things that are merely possible, in the sense that they can be neither corroborated nor denied conclusively. Othello can never know for sure that Desdemona is faithful, and so he must have faith in her (in the restricted and nonmystical sense that he must accept a belief that is reasonable but can never be categorically proven). In *The Winter's Tale*, it is equally *possible* that Hermione has actually slept with Polixenes, but Leontes turns this gratuitous possibility into a cornerstone for his thought and feeling. In the next act, he returns us explicitly to Camillo's diagnosis by referring to similar cognitive "foundations" that themselves cannot be questioned:

> If I mistake
> In those foundations which I build upon,
> The centre is not big enough to bear
> A school-boy's top. (2.1.100–3)

Two scenes later, Paulina also urges him to "remove / The root of his opinion, which is rotten / As ever oak or stone was sound" (2.3.88–90). By this time, however, Leontes has such a powerful emotional investment in his belief that his world becomes entirely circular. It is only the emotional shock of his son's death that finally enables him to break out of his vicious circle, at which point it is too late.

While these cognitive aspects throw some interesting light on the problem of jealousy in these plays, they still do not explain the central conundrum that lies before us. Why is it that Leontes and Othello, of all people, are so particularly inept at distinguishing what is merely possible from what is likely? And why does their jealousy become so incredibly intense and destructive? In *The Winter's Tale*, Polixenes analyzes the second question in some detail:

> This jealousy
> Is for a precious creature: as she's rare,
> Must it be great; and, as his person's mighty,
> Must it be violent; and, as he does conceive

He is dishonour'd by a man which ever
Profess'd to him; why his revenges must
In that be made more bitter. (1.2.451–57)

Polixenes offers no less than three complementary explanations here. The first is that Hermione is an incredible woman, a true nonpareil, and this impression is shared by other characters. Later in the play, Paulina declares to Leontes that

If, one by one, you wedded all the world,
Or from the all that are took something good,
To make a perfect woman, she you kill'd
Would be unparallel'd. (5.1.13–16)

The precise connection Polixenes sees between Hermione's perfection and Leontes' jealousy—that a "rare" woman will inspire "great" jealousy—is ambiguous, at least in terms of its emphasis. He could be saying either that Leontes is an extremely fortunate man who has reason to fear the loss of a wonderful woman he could never replace (which makes his jealousy derivative of his love). Or it could mean that Hermione's perfection is such that it is likely to attract many potential suitors (which suggests a more cynical need for careful mate guarding). It will be wise to allow this ambiguity to persist for a moment as we continue to explore Polixenes' analysis.

The second explanation offered by Polixenes seems more straightforward, that a powerful man is more likely to allow his feelings untrammeled expression because he gets away with it. The third potential cause, finally, is more concerned with hurt feelings: that Leontes feels betrayed by a person he has trusted and loved, which (together with shame and dishonor) is bound to add insult to injury. This brings us back to the earlier idea that Leontes' jealousy derives from his affection, but this time with a notable difference: the love that is spurned in this case is not his love for Hermione, but for Polixenes.

I do not mean to suggest, as some critics have done rather unconvincingly, that there is some sort of homoerotic or homosexual undercurrent between Leontes and Polixenes. (Whether their relationship can be described adequately as "homosocial" is a different issue, but it will not concern me here.) What we know for certain is that the two kings have been friends since childhood and place a great value on their relationship. But when the first act begins, there is an imbalance between them: Polixenes is anxious to leave, while Leontes is imploring him to stay. For most people—Elizabethans, Sicilians, or Swedes—such a scene can only continue for so long until it becomes a bit embarrassing (for both parties) as well as humiliating (for the one that does the pleading). Now if—and this can be no more than an "if" at this point—Leontes supposes that the depth of Polixenes' love will naturally be reflected in the urgency with which he seeks to prolong his stay, then the play opens with an affective imbalance between the two men. In that case Hermione's success in entreating Polixenes to stay must be regarded by Leontes as a blow in the face.

What I am suggesting, tentatively at this point, is that the love the Sicilian king feels for both Polixenes and Hermione has made him very vulnerable. Indeed, when we examine his reactions to his supposed cuckoldry more closely, it becomes quite obvious that he has come to think of his own affection or love as a fatal weakness. At the beginning of what has been described as "the obscurest passage in Shakespeare,"[76] Leontes defines his jealousy as rooted in love: "Affection! thy intention stabs the centre: / Thou dost make possible things not so held, / Communicat'st with dreams" (1.2.138–40). It is worth noting that Shakespeare once again associates jealousy with an unreasonable belief in mere *possibilities*. Leontes goes on to connect his love with strong feelings of vulnerability and shame: "How sometimes nature will betray its folly, its tenderness, and make itself a pastime / To harder bosoms!" (1.2.151–53). Feeling stupid and humiliated because he has loved and therefore opened himself up to betrayal, Leontes casts himself as a victim at the hands of Hermione and Polixenes. This is not the sort of thing one would expect from a callous, omnipotent, mate-guarding patriarch who merely seeks to protect his domestic chattel against potential theft.

It seems likely, then, that Leontes loves both Hermione and Polixenes deeply but fears that neither love may be fully requited. In that case things do not become easier when Hermione offers him this disappointing profession of conjugal love: "Yet, good deed, Leontes / I love thee not a jar o'th' clock behind / What lady she her lord" (1.2.42–44). What she offers her husband is merely the kind of average love that could reasonably be expected from any old wife. This brings Cordelia to mind, and the potential beggary in any love that can be weighed according to one's formal relationship: "I love your majesty / According to my bond, no more nor less" (*Lear* 1.1.92–93). Two acts later, when Hermione is placed on a grotesque trial by her jealous husband, the parallel with *Lear* becomes even more striking. At this point Hermione defines her affection (this time for Polixenes) explicitly in terms of duty and obedience:

> I do confess
> I lov'd him as in honour he requir'd,
> With such a kind of love as might become
> A lady like me; with a love, even such,
> So, and no other, as yourself commanded:
> Which, not to have done, I think had been in me
> Both disobedience and ingratitude
> To you, and toward your friend. (3.2.61–68)

As we saw in the discussion of *Lear,* the relationship between love and duty is intrinsically tense and conflicted for human beings. On the one hand, a love that is reduced to a duty ceases to be an emotion in any meaningful sense and becomes a formal routine or practice. On the other hand, love cannot be freely given in any absolute sense since it involves an element of obligation and commitment toward the other person. What Hermione's plight illustrates is how a more specific sociohistorical arrangement like the patriarchal family can exacerbate this tension between love and duty to the point where it undermines itself and fails to satisfy either party. For Leontes, the crux is that every time Hermione asserts and confirms her wifely duty and obedience as a loving wife she automatically occludes the emotional recognition he really seeks from her. How can he ever be certain of what she feels when it is her duty to love him? For Hermione, the situation is even more absurd and counter-productive, since the attempt to be loyal and to honor her husband's wishes is precisely what gets her into trouble.

As we have seen, we have good reason to endorse Polixenes' analysis of his friend's violent jealousy. I would now like to suggest that the same interpretation should be extended across the Shakespeare canon, to *Othello.* Most obviously, it seems clear that the jealousy in both plays concerns a woman of matchless beauty and virtue. Hermione is described repeatedly as a paragon of womanhood whose beauty is rivaled only by her daughter's, while Cassio informs us that Othello

> hath achieved a maid
> That paragons description and wild fame,
> One that excels the quirks of blazoning pens
> And in th'essential vesture of creation
> Does tire the inginer. (2.1.61–65)

Both Leontes and Othello are clearly very fortunate men. The regrettable downside of any good fortune, of course, is that it makes you vulnerable because you now have something precious to lose. This is basically Iago's analysis of jealousy in *Othello:*

> Poor and content is rich, and rich enough,
> But riches fineless is as poor as winter
> To him that ever fears he shall be poor.
> Good God, the souls of all my tribe defend
> From jealousy. (3.3.174–78)

In this passage, Iago points to a problem that goes even deeper than human nature, since it is shared by any social animal that must constantly negotiate its own desires and temporary triumphs in relation to the similar appetites of other individuals.

As I have tried to show, however, we should be wary of any critical attempt to turn either Leontes or Othello into mate-guarding beasts, proprietary patriarchs, or, for that matter, intrinsically insecure and self-loathing figures. In spite of their detestable actions, Shakespeare leaves us little doubt that their vulnerability is rooted in love rather than more callous or self-regarding considerations. Of course, a distinctly normative theorist of love can always chide Othello for the depth of his existential as well as emotional investment in his wife—"Excellent wretch! perdition catch my soul / But I do love thee! and when I love thee not / Chaos is come again" (3.3.90–92)—but such a charge is perhaps better directed toward the emotion rather than the character who feels it. To love *is* to become vulnerable to loss and pain, as Leontes realizes with great distress when he suspects that Hermione and Polixenes may be laughing behind his back. The deeper we love, the more vulnerable we become, and we need not define sexual jealousy as a specific evolved adaptation to accept this connection.

It may, of course, be disturbing to think that the difference between Othello and the average jealous man may be a matter of degree rather than kind. It may be more ideologically or emotionally comforting to convince ourselves that someone who loves truly will not be jealous and that some other factor—patriarchy, racism, and so on—is really to blame. But as we have seen, such a rejection of folk psychology cannot be applied to Shakespeare's play without considerable violence. We have no reason to dispute Othello's final account of himself as a man who "loved not wisely, but too well" and who therefore "threw a pearl away / Richer than all his tribe" (5.2.344, 347–48). As in *All's Well*, Shakespeare gives us a character who loves *too much*.

The second characteristic that is shared by Leontes and Othello—and outlined above by Polixenes—is that they are extremely powerful men with almost unrestricted authority. (Othello may not be king of Venice, but he *is* commander of Cyprus, endowed with supreme authority over the Venetian subjects on his island.) This means that there is no larger social or institutional check for their jealousy once it gets out of hand, and the same problem also afflicts their personal relationships, since their own wives are held back by the domestic ideal of obedience and duty. Since I have already discussed Hermione's near-equation of love with duty and obedience, an example from *Othello* will be enough to illustrate this point. When Othello lashes out for the first time against Desdemona and the latter decides to leave the room rather than "stay to offend" her husband, the dumbfounded Lodovico comments: "Truly, an obedient lady" (4.1.247). It is striking that both victims of jealous rage occupy an almost entirely defensive posture with respect to the monstrous accusations hurled at them, leaving two other women (Emilia and Paulina) to shower justified abuse on their husbands. Once again we recognize the central pattern from *King Lear,* where a lovesick autocrat allows his fury free expression, is never challenged head-on by his daughter or wife, and renders himself entirely immune to any other protesting voices.

This exalted position in society—where each is king of his own little dramatic world, metaphorically or otherwise—has another consequence for Othello and Leontes. Since they occupy the apex of a social structure, their fall becomes all the more dramatic and painful. In *The Winter's Tale,* Leontes soon wishes for servants whose eyes might "see alike mine honour as their profits" and worries about potential "scandal to the blood o'th' prince, my son" (1.2.310, 330), while Othello seeks to define himself as "an honourable murderer, if you will, / For nought I did in hate, but all in honour" (*Othello* 5.2.293–94). In fact, Othello appears to regard his own elevated social position as an instigating factor for jealousy. After rejecting skin color, lack of eloquence, and age difference as explanations for his wife's supposed transgression, he refers to cuckoldry as "the plague of great ones" (3.3.277). This again suggests that the noble Moor, at least, does not subscribe to the modern critical commonplace that he is a self-loathing or inherently insecure being. His basic problem is rather that he has been sufficiently attractive to attract a very attractive woman, who is likely to attract a substantial number of other attractive men.

We can conclude from this that the jealous man in these Shakespeare plays is not a discursive construct specific to the early modern period. He is a privileged and powerful human being who loves his wife deeply and who therefore has something very precious to lose. This situation will quite naturally be exacerbated in a specific culture like early modern England that places a particularly high premium on honor and that inserts its men and women into a formally unequal relationship where love becomes a matter of duty and obedience. But these are no more than specific variations on a much larger human theme where love or jealousy are neither immaterial substances that "transcend" social reality nor reducible to some crass cost-benefit analysis, social determinist dictate, or "sexual economy." When we say, as I think we should, that *Othello* presents us with a timeless theme in the history of our species, it is important to get all the prepositions right in this formulation. The drama of jealousy has always unfolded *in* history, not outside it.

But let us pause right here, just before we raise the biocultural flag and proceed to celebrate Shakespeare as the world's first literary exponent of gene-culture interactionism. For the question remains whether this string of psychological causes—for all its textual and theoretical support—can really be regarded as a *sufficient* cause for the singularly violent and destructive jealousies that Shakespeare depicts. Is it convincing to suppose that most powerful men who marry beautiful women whom they love deeply will sooner or later turn jealous to the point of murder? Hardly, for then we would expect our royal palaces or government buildings to be strewn with female bodies, and the homicide statistics in Shakespeare's society and our own would also be much higher.[77] It would seem, then, that we still have not addressed the fundamental question that must have been equally disturbing for Shakespeare's contemporaries as it is for us: how can it be that these men are transported so far beyond everyday pangs of jealousy into destructive or even murderous rage?

In my view, there are two reasons why this question must remain unanswered. First, we must not forget—as so many literary critics and critical theorists do today—that we are dealing with intentional artifacts bound by literary conventions. In the case of *Othello*, we are looking at a tragedy. As Robert Storey observes, tragedy educates its readers in three ways: it invites empathetic identification, it creates ambivalence about the emotional allegiance that results, and it enables a vicarious experience of catastrophe.[78] So while a moralist stands on the outside looking in, or rather, looking *at* the tragic protagonist, a tragedian or tragic reader explores how it feels on the *inside*. This vicarious experience enables us to explore deeply troubling things that we might well have to moralize heavily about in our everyday lives. Now if there were a clear answer to Othello's madness it would probably make the play less unsettling, and *Othello* is a brilliant tragedy because it is *extremely* unsettling. In the words of Hans-Georg Gadamer, "It is part of the reality of a play that it leaves an indefinite space around its real theme. A play in which everything is completely motivated creaks like a machine. It would be a false reality if the action could all be calculated out like an equation."[79]

As human beings, we have an innate desire—a so-called cognitive imperative—to explain atrocities like Desdemona's innocent death so that we may render our experience intelligible and manageable. What makes *Othello* so powerful and captivating is that it plays on this desire but refuses to satisfy it. The play both invites and frustrates our attempts at psychological explanation by presenting us with psychological causes that either prove too many (in the case of Iago's malice) or ultimately fail to add up (in the case of Othello's murder of his loved one). The empathetic identification Storey speaks of would be impossible unless we shared some common ground with Othello, but as the play progresses our desire to make sense of him, to explain him, increases in proportion to our growing sense of estrangement.

As Edward Pechter points out with considerable insight, "There is, finally, no satisfying explanation for the fall of Othello: we 'cannot speak / Any beginning to this peevish odds.' Not that we therefore abandon the quest for this absent origin; quite the contrary, as witness the massive monuments of interpretation on *Othello* and *Paradise Lost*."[80] What I have tried to do in this chapter, apart from setting a more general theoretical change of course, is to explain why this should be. Shakespearean jealousy is in fact richly motivated, but the explanations offered can never be satisfying in any deterministic sense. We are offered strong and convincing causes as well as brittle and unconvincing ones, but these do not add up to a *sufficient* cause for the atrocities that ensue.

One reason why the critical "monuments" Pechter speaks of have grown so large and distinctly Pisa-shaped in recent years is that the majority of their builders worked with the implicit assumption that a successful interpretation involves a faithful match between text and theory. Indeed, even those critics who have embraced extreme antirealist positions have not lost faith in their own ability to explain literary texts using theories about the human psyche or society. This brings us to the second reason why we cannot expect *Othello* to unravel its deepest mysteries before us.

To "explain" Othello's murder of his wife in a satisfying manner would be to show that his actions are actually quite plausible or even predictable given a certain conception of human nature or the specific situation he finds himself in. But even in real life, let alone art, we would be hard-pressed to find a concept of human nature that could serve such a purpose since this theory would have to deny the extraordinary complexity—both biological and social—that creates human universals as well as individual and cultural variation. Given their specific circumstances and the apparent universality of jealousy in human cultures, we could certainly have expected Othello or Leontes to become a little wary in the presence of admirable men like Polixenes and Cassio. But what Shakespeare treats us to in *Othello* and *The Winter's Tale* is not everyday jealousy or a stage version of the average Elizabethan man. He confronts us with the horrifying individual exception rather than the psychological rule.

The scary and interesting thing about Shakespearean jealousy, then, is that its deepest mystery cannot be explained away. We cannot assign it to a barbaric and unenlightened past, to a pathological insecurity that can be eradicated by equal doses of therapy and social change, or to some hardwired mate-killing module. And therein, I suppose, lies its perennial horror and fascination.

Conclusion

Of the many famous statements made about William Shakespeare over the last four hundred years, one cannot pass over John Dryden's in *On Dramatic Poesy* (1668):

> He was the man who of all moderns, and perhaps ancient poets, had the largest and most comprehensive soul. All the images of Nature were still present to him, and he drew them, not laboriously, but luckily; when he describes any thing, you more than see it, you feel it too. Those who accuse him of having wanted learning, give him the greater commendation: he was naturally learn'd; he needed not the spectacles of books to read Nature; he looked inwards, and found her there.[1]

What Dryden finds in Shakespeare is an amazing intuitive grasp of human nature in all its variety, coupled with a capacity to render these insights both easily and vividly in literary form. There is nothing mystical or otherworldly about this Shakespeare. Dryden describes an extremely talented and insightful writer whose unusually capacious intellect took humanity as its principal subject matter. When Shakespeare writes about love he is not merely recording the social constructions or limited fashions and perspectives of his own place and time; in the broadest and most inclusive sense, he is writing about *us*.

For many years now, such assertions have generated increasingly polarized responses from literary critics. One group (represented by a steadily shrinking minority of traditionalists) cites Dryden and Dr. Johnson with approbation and agrees that Shakespeare was indeed a genius with special recourse to human nature. When pressed to explain just what concept of human nature they use as their reference point, these readers usually resort to a gesture whose lameness almost rivals the grandeur they ascribe to Shakespeare: they point their interlocutor back to the plays, suggesting that a sufficient period of reverent immersion will enable him or her to perceive the same timeless truths as they do. While I share this reverence toward Shakespeare's genius, such unsupported assertions strike me as too reminiscent of a mystical séance. Literary value is certainly an elusive phenomenon, and one that we may never be able to reason about in any satisfactory manner,[2] but a proposition about human nature should clearly be more open to rational examination.

The other group, which prides itself on being more theoretically sophisticated and cutting-edge than the traditionalists, is characterized by a curious Pavlovian reflex. For as soon as they hear words like "human nature," "truth," "coherence," "genius," "tradition," "universality," and sometimes even "love," they cringe and reach for their guns as if some horrible beast were about to overrun them. On rare occasions they cringe for good reason, since some of these words can sometimes serve the oppressive functions that are ascribed to them. But as I have tried to suggest in this book, much of this instinctive reaction in the humanities to certain inadmissible key words—especially the arch-villains "biology" and "evolution"—has been based on a series of unfortunate misunderstandings.

The most frequent misconception, especially among historical materialists and postmodernists, is that the wicked concept of "human nature" must be something that "transcends" or floats above particular historical or cultural contexts. In this book I have tried to give the real reason why Shakespeare could not avoid tapping into a common humanity when he wrote about love: human nature does not *transcend* our lived reality but *suffuses* it. We humans do happen to belong to an identifiable species, and no amount of radical historicism or armchair philosophy can disguise the fact that Shakespeare was a human being who wrote principally about other human beings, with all the common ground and idiosyncrasies that this entails. Since my book rests on the conviction that literary critics should take this point more seriously, this concluding discussion will be structured around three premises that have guided my discussions of Shakespearean love.

My first and most basic guiding assumption has been that human nature is a necessary concept that is best conceptualized in terms of an interaction between genes and environments. This approach dissolves the traditional dichotomy between nature and culture, as well as the absurd postmodern idea that what we call "nature" is really a form of "culture." In keeping with this perspective, my discussion of love has explored the interaction between evolved dispositions and particular social and historical contexts. The practical usefulness of such a framework becomes obvious when we consider the Roman plays discussed in this book, where Shakespeare describes a painful tug-of-war between innate dispositions for parental love and cultural strictures. At first sight, *Coriolanus* seems to involve a lucid conflict between natural love for one's family and a culturally induced obsession with honor. But just as Shakespeare intimated in *The Winter's Tale*, what we term "culture" or "art" or "custom" is ultimately a form of nature: it is never separable from the fundamental human needs and dispositions that it expresses and responds to. We succumb to a seductive delusion, based on centuries of misunderstandings about the nature of human beings, if we think that the attempt to curb a particular passion is necessarily less "natural" than the passion itself. For one thing, such self-restraint would be utterly unthinkable without the peerless prefrontal cortex belonging to *Homo sapiens*, that curious self-regulating animal.

Thanks to this interactionist framework, I also hope to have raised some doubts about the widespread assumption among literature professors and social scientists that romantic love is a Western construction or invention. In large part, the resilience of this idea stems from a notorious unwillingness to define the object of study, except in the vaguest terms. If by "romantic love" we mean the rather improbable idea that there is only one person on this planet that can make me happy, and that truly loving this person means loving him or her forever, and that this should happen within the confines of a nuclear family, and so forth, then we are certainly dealing with an idiosyncratic ideal. But this account is no more than a caricature of the broader human impulse for amorous exclusivity and commitment that belongs to the passionate romantic merger. Some cultures honor romantic love, others seek to undermine it, others do not give it any recognition, and Western culture has so far positively fetishized it, but it still forms part of a universal emotional repertoire.

In *Troilus and Cressida*, Shakespeare seems to suggest that many of our qualms, suspicions, and complaints about romantic love should really be addressed to Father Time, a figure who holds nothing sacred. To love someone romantically is to want to be with that person forever . . . that is, at least for the time being. If love dies, can we really say that it was an illusion, a psychological idealization or overvaluation of the love object, and hence less real than its bitter aftermath? And since all our vows are made in the present tense but always concern an uncertain future, the marital vow in *Troilus and Cressida* becomes more than a symbolic expression of love. It also becomes a desperate attempt to infuse our honest desires with a moral, social, and rational permanence that our feelings themselves cannot supply.

In *All's Well*, which turns so very symmetrically from affective *overvaluation* to a corresponding *undervaluation*, Shakespeare once more examines the delicate relationship between individual appraisal and the social consensus, this time with an eye to their divergence. In this play, he raises complex questions that we also recognize from *King Lear*: Is love something that can be deserved? Can it even be a duty to love someone, be it a member of the opposite sex or a parent? As we have seen, such questions become particularly difficult since love itself involves a measure of obligation toward the loved one. Love cannot be compelled, but it can certainly compel us and restrict our freedom. *All's Well* also reminds us of how the same recognizable passion—romantic love—can be assessed very differently depending on our historical context: in an early modern context, Helena's single-minded pursuit of Bertram is understood as a "fault" because the emotion has not been hypercognized and idealized to a modern extent.

The second premise that has guided my book is that fictional works are characterized by a paradox of mimesis and make-believe. This is something of a theoretical truism, but what I have tried to show is that the biocultural approach—coupled with some hermeneutical awareness—is uniquely equipped to respect it, with manifest practical consequences for literary analysis.

Let us begin with the principle of mimesis, which dictates that Shakespeare's plays must mirror reality-as-other-people-understand-it in order to be intelligible as well as dramatically effective. Othello's murder of Desdemona, for example, will be shocking and tragic only if we already assume that such acts are not everyday events; people do not normally kill the ones they love. If we combine this idea with my first premise—that human nature is an interaction between genes and environment, and hence involves constants and regularities as well as historical particulars—then we can expect that readers in different epochs and contexts will have many points of agreement about what it is they have seen.

Those who are familiar with the many twists and turns of Shakespeare criticism in the twentieth century may balk at such a suggestion. Surely the only constant in this critical heritage has been disagreement, even over the most basic issues? But the literary-critical industry is clearly a special case here, given its extreme emphasis on *newness* that threatens to turn it into a kind of fashion industry rather than the cumulative research tradition it ought to be. Too often these wild swings of the pendulum have been taken as evidence that Shakespeare does not mirror human nature so much as his readers mirror their own private convictions in his plays. But as a respected friend and colleague of mine put it once, the principal objective of Shakespeare criticism cannot be to demonstrate that all past readers of Shakespeare have completely misunderstood his plays and that we are now suddenly in a position to expose these errors. Shakespeare criticism should not be an escape from common sense or received opinion,[3] but a patient and systematic working out of literary problems whose solutions may or may not coincide with other people's experience of the same plays. Why should the serious study of literature be devoid of the kind of cumulative validation and disproval that is taken for granted in so many other academic disciplines? Literary studies should certainly be pluralistic, but this pluralism should not be an excuse for not thinking things through.

In at least two of my readings, I hope to have vindicated the impressions of generations of theatergoers and lay readers against what can only be described as recent academic distortions. In both cases the critics in question have twisted Shakespeare's text considerably in order to demonstrate that what passes for "love" is really something much more sinister. But a substantial part of the tragedy in *Othello*, first of all, is that the protagonist *is* a kind and noble Moor who loves Desdemona deeply and devotedly; he is neither the proprietary patriarch nor the self-loathing auto-racist described by scores of literary critics. King Lear, for his part, does not invent his love test in order to humiliate and dominate his daughters or because he is trapped in a developmental phase that we normally associate with toddlers. On the contrary, Shakespeare's play gives us considerable evidence that Lear is a confused old man whose strength and sanity is fading, who is hungry for love, and who has every reason to worry about life after retirement: will my children be there for me now that I need them?

So far I have addressed the most obvious aspect of mimesis, which ensures that there will be firm points of contact between these fictional constructs and our flesh-and-blood reality. But in order to catch our interest and engage our emotions, fictional works cannot be painted in drab colors or remind us of boring facts about our everyday existence It is a substantial part of the dramatist's job description to create conflicts, and Shakespeare's works will naturally gravitate toward what is exceptional and unusual. This means that no matter how convincing and theoretically grounded our assumptions about human nature may be, they can never be expected to be directly explanatory: they can only serve as a kind of framework or backdrop against which the literary text is measured.

Perhaps the most striking example in this study is the extraordinary tug-of-war between parental instincts and honor worship in *Titus Andronicus*. In this play, Shakespeare and Peele depict parental impulses that seem stronger and more un compromising than those posited by a modern authority on the subject, the anthropologist Sarah Hrdy. The play also treats us to cultural pressures that must be regarded as exceptional by any standard, since Titus gladly sacrifices not two, but twenty-two, sons in the wars against the Goths. In both instances, the play seizes on facts of human existence (the depth of human parental affections, the shaping power of culture) and polarizes them for maximum dramatic effect.

Ultimately, the capacity of literary make-believe to stretch the bounds of mimetic credibility reaches a point where we feel that the bond between fiction and reality has been broken. Such moments are relatively rare in Shakespeare, most likely because he endorsed the literary ideal espoused by Prince Hamlet: not to "o'erstep" the "modesty of nature" (3.2.20). If we go back once more to *Troilus and Cressida*, we have seen that Shakespeare condenses the traditional love story so drastically that only a day passes between mutual protestations of undying love and Cressida's betrayal. This development is bound to strike any reader or theatergoer in any century as grossly improbable, and it contributes strongly to the sense of abstract disillusionment that permeates Shakespeare's play in its entirety. Our disillusionment with love in this play springs largely from our disorientation. It is this departure from our predictable and stable conception of reality—or rather, its heightening and intensification—that enables the play to turn the tables on its audience and make them question their own preconceived assumptions.

In *Othello*, likewise, it is hard to watch the protagonist's rapid development from kind lover to jealous murderer without consternation and outrage. Hence all the critical attempts to explain the cause(s) of Othello's fall: that his development was more or less inevitable, given his skin color, age, flawed love, and so forth. But as we have seen, what Shakespeare presents in this play is not a predictable psychological response but an exceptional case by any psychological standard. Once more we see the importance of treating any conception of human nature, from social psychology to evolutionary theory, as an analytical framework rather than an explanatory theory for literary texts.

My third and final theoretical premise has been that the study of literature should be rescued from the ideological reductivism that has plagued our discipline for some time now. Critics of various creeds and convictions have hijacked the word "relevance" and managed to convince their colleagues and students that readings of Shakespeare will only speak to our present situation if they are politically "enabling" and "progressive" (the radical version) or, somewhat more infrequently, "edifying" (the conservative version). Like the widespread fear of biological explanation, such literary instrumentalism involves a strange consensus between opposing ends of the political spectrum, where all readings are obliged to contribute directly to building a better society or building the character.

Lest this be misunderstood, I want to stress once again that politics and morality are vital subjects for the humanities since they raise the question of how we should live. But in this book I have pointed to numerous examples of what can happen when ideological commitment takes precedence over the desire for understanding. According to some feminist theorists, for example, Bertram in *All's Well* even becomes a woman hater because he doesn't want to marry a particular woman. Furthermore, it is not enough to loosen the more specific grasp of political preconceptions on the literary works themselves; we must also do the same for their perennial subject matter, human nature. Instead of ensconcing ourselves in the narrow corridors of language idealism and dogmatic culturalism, the humanities should take an active and constructive part in the dialogue between the social sciences and the life sciences about our common humanity.

In short, the biocultural approach promises new avenues of research in one of the most crowded fields of literary criticism, bringing new tools to old questions about literature and human nature. A book of this kind can only hope to perform some of the necessary groundwork. But if more people in Shakespeare studies are prepared to accept and employ the interactionist consensus that is now slowly spreading from the life sciences to the social sciences, then this can provide us with a much-needed common ground that will enable us to agree as well as disagree more meaningfully and constructively than has previously been the case. Once we accept that all aspects of human experience have strong biological as well as cultural components—regardless of our personal views in matters of politics or morality—then we can raise intriguing new questions about the complex interaction among human nature, specific sociocultural contexts, and the world of fiction. In the long run, this may also help us bridge the regrettable gap between the academic study of Shakespeare and the surrounding world where human beings continue to live, die, and fall hopelessly in love with one another.

Notes

Introduction

1. Tolstoy, "What is Art?" 121- 333.
2. Tolstoy, "Shakespeare and the Drama," 394.
3. Ibid., 451.
4. My source is Michael Massing's review of Stephen Prothero's *American Jesus*. Massing, "America's Favorite Philosopher," 7.
5. Darwin, *The Autobiography*, 138, 139. In a fine article on Darwin's response to his daughter's death, George Levine speculates that "it wasn't science itself that made Shakespeare nauseating to Darwin. He never would have imagined that science and literature are incompatible and his own career shows a mutual shaping of those forces. Science made literature unendurable because science was already deeply informed by the moral implications and the emotional intensities of literature." Levine, "Darwin and Pain," 97–118.
6. A recent case for the complementarity of science and art is offered by the moral philosopher Mary Midgley in *Science and Poetry*.
7. Darwin, *Expression of Emotions*.
8. While this endeavor has only recently become feasible thanks to important new developments in a range of academic disciplines, the idea that we must understand Shakespeare as a human being as well as an Elizabethan is not new. In the 1940s, Theodore Spencer drew the following conclusion toward the end of *Shakespeare and the Nature of Man*: "But Shakespeare was in touch with something more than his age, and if we are to come back to our starting-point and try to arrive at a final view of his work as a whole, we must see it as a reflection of deeper truths than any that can be described by a local and temporary picture of the cosmos, of psychology, or of the state. Beneath any view of man's nature, at the very basis of human experience, are the elementary facts of birth, of life and of death. The rhythm of their sequence and renewal lies behind all our knowledge and emotions, and it is the rhythm that we share with all living nature, with animals and grass. . . . And if we think of Shakespeare's work in relation to this essential pattern, this fundamental rhythm, we shall have, perhaps, a view of the sequence of his plays that will both underlie and transcend any view that we can obtain by thinking of his work merely in relation to the ideas of his time." *Shakespeare and the Nature of Man*, 222.

9. There is still no consensus about the best rubric for this fledgling field, but some recent contenders have been "biopoetics," "biocultural studies," "Darwinian literary criticism," and "adaptationist literary studies." The literature is growing so fast that it already defies any brief summary, but two founding texts are Carroll's *Evolution and Literary Theory* and Storey's *Mimesis and the Human Animal*. For recent and representative contributions to Darwinian literary criticism, see Carroll's *Literary Darwinism* and *Literary Animal*, Gottschall and Wilson, eds. Joseph Carroll gives a detailed survey of evolutionary-psychological approaches to literature in "Evolutionary Pyschology and Literature." Boyd, finally, gives a rewarding and accessible account of the potentials of a biocultural approach to literature in "Literature and Evolution."

There are important points of convergence between this movement and the cognitive approach to literature, or at least with those cognitive critics who have renounced the post-structuralist and strong constructivist heritage in the humanities. For an overview of affinities and differences between "cognitive" and "cognitive-evolutionary" criticism and theory from the perspective of the former school, see Hart, "Epistemology of Cognitive Literary Studies." A pioneering cognitive study of Shakespeare that employs a welcome interactionist perspective on the mind but attempts to reconcile post-structuralist theory with modern neuroscience is Crane's *Shakespeare's Brain: Reading with Cognitive Theory*. Unfortunately, the polemical chapter on evolution and literature in Hogan's otherwise commendable *Cognitive Science, Literature, and the Arts* misses the mark, both theoretically and in its choice of adversaries; see Gottschall's review essay "Literary Studies, Universals, and the Sciences of the Mind."

Finally, Joseph Carroll and Nancy Easterlin have outlined the relationship between an evolutionary and an ecocritical approach to literature; see Carroll, "Ecology of Victorian Fiction," and "Organism, Environment and Literary Representation," and Easterlin, "'Loving Ourselves Best of All.'"

10. When Tolstoy prophesied Darwin's eventual disappearance from the public scene, he also named a successor—Friedrich Nietzsche—whose teachings, "though perfectly absurd, unthought-out, obscure, and bad in their content, correspond better to the present-day outlook on life" ("Shakespeare and the Drama," 451). From the perspective of the humanities, at least, Tolstoy turned out to be right. Nietzsche's philosophy became a crucial literary-theoretical influence in the late twentieth century, while Darwinism remained anathema.

11. Wells, *Shakespeare's Humanism*, 197. This excellent book is worth reading in full, but pages 192–99 are particularly relevant for the aspiring literary evolutionist. See also the introduction to *Neo-Historicism*, Wells, Burgess, and Wymer, eds., 1–27; and Wells's positive remarks on evolutionary psychology in *Shakespeare on Masculinity*, 204–5n88. Essentially the same point has been made previously by Easterlin: "Humanists and social scientists, including literary theorists, who

ignore the implications of evolutionary theory and biology do so at the cost of the increasing irrelevance of their disciplines. To be meaningful, the discussion of the artifacts of human culture must be framed by our knowledge of human beings, not by artificial or incomplete notions of our world and our social experience." "Making Knowledge," 136.

12. Harold Bloom, *Invention of the Human*, 11.

13. Samuel Johnson, "Preface to Shakespeare," 62.

14. This is one of five characteristics of the New Historicism, as listed by H. Aram Veeser in his influential introduction to *New Historicism*, xi.

15. Allan Bloom, *Love and Friendship*, 1–2. Bloom gives voice to similar ideas further on in his study (e.g., see pgs. 138, 142), but his only critique of a specific biological argument concerns the ethologist Konrad Lorenz, whose groundbreaking contributions to the study of human behavior were made many decades ago.

16. Allan Bloom, *Love and Friendship*, 1.

17. Peter Singer, one of several philosophers who have lamented the tendency of the political left to vilify evolutionary accounts of human nature, does not fail to make this connection: "It is intriguing how two very different ideologies—Christianity and Marxism—agreed with each other in insisting on the gulf between humans and animals, and therefore that evolutionary theory cannot be applied to human beings." *Darwinian Left*, 28. For another critique from the left (this time of the anti-biological, anti-universal, and anti-essentialist orientation of postmodernism), see Eagleton, *After Theory*, chapters 5 and 6. Among other things, Eagleton notes that Marx—unlike many of his followers—was far from a radical culturalist since he concerned himself with our "species being."

18. Pechter, *"Othello" and Interpretive Traditions*, 21–22.

19. These examples are taken from Donald E. Brown's famous characterization of "the universal people" in *Human Universals*, chapter 6. A straightforward theoretical "application" of the kind I am questioning—but of evolutionary principles rather than human universals—is offered by Nanelle and David Barash in *Madame Bovary's Ovaries*.

20. With the exception of *King Lear* in chapter 3, all references to Shakespeare's works are taken from *The Arden Shakespeare: Complete Works*.

21. Bock, *Human Nature Mythology*, 108.

22. Dover, "Human Nature: One for All and All for One?" in Wells and Mc-Fadden, *Human Nature*, 82–102, esp. 83, 94.

23. On this point, see Hogan, "Literary Universals," esp. 228, and *Mind and Its Stories*. I want to stress a major difference between Hogan's and my own usage of these terms: Hogan is interested in *cultural* universals, which means that a phenomenon that is exhibited by all cultures (but not all human beings) can rightly be termed an *absolute*. Given my own concern with *human* universals, I would term the same phenomenon *statistical*; in order to become *absolute* it would have to apply to

all human beings. While the term "universal" can be potentially misleading when referring to statistical patterns that allow for significant exceptions, it is still more useful than alternative terms such as "pan-cultural" (which is too weak, suggesting only that a trait or behavior exists in all cultures) or "monomorphic" (which is too strong, suggesting that it is exhibited by all humans).

24. Experts have so far been hard-pressed to uncover any timeless laws in biology—which seems reasonable, since life forms evolve over time as a result of unpredictable mutations—but this has not prevented biologists from making broad generalizations about the phenomena they study. On this point, see Waters, "Causal Regularities."

25. Mikel Dufrenne, cited in Magliola, *Phenomenology and Literature*, 146. Compare Wells's remark that if "there were no universal passions and humours, we would have no means of evaluating literature from another age or another culture: a text would have value only for the community in which it was produced." *Shakespeare's Humanism*, 192.

26. For a sharp and enjoyable set of reckonings with postmodern theory and some tentative suggestions on how to transcend it, see Patai and Corral, *Theory's Empire*. McAlindon offers a trenchant critique of radical Shakespeare criticism in *Shakespeare Minus 'Theory.'*

27. Grady, "Shakespeare Studies," 116.

28. Ibid., 114.

29. Boyd, "Literature and Evolution," 17.

30. Nordlund, "Consilient Literary Interpretation."

31. Charney, *Love and Lust*, 4.

32. Ehrlich, *Human Natures*, 123. This is a funny anecdote, but it would be a mistake to discount its disturbing implications. Ehrlich appends a telling footnote: "Today, those radical students are doubtless tenured deconstructionist professors in departments of English language and literature" (372n112).

33. Hrdy, *Mother Nature*, 232.

34. The nature of Shakespeare's characters was debated in the *Shakser* Listserv in April and May, 2006; see http://www.shaksper.net/archives/2006/index.html for a list of all postings. Compare Stanley Cavell's remark on the distaste for character study:

> I think that one reason a critic may shun direct contact with characters is that he or she has been made to believe or assume, by some philosophy or other, that characters are not people, that what can be known about people cannot be known about characters, and in particular that psychology is either not appropriate to the study of these fictional beings or that psychology is the province of psychologists and not to be ventured from the armchairs of literary studies. But is any of this more than the merest assumption;

unexamined principles which are part of current academic fashion? (*Disowning Knowledge*, 40)

35. Harold Bloom, *Invention of the Human*, 16. See also A. D. Nuttall's distinction between opaque and transparent critical language and his illuminating revision of the critical concept of mimesis more generally, in *New Mimesis*.

36. A promising account of this process, and one that I am still digesting, is offered by Alan Palmer in *Fictional Minds*.

37. Arnhart, *Darwinian Natural Right*, 102.

Chapter 1

1. Fromm, *Art of Loving*, 14.

2. Mary Midgley makes this simple point, in the context of moral philosophy, in *Beast and Man*, 166. Compare Donald Symons's remark that "every theory of human behavior implies a human psychology. . . . And every psychological theory implies a human nature." "Use and Misuse of Darwinism," esp. 141.

3. It is, I think, telling that the editors of a recent volume of humanities essays on the "fragile category of the 'human'" in early modern culture could afford to dismiss Darwin's relevance to such questions in a summary subclause. See Fudge, Gilbert, and Wiseman's introduction to *At the Borders of the Human*, 1.

4. Eagleton, *After Theory*, 121.

5. Hjort and Laver, introduction to *Emotion and the Arts*, 3–19, esp. 7–9.

6. Paul Griffiths—who actually distinguishes between three kinds of constructivism—defines this version as "trivial." *What Emotions Really Are*, 138–65.

7. Easterlin, "Making Knowledge," 131.

8. Cornelius, *Science of Emotion*, 326.

9. Culler, *Literary Theory*, 68.

10. Malik, *Meaning of Race*, especially chapter 9.

11. Wilson, *Sociobiology*, 6.

12. There is no space in the present book for a detailed discussion of this debate. So far, the most incisive and comprehensive academic survey of the sociobiology debate is Segerstråle's *Defenders of the Truth*. A popular and highly simplified version can be found in Anthony Brown's *Darwin Wars*. The most famous critics of the research program Evolutionary Psychology (EP) collaborated on a collection entitled *Alas, Poor Darwin*, ed. Hilary Rose and Stephen Rose. Unfortunately, many of these essays mix good points with what can only be described as misrepresentations of their opponents and unjustified sarcasm. See also Stephen Rose, *Lifelines*.

13. Edward O. Wilson, *Consilience*, 138.

14. For bibliographic references, see the introduction, note 9, above.

15. Elster, *Alchemies of the Mind*, 48.

16. Irving Singer, *Nature of Love*, vol. 2, xv.

17. Burton, *Anatomy of Melancholy*, 3.1.2.1: 16.

18. Irving Singer, *Nature of Love*, vol. 3, 431–32.

19. Solomon, "Politics of Emotion," esp. 18.

20. Academic inquiry into the emotions has virtually exploded in the last couple of decades. A good introduction to some major theoretical perspectives can be found in Cornelius, *Science of Emotion*. The real bible in this area, however, is *Handbook of Emotions*, edited by Michael Lewis and Jeannette M. Haviland-Jones.

21. See Griffiths, *What Emotions Really Are*.

22. Paul Ekman, textual commentary in Darwin, *Expression of Emotions*, 212.

23. Aristotle, *Nichomachean Ethics*, vol. I, part 3, 4–5, sec. 1094b.

24. Johnson-Laird and Oatley, "Cognitive and Social Construction," 459.

25. Sternberg, *Cupid's Arrow*.

26. Hatfield and Rapson, *Love and Sex*, 3.

27. Translated by F. L. Lucas, cited in Rhodes, *Necessity for Love*, 5. A more prosaic translation of the entire fragment—preserved in Longinus's *On Sublimity*—is offered by David A. Campbell in the Loeb edition: "He seems as fortunate as the gods to me, the man who sits opposite you and listens nearby to your sweet voice and laughter. Truly that sets my heart trembling in my breast. For when I look at you for a moment, then it is no longer possible for me to speak; my tongue has snapped, at once a subtle fire has stolen beneath my flesh, I see nothing with my eyes, my ears hum, sweat pours from me, a trembling seizes me all over, I am greener than grass, and it seems to me that I am little short of dying. But all that can be endured, since . . . even a poor man . . . " *Greek Lyric I*, 79–80.

28. The distinction between passionate and companionate love was developed by Ellen Berscheid and Elaine Walster (married name Hatfield) in *Interpersonal Attraction* (1969; 2nd ed. 1978) and received more extensive treatment in Walster and Walster, *A New Look at Love* (1978). See also Hatfield, "Passionate and Companionate Love."

29. Interviewed by the anthropologist Marjorie Shostak, cited in Hatfield and Rapson, *Love and Sex*, 205. I have removed the italics in my source.

30. Sternberg, "Triangulating Love," esp. 126. Sternberg's term for the full integration of passion, intimacy, and commitment is "consummate love."

31. Helen Harris, "Rethinking Polynesian Heterosexual Relationships." The criteria cited here are mainly derived from Tennov's *Love and Limerence*. For a helpful survey of various theoretical approaches to romantic love, see Hendrick and Hendrick, "Romantic Love."

32. Bloch, *Medieval Misogyny*, 8. Like many modern scholars who contend that romantic love is a Western invention or social construction, Bloch appears

to base his argument mainly on ideas published in the 1930s and 1950s by C. S. Lewis (*The Allegory of Love*, 1936) and Denis de Rougemont (*Love in the Western World*, 1939).

33. Burton, *Anatomy of Melancholy*, 3.2.3.1: 164.

34. Tennov, *Love and Limerence*. The term "crystallization" originally comes from Stendhal's *De l'amour*, where it designates the fifth stage of passionate love: "That process of mind which discovers fresh perfections in its beloved at every turn of events." Cited in Brehm, "Passionate Love," esp. 234.

35. Irving Singer, *Nature of Love*, vol. 3, xii.

36. On this point, see Barrell, *Poetry, Language and Politics*, 23–25.

37. Compare Belsey's observation that "in the early modern period love and lust are not consistently used as antitheses: on the contrary, both terms are synonyms for desire, each innocent or reprobate according to the context, and occurring interchangeably without apparent irony" ("Love as Trompe-l'Oeil," esp. 266). Belsey claims that the emergence of a radical distinction in English between sexual "lust" and true "love" evinces a gradual social purification of desire and sexuality within the confines of the nuclear family, thus participating in the "construction of family values" (276). As we will see further on, there are problems with the latter contention since the nuclear family appears to have been in place as early as the fourteenth century.

38. Radcliffe Richards, *Human Nature after Darwin*. To avoid misunderstandings, I should point out right away that my discussion will flesh out Radcliffe Richards's second "boundary" by distinguishing between scientific and historical materialism.

39. Ehrlich, *Human Natures*, 214.

40. Lampert, *Evolution of Love*, 6.

41. As early as in 1983, Michael Liebowitz at Columbia University identified a link between romantic attraction and elevated levels of certain neurotransmitters, as well as a corresponding connection between the calm and loving feelings of attachment and the natural opiate serotonin. Later research has fleshed out the picture as follows (with apologies for inevitable simplification): the stage of attraction involves a cocktail of endogenous phenethylamine (PEA), norepinephrine, dopamine, and serotonin, while feelings of attachment or affiliation involve endorphins, oxytocin, and vasopressin.

42. Griffiths, *What Emotions Really Are*, 155.

43. Charnes, "What's Love Got to Do with It?" 1–5.

44. Levin, "Bashing the Bourgeois Subject." Levin's complaint drew a sardonic response from one of the critics he attacked, Catherine Belsey, where she used the most formidable and unfalsifiable of all polemical tools. She delivered a sweeping psychoanalysis of Levin's mind, attributing his jocular tone and repetition of sentence structures to deep underlying anxieties about his imminent

loss of subjecthood (Belsey, "The Subject in Danger"). Levin's contributions to the literary-theoretical debate in the 1990s have since been collected in *Looking for an Argument*.

45. Levin, "On Defending Shakespeare," 50–55.

46. Charnes, "Near-Misses," esp. 58.

47. In a recent essay that pays tribute to de Beauvoir, Marilyn Friedman lists ten reasons why women should be wary of romantic love and its attendant merger of identities. See "Romantic Love and Personal Autonomy."

48. Attempts have been made to improve the definition of constructivism so that it might become less vague. With regard to the emotions, see Griffiths, *What Emotions Really Are*, 138–65. David Sloan Wilson makes a welcome and detailed case for "Evolutionary Social Constructivism" in Gottschall and Wilson, *Literary Animal*, 20–37. For a general discussion of social constructivism "from the inside," which is friendly but critical of its vagueness, see Ian Hacking, *The Social Construction of What?*

49. It has become standard procedure to distinguish between two uses of the term "evolutionary psychology," where one designates a specific research program initiated by John Tooby and Leda Cosmides in California, and the other denotes a more general inquiry into the evolutionary foundations of mental processes and behaviors. Throughout my discussion I will use "evolutionary psychology" mainly in the second sense and distinguish my occasional use of the first by means of capital letters.

50. Ekman, "Argument for Basic Emotions."

51. Argyros, *Blessed Rage for Order*, 104.

52. I borrow this expression from Ehrlich's *Human Natures*, where it denotes a trait that was once adaptive but has now lost its adaptive function.

53. Barbara Smuts, *Sex and Friendship in Baboons* (New York: Aldine, 1985), 223; cited in de Waal, *Good Natured*, 156.

54. Arnhart discusses the principle of evolutionary parsimony in *Darwinian Natural Right*, 22–23.

55. Thomas Lewis, Fari Amini, and Richard Lannon, *General Theory of Love*, 41.

56. As Alan C. Gross points out, the role of analogy in science is "not probative, but heuristic"—that is, it is not concerned with confirming the process or mechanism of a phenomenon but with *finding* it. *Rhetoric of Science*, 27–29. Stephen Rose likewise stresses the difference between analogy and homology, where the latter "implies a deeper identity, derived from an assumed common evolutionary origin. This assumption of a shared history implies common mechanisms." Rose, *Lifelines*, 34.

57. From a gene's-eye perspective, anything an organism does to ensure personal survival and/or that of genetic relatives will contribute to its "inclusive

fitness." According to Hamilton's rule, organisms can be expected to behave altruistically whenever the benefit to genetic kin exceeds the costs to the self. This explains, for example, why insect societies exhibit behaviors that might be regarded as genetically suicidal from the individual's perspective. The bee that does not reproduce and perishes in defense of its hive incurs a considerable personal fitness cost that is nevertheless outweighed, mathematically speaking, by its contribution to the survival of genetic kin. The key factor that makes this possible is the close genetic relatedness of these social insects to other members of their society.

58. John Bowlby, *Attachment and Loss*, vol.1, 183.

59. Cited in Cornelius, *Science of Emotion*, 198.

60. Shaver, Hazan, and Bradshaw, "Love as Attachment."

61. "Within our folk psychology, there is a tendency to assume that the attachment behavior of an infant is a rudimentary form of 'love.' From a processual perspective, such assumptions are precarious. There are, for example, many types of 'love' in our own society—romantic, caretaker, sibling, friendships. . . . Moreover, by the time an infant has reached adulthood she or he has undergone a variety of changes associated with puberty, rites of passage, neurophysiological and cognitive development, adolescence, and socialization in general. Researchers must examine each emotional phenomenon separately to discover the processes by which it is generated. While it is probable that some of the cognitive models, cultural norms, and physiological mechanisms associated with early attachment behavior influence these later 'love' systems . . . , most likely each phenomenon can be characterized by a distinct coherence of factors." Hinton, "Outline of a Bioculturally Based, 'Processual' Approach to the Emotions," esp. 312.

62. Diamond, "What Does Sexual Orientation Orient?" esp. 179–80.

63. For what appears to be an exhaustive table of the characteristics shared by childhood attachment and romantic love, see Shaver, Hazan, and Bradshaw, "Love as Attachment," 74–75, Table 4.

64. See, for example, Bristol, "What Freud Taught Us."

65. Konner, *The Tangled Wing*, 298.

66. Bartels and Zeki, "Neural Basis of Romantic Love."

67. Bartels and Zeki, "Neural Correlates of Maternal and Romantic Love."

68. Fisher, Aron, and Brown, "Romantic Love," esp. 59–60. See also Fisher, Aron, et al., "Defining the Brain Systems of Lust."

69. Diamond, "What Does Sexual Orientation Orient?" 173, 176.

70. Gillis, *For Better, for Worse*, 37.

71. Person, "Romantic Love," 383.

72. Jankowiak and Fischer, "Cross-Cultural Perspective."

73. See, for example, Jankowiak, *Romantic Passion*.

74. Hogan, *Mind and Its Stories*.

75. Gottschall and Nordlund, "Romantic Love."

76. Geoffrey Miller discusses different theories of sexual selection in *The Mating Mind*.

77. However, sexual selection is not the only factor behind sexual dimorphism, as Hrdy explains in *Mother Nature*, 47–50.

78. Today there is a vast general literature on biological sex differences between men and women—some of which is excellent, some indifferent, and some awful. Fortunately, the last decade has seen a marked increase in quality, with the publication of a number of important and reliable works as the science itself has come into maturity. For accessible general introductions, see Blum's thoughtful *Sex on the Brain;* Zuk's important corrective to simplified analogies between humans and other animals, *Sexual Selections;* and Fisher's speculative but enjoyable *Anatomy of Love*. For substantial and technical texts that are still accessible to nonscientists, see Low's challenging discussion from the perspective of behavioral ecology in *Why Sex Matters;* Geary's excellent fusion of ultimate and developmental perspectives in *Male, Female;* and Anne Campbell's vindication of the evolutionary perspective in *Mind of Her Own*. I also want to mention two textbooks that put the science of genes, hormones, and reproductive ecologies into perspective by placing it alongside other theoretical perspectives: Lippa, *Gender, Nature, and Nurture* and Archer and Lloyd's *Sex and Gender*.

79. For an overview of iniquitous gender arrangements across the planet, see Stearns, *Gender in World History*.

80. As I intimated in the introduction, the traditional distinction between descriptive and normative statements is important but also very complex. Traditionally, many researchers into human nature have waved off ideological objections with reference to the so-called naturalistic fallacy: that one cannot generate a normative statement from a descriptive statement. Unfortunately, this supposed fallacy has itself been exposed convincingly as a fallacy—and therefore dubbed "the naturalistic fallacy fallacy"—by John Searle in *Speech Acts*. It seems more fruitful to accept that the descriptive and the normative overlap to some degree without seeking to reduce one into the other. All normative statements must have a descriptive foundation (on what else could we base our values?), and our descriptive statements require some sort of motivation that is based on values (why else would we speak?).

81. Panksepp, "Emotions as Natural Kinds," 148.

82. Rogers, *Sexing the Brain*, 86. Rogers, an Australian neuroscientist, appears to make this admission somewhat reluctantly since she is critical of hormonal and physiological reductionism.

83. Cahill, "Why Sex Matters for Neuroscience," 1, 8.

84. Trivers, "Parental Investment." Trivers revised "Bateman's principle," which predicted a universal correlation between sexual behavior and reproductive

effort, but he explained it differently, in terms of energy investment in sex cells. Trivers's theory has also been reformulated and sharpened by Donald Symons and others in terms of *typical* and *minimum* parental investment: "Humans are like other mammals in that a male's minimum possible parental investment is very small, but different from other mammals in that a male's typical parental investment is very large" (Kenrick, Sadalla, and Trost, "Evolution, Traits, and the Stages of Human Courtship," esp. 215).

85. Darwin, *Descent of Man*.

86. For an excellent corrective to simplified assumptions about male and female among primates, see Hrdy, *Mother Nature* (1999).

87. Geary, *Male, Female*, 129.

88. For an overview of sex differences in cognition—including language competence, facial processing, theory of mind, spatial ability, and so forth—that pays attention to both genetic and developmental aspects, see Geary, *Male, Female*, chapter 8. For critical views regarding the science of biological sex differences, see Rogers, *Sexing the Brain*, and Anne Fausto-Sterling, *Sexing the Body*.

89. The Darwinian feminist Barbara Smuts examines six hypotheses about the origin of male intersexual dominance in "Evolutionary Origins of Patriarchy"; see also Wilson and Daly, "Man Who Mistook His Wife."

90. See, for example, Anne Fausto-Sterling's otherwise thoughtful and constructive argument in "Beyond Difference." Such distortions of Blackwell's achievement are lamented from a feminist perspective by Griet Vandermassen: "Reading feminist accounts of Blackwell's critique, one is struck—again—by the authors' inability to distinguish between the scientific and the ideological character of a theory." "Sexual Selection," 14.

91. Blackwell, *Sexes Throughout Nature*, 33–34.

92. Spiro, *Culture and Human Nature*, 70.

93. Charney, *Love and Lust*, 167.

94. In their widely publicized 1991 twin study, Michael Bailey and Richard Pillard found that if one identical twin was a self-professed homosexual then there was a 52 percent chance that the other twin would have the same sexual orientation. These telling figures are recognized even by self-proclaimed critics of genetic determinism such as Lesley Rogers and Anne Fausto-Sterling, both of whom prefer to see the study as showing that homosexuality is roughly 50 percent environmental in origin. See Rogers, *Sexing the Brain*, 66, and Fausto-Sterling, *Myths of Gender*, 257.

95. Fisher, *Anatomy of Love*, 167.

96. Midgley, *Beast and Man*, 282.

97. McEwan, *Enduring Love*, 14.

98. Hrdy, *Mother Nature*, 212.

99. Storey, *Mimesis and the Human Animal*, 30.

100. Lazarus and Lazarus, *Passion and Reason*, 111.

101. My discussion of Triandis is indebted to Hatfield and Rapson, *Love and Sex*, 12–13, who add some useful qualifications to this admittedly schematic distinction: for example, individual personality differences may be more powerful than cultural differences in shaping behavior, and people sometimes assimilate rapidly from one culture to another. On the application of Triandis to cultural styles of loving, see also Dion and Dion, "Romantic Love," esp. 279–86.

102. As Ralph Houlbrooke puts it, marriages ranged from "the arranged at one end to the completely free at the other," and it is "clear from a large body of evidence that the duty of compliance with parental wishes was never inculcated with uniform success even in wealthy families. There was a widespread belief among would-be marriage partners that freedom of choice was their right." *English Family*, 69, 71.

103. Shaver, Wu, and Schwartz (1991); discussed in Hatfield and Rapson, "Love and Attachment Processes."

104. Jankowiak, introduction to *Romantic Passion*, 17n2.

105. Heelas, "Emotion Talk Across Cultures." This distinction, which does not dispute the biological basis for emotional experience, is a good example of how social constructivism can enrich our understanding of human emotions without overstating its case.

106. Irving Singer, *Nature of Love*, vol. 2, 22–23.

107. Ibid., vol. 2, 35.

108. Ibid., vol. 2, 70.

109. In spite of his questionable equation of passion with adultery, Denis de Rougemont's remarks on the narcotic ideal of romantic passion in Western culture strike me as ruthlessly to the point:

> Just think about our enthusiasm for the novel, and for films adapted from novels; or the idealized eroticism that suffuses our entire culture, our education, and the images that surround us; or indeed our escapism that is exacerbated by the ennui of living in a mechanized society. Everything inside us and around us glorifies passion. We think of it as the promise of a richer life, as a transfiguring power, as something that lies beyond both happiness and suffering, a burning bliss. . . . And yet the amorous passion is really a matter of suffering. . . . Have we become so self-deluded and "mystified" that we no longer recognize this? (*L'Amour et l'Occident* [Love in the Western World], 2. Translation mine.)

110. Midgley, *Beast and Man*, 182–83.

111. Regis, "Madness of Excess," esp. 141.

112. Spiro, *Culture and Human Nature*, 35.

113. The materialist gentleman in question was called John Derpier; see Keith Thomas, *Man and the Natural World*, 122.

114. See Stearns, "History of Emotions."

115. Beall and Sternberg, "Social Construction of Love."

Chapter 2

1. McAlindon, *Shakespeare Minus 'Theory,'* 136.

2. See Tayler, *Nature and Art in Renaissance Literature*, for an instructive literary-philosophical survey of how these concepts were used from the Greeks to the Elizabethans.

3. Carroll, *Evolution and Literary Theory*, 405.

4. This is not the only current renaissance of Renaissance ideas. Throughout the twentieth century, psychologists smiled condescendingly at the Galenic conception of temperament that was so central to Shakespeare's intellectual heritage—only to find that humans are born with a temperamental bias toward certain personality traits. See Kagan, *Galen's Prophecy*.

5. Montaigne, *Essays*, vol. 2, chap. 8, p. 67.

6. Cressy, "Foucault, Stone, Shakespeare."

7. Postman, *Building a Bridge*, chapter 7 and appendix 3.

8. Pollock, *Forgotten Children*, 23.

9. For Postman, by contrast, "these paintings are entirely accurate representations of the psychological and social perceptions of children prior to the seventeenth century." *Building a Bridge*, Appendix 3, 186.

10. On the latter point, see Robert LeVine, "Child Rearing as a Cultural Adaptation" (1977), cited in Pollock, *Forgotten Children*, 51. Pollock adds: "With 80 to 85 per cent of all babies surviving, at least for a few years, it would have been impossible for mothers to avoid getting attached to their children" (51).

11. Shakespeare, *Winter's Tale*, 1.2.166.

12. For early critiques of Pollock and other historians who stress historical continuity, see Bellingham, "History of Childhood," *Journal of Family History* 13 (1988); Morgan, *The Family, Politics, and Social Theory* (1985), and Casey, *The History of the Family* (1989).

13. Orme, *Medieval Children*, 5.

14. Sulloway, *Born to Rebel*, 89.

15. Harry Harlow's life and achievement has recently become the subject of a thoughtful and informative biography, *Love at Goon Park*, by the science journalist Deborah Blum.

16. Dissanayake, *Art and Intimacy*, chapter 1.

17. Hrdy, *Mother Nature*, 159.

18. De Waal, *Good Natured*, 123.

19. The Titi monkey is an interesting exception: a small, monogamous, tree-living species the females of which seem less interested in their offspring than in their mates, the latter of which carry the infants on their backs. This sex-role reversal is entirely in keeping with the predictions of parental investment theory.

20. Hrdy, *Mother Nature*, 205.

21. Geary, *Male, Female*, 103–4.

22. Ibid., 103.

23. Anne Campbell, *Mind of Her Own*, 63.

24. Carroll, *Evolution and Literary Theory*, 362.

25. Nuttall, *New Mimesis*, 100.

26. Miola, *Shakespeare's Rome*, 9, 17.

27. Nuttall, *New Mimesis*, 101.

28. Ronan, *Antike Roman*, 21.

29. Coppélia Kahn, *Roman Shakespeare*, 22n6.

30. Vickers, *Shakespeare, Co-Author*, chapter 3, 148–244.

31. On this point, see Klause, "Politics, Heresy and Martyrdom"; and Swärdh, *Rape and Religion in English Renaissance Literature*.

32. Ronan, *Antike Roman*, 31.

33. Miola, *Shakespeare's Rome*, 49.

34. Boyd, "Mutius," esp. 208.

35. *Honor/honors*: lines 7, 39, 42, 45, 52, 70, 153, 159, 160, 181, 201, 217, 256, 263, 279, 382, 421, 441, 471, 480, 482. *Honorable*: lines 220, 243. *Honored*: lines 249, 432. *Dishonor*: lines 13, 300, 308, 440. *Dishonored*: lines 345, 350, 370, 390, 430, 437.

36. For a historical overview of the concept of honor in early modern England, see Mervyn James, *Society, Politics and Culture*, chapter 8, "English Politics and the Concept of Honour, 1485–1642," 308–415.

37. See the first part of the second definition of "honor" in the *Oxford English Dictionary*.

38. See Boyd, "Common Words," esp. 301–2. There is a small discrepancy between Boyd's figures and mine since we have used different editions of the play, but the difference is only marginal and has no effect on the larger statistical patterns.

39. Ronan, *Antike Roman*, 42.

40. Edward O. Wilson, *On Human Nature*, 89.

41. Stewart, *Honor*, 21.

42. Barber, *Theme of Honour's Tongue*.

43. Stewart, *Honor*, 48.

44. Cited in Keith Thomas, *Man and the Natural World*, 64. Erica Fudge discusses the fragile dividing line between animals and humans in *Perceiving Animals*.

45. "There has been much work in evolutionary psychology both on the necessity and mechanisms of the emotions driving revenge, on the cross-cultural presence of revenge, on the culturally different thresholds of revenge, and the tension between the impulse to revenge and the cultural constraints on revenge, especially in state societies." Boyd, "Literature and Evolution," 13.

46. For a different but compatible perspective on Aaron the Moor and parental love as a human universal, see Brian Boyd, "Kind and Unkindness." In this excellent reading Boyd suggests that the character of Aaron enabled Shakespeare "to explore the very basis of the revenge plot—pity for one's own, pitilessness for others—and to probe its implications as searchingly as he could. No other revenge play examines so insistently our human habit of identifying with our own and our human hesitation about seeing others as also, in some measure, our own."

47. Kernan, *Shakespeare, the King's Playwright*, 135.

48. These critics include Gurr, "*Coriolanus* and the Body Politic"; Richard Wilson, "Against the Grain"; Patterson, *Shakespeare and the Popular Voice*; and Kiernan, *Eight Tragedies of Shakespeare*.

49. "In the tense political situation that existed between Whitehall and St. James' Palace in 1608–9, praise of 'Heroique Minds' could mean only one thing: it was a coded indication that you subscribed to the ideals of militant Protestantism and that you were a supporter of its charismatic and bellicose young patron." Wells, *Shakespeare on Masculinity*, 155. Wells argues convincingly, however, that *Coriolanus* constitutes Shakespeare's "last and most emphatic denunciation of heroic values" (176).

50. McFarland, "The Image of the Family in *King Lear*," esp. 106.

51. Coppélia Kahn, *Roman Shakespeare*, 147.

52. Dreher, *Domination and Defiance*, 8, 9.

53. Bryan, "Volumnia." Bryan's contention that a conservative Shakespeare is warning us about the capacity of unnatural mothers to cause social disorder seems much less convincing, especially since Volumnia identifies her own and her son's interests so closely with those of Rome. In *Rome and Romans According to Shakespeare*, Michael Platt even suggests "Mrs. Body Politic" as an appropriate nickname for her, and Coppélia Kahn comes to similar conclusions in *Roman Shakespeare*. As in *Titus*, Shakespeare seems more interested in how Roman parents—male or female—can become so obsessed with honor and social status that they inflict a good deal of suffering on their children.

54. Platt, *Rome and Romans*, 116.

55. Nuttall, *New Mimesis*, 118.

56. For a fairly radical reassessment by an independent scholar, see Judith Rich Harris, *The Nurture Assumption* and *No Two Alike*.

57. Sulloway, *Born to Rebel*, 95.

58. Nuttall, *New Mimesis*, 116.

59. Platt, *Rome and Romans*, 89.

60. McFarland, "Individual and Society," esp. 130.

61. Ide, *Possessed with Greatness*, 185.

62. Ibid., 168.

63. On this point, see Brockbank's introduction to the second Arden edition of the play, 33.

64. O'Hear, *Beyond Evolution*, 173.

65. Hrdy, *Mother Nature*, 94.

66. An incomplete attempt to explain suicide bombing in evolutionary terms is made by Jay D. Glass in *Soldiers of God*.

Chapter 3

1. Since *King Lear* poses particularly difficult problems for modern editors—should we conflate the Quarto and Folio versions or regard them as two different versions of the same story?—the page references in this chapter are taken from the Arden third edition of the individual play, rather than from the *Complete Works*. The advantage with this edition is that it conflates the Quarto and Folio but also indicates the differences between them in the running text—rather than in a separate section of textual notes—which makes it easy to preserve this information in citations.

2. Spiro, *Culture and Human Nature*, 23.

3. Dissanayake, *Art and Intimacy*, 45.

4. De Waal, *Good Natured*, 187.

5. Mock and Parker, *Evolution of Sibling Rivalry*, 8.

6. Cited in Leites, *Puritan Conscience and Modern Sexuality*, 41.

7. Montaigne, *Essays*, vol. 2, chap. 8, p. 67.

8. Elster, *Alchemies of the Mind*, 76–107.

9. Wright, *Passions of the Mind*, 227. Wright's text was published three years earlier, in 1601, but Newbold regards the second edition as more authoritative.

10. Burton, *Anatomy of Melancholy*, 3.1.3.1: 29. Italics mine.

11. MacFarlane, *Marriage and Love in England*, 108.

12. Ibid., 113.

13. Donne, "Anatomy of the World," vol. 1, 1096: lines 213–15.

14. Cited in McLuskie, "Patriarchal Bard," esp. 144.

15. McFarland, "Image of the Family," 102–3.

16. Sulloway, *Born to Rebel*, 65–66.

17. Bradshaw, *Misrepresentations*.

18. McLuskie, "Patriarchal Bard," 143.

19. Boose, "Family in Shakespeare Studies," esp. 725.

20. Blissett, "Recognition in *King Lear*," esp. 104.

21. Berger, "Lear Family Romance," 33.

22. Not surprisingly, most "incestuous" readings of *Lear* ground themselves in psychoanalytic theory. Examples apart from those cited in the running text include Crick, "Lear and Cordelia's Tragic Love"; Bleichner, "*King Lear, King Leir*"; Ford, *Patriarchy and Incest*; and Asp, "'The Clamor of Eros.'"

23. In an interview for *The Atlantic*, Jane Smiley actively encourages a revisionist rereading of *King Lear* in terms of incest; http://www.theatlantic.com/unbound/bookauth/ba980528.htm.

24. McCabe, *Incest, Drama and Nature's Law*, 177.

25. Dreher, *Domination and Defiance*, 69.

26. In the introduction to *Ten Theories of Human Nature*, Leslie Stevenson defines two characteristics of a *closed* intellectual system: (1) not allowing any evidence to count against the theory, and (2) answering criticism by analyzing the motivations of the critic in terms of the theory itself. See also pages 162–67 for a balanced critique of Freud's legacy. Stevenson and Haberman, *Ten Theories of Human Nature*, 13. For an interesting account of what can happen when you have the audacity to question central aspects of Freud's heritage, see Crews, "Confessions of a Freud Basher."

27. Sigmund Freud, "On the Universal Tendency to Debasement in the Sphere of Love," cited in Evans, *Love*, 109.

28. Schlegel, excerpt from *Lectures on Dramatic Art and Literature*, 32.

29. Dreher, *Domination and Defiance*, 72–73.

30. Coppélia Kahn, "The Absent Mother," 33–49, esp. 40.

31. Cunningham, "*King Lear*," esp. 25.

32. Cavell, "Avoidance of Love," in *Disowning Knowledge*, 39–123, esp. 57.

33. One difference between the Folio (1623) and Quarto (1608, 1619) editions of the play is that the "Folio Lear" explains the rationale behind his division of the kingdom: it is done to prevent a future civil war (1.1.39–44), and Lear stresses that he is now relinquishing his power, territorial rights, and duties as sovereign (48–50). As far as I can gather, however, these and other textual discrepancies have only marginal consequences, if any, for my argument here.

34. Cited in Reibetanz, *Lear World*, 20.

35. Berns, "Gratitude, Nature, and Piety," esp. 30.

36. Berger, "Lear Family Romance," 31.

37. Dodd, "Impossible Worlds," esp. 489.

38. Reibetanz, *Lear World*, 19.

39. Bullough, *Narrative and Dramatic Sources*, vol. 7, 287.

40. Leggatt, "Madness," esp. 127.

41. Frye, *"King Lear,"* esp. 102–3.

42. Danby, *Shakespeare's Doctrine of Nature,* 116.

43. Hoeniger, *Medicine and Shakespeare,* 317.

44. Dodd, "Impossible Worlds," 479.

45. Alvin B. Kernan, *Shakespeare, the King's Playwright.*

46. McFarland, "Image of the Family," 100.

47. Berns, "Gratitude, Nature, and Piety," 32.

48. Paul Kahn, *Law and Love,* 5, 7.

49. In *The Art of Loving,* Erich Fromm argues that the *responsibility* that belongs to love must be distinguished from *duty* because the former is "an entirely voluntary act" (29).

50. Cited in Houlbrooke, *English Family,* 42.

51. Berns, "Gratitude, Nature, and Piety," 28–29.

52. Montaigne, *Essays,* vol. 2, chap. 8, p. 70.

53. Paul Kahn, *Law and Love,* 56.

54. Ibid., 135.

55. Dylan Evans, previously a respected authority on Lacan, has written an instructive and enjoyable account of his own wholesale rejection of the French psychoanalyst. See "From Lacan to Darwin," in Gottschall and Wilson, *Literary Animal,* 38–55.

56. Many attempts have been made to construct a taxonomy of the complex meanings of "nature" in *King Lear:* see, for example, Danby's thematic reading in terms of two opposing interpretations of nature: one *orthodox* (reminiscent of Francis Bacon and Thomas Hooker, seeing nature as a benevolent and stable source of social norms) and one *malignant* (reminiscent of Thomas Hobbes, which is both individualistic and atomistic). (See *Shakespeare's Doctrine of Nature.*) Frye finds nature represented on four different levels in accordance with Elizabethan doctrine: *heaven* (represented in *Lear* by impotent pagan gods), a *higher human order of nature* (represented by a social world of love, loyalty, and authority), a *lower, "fallen," physical nature* (represented by man as animal), and finally a *demonic world* (represented as hell). (*"King Lear,"* 101–21.) Focusing more closely on Shakespeare's word usage, Berns classifies it very usefully under five different headings:

Nature sometimes means (1) the general order of the social, political, and cosmic whole within which the activity of any one person or group can only be a part; (2) the constitution, or character, of an individual as a whole, that is, the unity arising from both endowment and habit; (3) the original endowment of an individual with the powers directed, but not necessarily compelled, towards definite ends, or purposes. This is the meaning expressed most often by Lear. Nature also means (4) the original endowment of an individual with powers supplied to be used howsoever their possessor wills. This is the meaning expressed most powerfully by Edmund. (5) Nature is twice personified as a goddess: once by Lear conflating meanings 1 and 3, and once by Edmund conflating meanings 1 and 4. ("Gratitude, Nature, and Piety," 39)

57. Tayler, *Nature and Art*, 51. Chapter 2 of Tayler's study gives an excellent survey of the classical backgrounds to Renaissance ideas about the relationship between the natural and the artificial.

58. See the twelfth definition of "charge" in the *Oxford English Dictionary*.

59. See the first part of the eighth definition of "charge" in the *Oxford English Dictionary*.

60. See the first part of the tenth definition of "charge" in the *Oxford English Dictionary*.

61. There are three more examples of the construction "at X's charge" in Shakespeare's plays, all of which occur in an economic context: *Henry IV, Part I* (1.3.78); *Merchant of Venice* (4.1.364–65); and *All's Well That Ends Well* (2.3.115).

62. Berger, "The Gloucester Family Romance," esp. 57.

63. Frye, "*King Lear*," 109–10.

64. Montaigne, *Essays*, vol. 1, chap. 27, p. 202.

65. Writing from an explicitly Christian perspective, Rowland Cotterill demonstrates considerable intellectual integrity in his assertion that "Shakespeare's plays offer no distinctively Christian practical wisdom. If Christian truth is to be seen as drawing support from events or characters in these and other plays of Shakespeare, the truth will have to be brought to the plays; it will not convincingly or distinctively be derived from them." ("Shakespeare and Christianity")

66. Elton, "*King Lear*" and the Gods, 338.

67. Dilman, *Love*, 122–24.

68. Fromm, *Art of Loving*, 48.

Chapter 4

1. Houlbrooke, *English Family*, 78.

2. There is a fairly broad anthropological consensus that marriage is a cultural universal, but the term is difficult to define satisfactorily, and there is considerable variation between different cultures. For an accessible introduction to these problems, see Leach, *Social Anthropology*, chapter 6, "Marriage, Legitimacy, Alliance."

3. Montaigne, *Essays*, vol. 1, 27: 200; vol. 3, chap. 5, pp. 72, 77.

4. A salient example of this distinction in Shakespeare's works is *Henry IV, Part 1*, where Margaret of Anjou marries the King while having a secret affair with the Earl of Suffolk (see 5.3.45–130 in particular).

5. Gillis, *For Better, for Worse*, 73.

6. Hawkes, "Love in *King Lear*."

7. Charney, *Love and Lust*, 209–10. Charney argues for clear generic tendencies in Shakespeare's portrayal of women, whose freedom and initiative in the comedies gives way to a "more constricted role" in the problem plays; the tragedies contain negative or bland portraits of women; and the romances involve a "distinct revival of the positive and lyric qualities of women." While there is much to be said for this generalization, it is far from watertight. For example, the claim that the heroines in the problem plays move "into a more constricted role" (210) holds true for Cressida and Isabella, but certainly not for Helena.

8. Hopkins, *Shakespearean Marriage*, 33.

9. Ehrlich, *Human Natures*, 194.

10. Gillis, *For Better, for Worse*, 52.

11. For an excellent attempt to define the nature of Shakespeare's problem plays, see the first chapter in Vivian Thomas, *Moral Universe*.

12. Pearson, *Elizabethan Love Conventions*, 20.

13. Lyons, *Ambiguity of Love's Triumph*, 83.

14. O'Rourke, "'Rule in Unity,'" esp. 149.

15. Neely, *Broken Nuptials*, 6.

16. See, for example, O'Rourke's assertion in "'Rule in Unity'": "If her idealization of him is less firm than his of her, this is not the revelation of individual character but the result of the different promises made to men and women in a patriarchal culture" (155).

17. As Anne Campbell points out, there may even be a connection here between sexual behavior and a general male proclivity for risk taking (*Mind of Her Own*, 86–87).

18. Ovid, *Art of Love*, 153.

19. Bacon, "Of Love," *Essayes*, 32.

20. Kermode, *Shakespeare's Language*, 129.

21. In Norman Rabkin's formulation, "value" in *Troilus and Cressida* is "a function of time." *Shakespeare and the Common Understanding*, 53.

22. Lyons, *Ambiguity of Love's Triumph*, 69.

23. I discuss the torrent of visual comparisons in the first scene of *Troilus and Cressida* in chapter 4 of *The Dark Lantern*.

24. Vivian Thomas, *Moral Universe*, 130.

25. Grene, *Tragic Imagination*, 72.

26. Kaula, "'Mad Idolatry,'" esp. 33. See also Barfoot's discussion of how the play's diction and imagery draws together the strands of mercantile and food imagery, tasting, and valuing in "*Troilus and Cressida*." Mead reminds us, equally pertinently, that Shakespeare belonged to a historical period "in which the substance of money was shifting in common understanding from coin specie of

'intrinsic' worth to a representational signification." See "'Thou Art Changed,'" esp. 238 39.

27. Whether or not Shakespeare himself read Plato, there is a close similarity between the exchange between Achilles and Ulysses in 3.3 and a discussion in Plato's *Alcibiades* that centers on the necessary dependence of self-knowledge on social reflection.

28. Yoder, "'Sons and Daughters,'" esp. 16–17.

29. Girard, *Theater of Envy.*

30. Girard's triadic conception of desire was instrumental when Sedgwick developed her well-known theory of homosocial desire in *Between Men.* In spite of Girard's polemical engagement with psychoanalysis, there are obvious similarities between his relational concept of desire and the work of Jacques Lacan. Girard's perspective can also be compared usefully to these psychoanalytical remarks by Bristol:

> The adult psychopathology of triangular love requires the condition of a real or imagined third party to enable the lover to love. It is a remnant of oedipal love, and the opposite of the lover dyad that is a twosome in structure and function. Some regard the latter as true romantic love, that is the absence of the disruptive influences of anger, jealousy, or competition with a feared superior rival. Thus defined, true love is impossible in the Oedipus complex and its failure is the motive force in adolescence and young adulthood to search again for dyadic love. ("What Freud Taught Us," 221)

31. Ovid, *Art of Love*, 97.

32. Girard, "Politics of Desire," esp. 197.

33. Girard, *Theater of Envy*, 153. Girard seems to infer Pandarus's quasi-incestuous love for Cressida from the way he praises her to Troilus.

34. Kirsch, *Experience of Love*, 43.

35. Irving Singer, *Nature of Love*, vol. 2, 236.

36. Grene, *Tragic Imagination*, 78.

37. Cook, *Making a Match*, 224, 223.

38. In his edition of the play, R. A. Foakes thinks Troilus's "basic attitude to love" can be defined as "gratification of the senses." Introduction to *Troilus and Cressida*, 16.

39. The only question mark concerns *empathy*, which is usually bundled together with the "emotional dependency" that Troilus clearly exhibits. But as we will see shortly, in the section on *All's Well*, the relation between romantic love and empathy is actually more complex than previous theorists have allowed.

40. See Wright, *The Moral Animal*, esp. chapters 3 and 13.

41. Adelman, *Suffocating Mothers*, 49.

42. Yoder, "'Sons and Daughters,'" 20–21.

43. The passage is summarized effectively in Wells, *Shakespeare's Humanism*, 128.

44. Thomas, *Moral Universe*, 52.

45. Ibid., 61.

46. Adelman, *Suffocating Mothers*, 46.

47. Thomas, *Moral Universe*, 49.

48. Geoffrey Chaucer, Robert Henryson, and William Caxton had all written about Troilus and Cressida, and the "scraps of available information indicate that 'the matter of Troy' was in vogue on the Elizabethan stage of 1598–1602. The Lord Admiral's Men had performed a play in 1598 which Philip Henslowe refers to as 'troye'; Henry Chettle and Thomas Dekker were paid for their 'troylles & creseda' in the spring of 1599; and the Admiral's Men had three other Troy-related dramas in the 1599 repertory: *Agamemnon*, *Troy's Revenge*, and *Orestes' Furies*." Ide, *Possessed with Greatness*, 20.

49. Allan Bloom, *Love and Friendship*, 103.

50. Lyons, *Ambiguity of Love's Triumph*, 84.

51. Hoeniger, *Medicine and Shakespeare*, 293.

52. In his forthcoming *Rape of Troy*, Jon Gottschall explains this ancient puzzle as follows: the works of Homer reflect a historical reality where systems of female slave-concubinage and excess female mortality had led to a shortage of women, which in turn generated a vicious circle of fierce male-male competition for access to the opposite sex. As Gottschall notes, such a destructive social imbalance could explain much of the fatalism and pessimism that suffuses the *Iliad*.

53. Another Shakespearean instance of such gender role reversal is the narrative poem *Venus and Adonis*, where a lusty goddess courts a reluctant young man.

54. For the latter contention, see Desens, *Bed-Trick in English Renaissance Drama*, 141.

55. Dreher, *Domination and Defiance*, 136, 138–39.

56. See Stanton, "All's Well in Love and War." In her introduction to the Oxford edition of the play, Susan Snyder argues convincingly for a more balanced view, but she still contends that the "key" to the critical division regarding Helena's moral stature "is the upsetting of the gender role system created by having the woman rather than the man take the sexual initiative" (31). This approach reduces the play's moral problem to a gender problem, and thus fails to consider the more basic question of whether it is right to treat *any* human being as a commodity that can be bought and sold against his or her will.

57. Neely, *Broken Nuptials*, 65, 70, 71.

58. Findlay, *Feminist Perspective*, 96.

59. The exact placement of the King's fistula in *All's Well* is a crux that has occupied people inside and outside the discipline of literary studies. According to Hoeniger, "Shakespeare decided to play a little with his audience: 'if you were amused because you thought that the King had *fistula in ano* you were wrong; he actually had fistula in the hand, and there was no need for him to expose himself'" (*Medicine and Shakespeare*, 297). For the view that Shakespeare placed it elsewhere, and even perused a contemporary treatise on the subject, see Cosman, "All's Well That Ends Well."

60. Dreher, *Domination and Defiance*, 138–39.

61. This discussion is indebted to a series of informal conversations with my colleague and friend Christer Larsson on the nature of emotion.

62. Thomas, *Moral Universe*, 48.

63. Bartels and Zeki, "The Neural Correlates of Maternal and Romantic Love," 1155, 1164.

64. Cook, *Making a Match*, 18.

65. Middleton, *Women Beware Women*.

66. Kastan, "Limits of Comedy," esp. 580.

67. Bertram uses a broad number of formal arguments to nullify his marriage: *disparagement, coercion, nonconsummation, lengthy separation, and failure to comply with marriage contract*. See Ranold, "Betrothals."

68. Smallwood, "Design," esp. 46–47, 55.

69. Cook, *Making a Match*, 65.

70. Harmon, "'Lawful Deeds,'" esp. 124, 125.

71. Lyons, *Ambiguity of Love's Triumph*, 114.

72. Dennis, "Meaning of Agape," esp. 75.

73. Kastan, "Limits of Comedy," 583–84.

74. Arnhart, *Darwinian Natural Right*, 80.

Chapter 5

1. The theoretical section of this chapter and part of the literary reading are based on my article "Theorising Early Modern Jealousy."

2. Breitenberg, *Anxious Masculinity*.

3. Charney, *Love and Lust*, 55.

4. Allan Bloom, *Love and Friendship*, 109–10.

5. Burton, *Anatomy of Melancholy*, 273.

6. Cited in Vaughan, *Contextual History*, 76.

7. Montaigne, *Essays*, vol. 3, chap. 5, p. 88.

8. Ovid, *Art of Love*, 104.

9. I am assuming, in accordance with a broad critical consensus and widespread public opinion, that jealousy is a central issue in both plays under consideration here. Fernie has contended that "it is shame, not jealousy, that is the signal and unifying passion of *Othello*" in *Shame in Shakespeare*, 19, but this claim—convincing or not—is only indirectly relevant to my purposes here, since I am not seeking to defend the notion of jealousy as a unifying subject in either play.

10. Rossiter, *Angel with Horns*, 189.

11. Wachterhauser, Introduction to *Hermeneutics and Truth*, 6.

12. For a recent replication in a fairly egalitarian country, see Wiederman and Kendall, "Evolution, Sex, and Jealousy."

13. Mary Beth Rose, *Expense of Spirit*.

14. As Laslett points out, it seems "rather hazardous to judge the relative prevalence of sexual deviation from changes in the tone of admonitory literature, confessional handbooks, or any source emanating from the respectable themselves, especially the ecclesiastics." Introduction to *Bastardy and Its Comparative History*, 59. Modern historians of emotion have also stressed that we must distinguish between so-called feeling rules (that is, normative emotional standards) and "emotional experience itself"—see Stearns, "History of Emotions," 20.

15. Cited in Amussen, *Ordered Society*, 45.

16. See, for example, Donald E. Brown, *Human Universals*, and David Buss, *Dangerous Passion*.

17. Fisher, *Anatomy of Love*, 270–71.

18. Dennett, *Darwin's Dangerous Idea*, 486. Conversely, it is just as mistaken to suppose, as Rom Harré and other constructivists do, that cross-cultural variation is evidence that a trait is cultural and cannot be subjected to evolutionary explanation (see Griffiths, *What Emotions Really Are*, 160).

19. Hupka, "Arousal of Romantic Jealousy," esp. 254, 262.

20. Spiro, *Culture and Human Nature*, 23.

21. Miller, *Mating Mind*, 337.

22. Winslow, et al., "Central Vasopressin in Pair Bonding"; Panksepp and Panksepp, "Seven Sins," esp. 121–22.

23. Hrdy, *Mother Nature*, 85.

24. Buss, *Dangerous Passion*, 171; see also Johnston, *Why We Feel*, 136.

25. Montaigne, *Essays*, vol. 3, chap. 5, p. 128.

26. Wilson and Daly, "Man Who Mistook His Wife," 301.

27. Buss, *Dangerous Passion*, 207.

28. Hupka, "Arousal of Romantic Jealousy," 257.

29. Sidanius and Pratto, *Social Dominance*, chap. 10, p. 298.

30. Winslow, et al., "Central Vasopressin in Pair Bonding."

31. Dickemann, "Paternal Confidence," esp. 313.

32. MacFarlane, *Marriage and Love*, 147.

33. Gillis, *For Better, for Worse*, 15.

34. Brodsky, "Widows in Late Elizabethan London," esp. 146.

35. Marriage was not an obvious option for the great majority of young men and women "who had no secure expectation of property, and whose chances of founding an establishment were so much affected by economic vicissitudes" (Laslett, *Bastardy and Its Comparative History*, 58). For other considerations, see Bacon, "Of Marriage and Single Life," in *Essayes*, 24–26.

36. Ingram, *Church Courts*, 146.

37. On this point, see Leites, *Puritan Conscience*; for literary perspectives, see Mary Beth Rose, *Expense of Spirit*.

38. Amussen, *Ordered Society*, 39, 149.

39. Gillis, *For Better, for Worse*, 34.

40. MacFarlane, *Marriage and Love*, 297.

41. See Gowing, *Domestic Dangers*, and Foyster, *Manhood in Early Modern England*, 78, 122.

42. Ingram, *Church Courts*, 130.

43. MacFarlane, *Marriage and Love*, 147.

44. Edward Coke, cited in Findlay, *Illegitimate Power*, 24.

45. This discussion is indebted to the expertise of Urban Morén, who is currently conducting doctoral research at Uppsala University on sexual subtexts related to syphilis in *The Winter's Tale*.

46. Vaughan, *Contextual History*, 78. The formulation is Vaughan's and not Wright's.

47. Adamson, *"Othello" as Tragedy*, 4.

48. Kenneth Gross, *Shakespeare's Noise*, 103.

49. Cowhig, "Othello's Race"; Rubinstein, "Bourgeois Equality."

50. Hogan, "*Othello*, Racism, and Despair."

51. Newman, "'And Wash the Ethiop White,'" esp. 153.

52. Kirsch, *Experience of Love*, 32–33.

53. There is, in other words, little support for Loomba's recent assertion—in overt opposition to any reading based on human nature or human universals—that "Shakespeare goes out of his way to draw attention to Othello's colour and race." "Human Nature or Human Difference?" esp. 156.

54. Loomba, "Sexuality and Racial Difference," esp. 165.

55. Barthelemy, "Ethiops Washed White," esp. 95.

56. Marilyn French, *Division of Experience*, 212.

57. Drakakis, "The Engendering of Toads."

58. Barthelemy, "Ethiops Washed White," 91.

59. Neely, "Women and Men in *Othello*," esp. 81.

60. Burton, *Anatomy of Melancholy*, 3.3.2: 282.

61. Levin, "Feminist Thematics," esp. 127–28.

62. Richmond, "Audience's Role," esp. 98, 99.

63. Traub, *Desire and Anxiety*, 36.

64. Cited in Rossiter, *Angel with Horns*, 201.

65. Calderwood, "Appalling Property," esp. 361.

66. Bevington, "Portrait of a Marriage."

67. Calderwood, "Appalling Property," 360.

68. Adamson, *"Othello" as Tragedy*, 125.

69. Harold Bloom, *Invention of the Human*, 450.

70. Bradshaw, *Misrepresentations*, 184.

71. Adamson, *"Othello" as Tragedy*, 131.

72. Harold Bloom, *Invention of the Human*, 639.

73. Cavell, *Disowning Knowledge*, chapter 6.

74. Sokol, *Art and Illusion*, 32.

75. Ibid., 44.

76. Pafford, Appendix 1 to Shakespeare, *Arden*, 165.

77. It should perhaps be pointed out that such crimes of passion were not common in the early modern period and that homicide rates were not extremely high compared to those in some modern Western countries. According to Sharpe, homicide rates in Essex fell from seven per hundred thousand inhabitants in the late sixteenth century to 2.8 in the late seventeenth century; see *Early Modern England*, 111. In comparison, rates in the United States have averaged between five and ten in the second half of the twentieth century.

78. Storey, *Mimesis and the Human Animal*, 138.

79. Gadamer, *Truth and Method*, 498.

80. Pechter, *"Othello" and Interpretive Traditions*, 105.

Conclusion

1. Dryden, "Of Dramatic Poesy, an Essay," esp. 79–80.

2. As Lyas points out, it may be impossible to give deductive reasons for aesthetic judgment in the sense of justifying it, but this does not make art criticism irrational or subjective. See "The Evaluation of Art." I fully agree with Dissanayake that "in a naturalist aesthetics, learned criteria of quality and learned responses to beauty will nevertheless rest upon evolved universal predispositions," and it is also quite possible that "some aesthetic experiences and ways can be demonstrated to be qualitatively superior to others" (*Art and Intimacy*, 208). The only question, as I see it, is *how?*

3. For a damaging view of literary theory as the antithesis of common sense, see Culler, *Literary Theory*.

Works Cited

Adamson, Jane. "Othello" as Tragedy: Some Problems of Judgment and Feeling. Cambridge, U.K.: Cambridge University Press, 1980.

Adelman, Janet. Suffocating Mothers: Fantasies of Maternal Origin in Shakespeare's Plays, "Hamlet" to "The Tempest." London: Routledge, 1992.

Amussen, Susan Dwyer. An Ordered Society: Gender and Class in Early Modern England. Oxford: Blackwell, 1988.

Archer, John, and Barbara Lloyd. Sex and Gender. 2nd ed. Cambridge, U.K.: Cambridge University Press, 2002.

Argyros, Alexander. A Blessed Rage for Order: Deconstruction, Evolution, and Chaos. Ann Arbor: University of Michigan Press, 1991.

Aristotle. Nichomachean Ethics. Translated by Roger Crisp. Cambridge, U.K.. Cambridge University Press, 2000.

Arnhart, Larry. Darwinian Natural Right: The Biological Ethics of Human Nature. New York: State University of New York Press, 1998.

Asp, Carolyn. "'The Clamor of Eros': Freud, Aging, and King Lear." In Memory and Desire: Aging, Literature, Psychoanalysis, edited by Kathleen Woodward and Murray M. Schwartz, 192–204. Bloomington: Indiana University Press, 1986.

Bacon, Francis. The Essayes or Counsels, Civill and Morall. 1597–1625. Edited by Michael Kiernan. Oxford: Clarendon, 1985.

Barash, Nanelle R., and David P. Barash. Madame Bovary's Ovaries: A Darwinian Look at Literature. New York: Delacorte Press, 2005.

Barber, Charles. The Theme of Honour's Tongue: A Study of Social Attitudes in the English Drama from Shakespeare to Dryden. Gothenburg Studies in English 58. Göteborg: Acta Universitatis Gothoburgensis, 1985.

Barfoot, C. C. "Troilus and Cressida: 'Praise Us as We Are Tasted.'" Shakespeare Quarterly 39, no. 1 (1988): 45–57.

Barkow, Jerome H., Leda Cosmides, and John Tooby, eds. The Adapted Mind: Evolutionary Psychology and the Generation of Culture. Oxford: Oxford University Press, 1992.

Barrell, John. Poetry, Language and Politics. Manchester, U.K.: Manchester University Press, 1988.

Bartels, Andreas, and Semir Zeki. "The Neural Basis of Romantic Love." Neuroreport 11, no. 17 (2000): 3829–34.

———. "The Neural Correlates of Maternal and Romantic Love." NeuroImage 21 (2004): 1155–66.

Barthelemy, Anthony Gerard, ed. *Critical Essays on Shakespeare's "Othello."* New York: G. K. Hall, 1994.

———. "Ethiops Washed White: Moors of the Non-Villainous Type." In Barthelemy, *Critical Essays*, 91–103.

Beall, Anne E., and Robert J. Sternberg. "The Social Construction of Love." *Journal of Social and Personal Relationships* 12, no. 3 (1995): 417–38.

Bellingham, Bruce. "The History of Childhood Since the 'Invention of Childhood': Some Issues of the Eighties." *Journal of Family History* 13, no. 1(1988): 347–58.

Belsey, Catherine. "Love as Trompe-l'Oeil: Taxonomies of Desire in *Venus and Adonis.*" *Shakespeare Quarterly* 46, no. 3 (1995): 257–76.

———. "The Subject in Danger: A Reply to Richard Levin." *Textual Practice* 3, no. 1 (1989): 87–90.

Berger, Harry, Jr. "The Gloucester Family Romance." In Erickson, *Making Trifles of Terrors*, 50–69.

———. "*King Lear*: The Lear Family Romance." In Erickson, *Making Trifles of Terrors*.

Berns, Lawrence. "Gratitude, Nature, and Piety in *King Lear*." *Interpretation* 3, no. 1 (1972): 27–51.

Berscheid, Ellen, and Elaine Walster. *Interpersonal Attraction*. 1969. 2nd ed. Reading, Mass.: Addison-Wesley, 1978.

Betzig, Laura, ed. *Human Nature: A Critical Reader*. Oxford: Oxford University Press, 1997.

Bevington, David. "*Othello*: Portrait of a Marriage." In Kolin, *"Othello": New Critical Essays*, 221–31.

Blackwell, Antoinette. *The Sexes Throughout Nature*. New York: G. P. Putnam's Sons, 1875.

Bleichner, Mark J. "*King Lear, King Leir*, and Incest Wishes." *American Imago* 45 (1988): 309–25.

Blissett, W. F. "Recognition in *King Lear*." In *Some Facets of "King Lear": Essays in Prismatic Criticism*, edited by Rosalie L. Colie and F. T. Flahiff, 103–16. Toronto: University of Toronto Press, 1974.

Bloch, R. Howard. *Medieval Misogyny and the Invention of Western Romantic Love*. Chicago: University of Chicago Press, 1991.

Bloom, Allan. *Shakespeare on Love and Friendship*. Chicago: University of Chicago Press, 2000.

Bloom, Harold. *Shakespeare: The Invention of the Human*. New York: Riverhead/Penguin, 1998.

Blum, Deborah. *Love at Goon Park: Harry Harlow and the Science of Affection*. Chichester: Wiley, 2003.

———. *Sex on the Brain: The Biological Differences between Men and Women*. New York: Viking, 1997.

Bock, Kenneth. *Human Nature Mythology.* Urbana: University of Illinois Press, 1994.

Bonfield, Lloyd, Richard M. Smith, and Keith Wrightson, eds. *The World We Have Gained: Histories of Population and Social Structure. Essays Presented to Peter Laslett on His Seventieth Birthday.* Oxford: Blackwell, 1986.

Boose, Lynda E. "The Family in Shakespeare Studies; or—Studies in the Family of Shakespeareans; or—the Politics of Politics." *Renaissance Quarterly* 40, no. 4 (1987): 707–42.

Bowlby, John. *Attachment and Loss.* Vol. 1, *Attachment.* 1969. Reprint, London: Pimlico/Random House, 1997.

Boyd, Brian. "Common Words in *Titus Andronicus:* The Presence of Peele." *Notes and Queries* 42, no. 240 (1995): 300–7.

———. "Kind and Unkindness: Aaron in *Titus Andronicus.*" In *Words that Count: Early Modern Authorship: Essays in Honor of MacDonald P. Jackson.* Edited by Brian Boyd. 51–77. Newark: University of Delaware Press, 2004.

———. "Literature and Evolution: A Bio-cultural Approach." *Philosophy and Literature* 29, no. 1 (2005): 1–23.

———. "Mutius: An Obstacle Removed in *Titus Andronicus.*" *Review of English Studies* 55, no. 219 (2004): 196–209.

Bradshaw, Graham. *Misrepresentations: Shakespeare and the Materialists.* Ithaca: Cornell University Press, 1993.

Brehm, Sharon S. "Passionate Love." In Sternberg and Barnes, *Psychology of Love,* 232–63.

Breitenberg, Mark. *Anxious Masculinity in Early Modern England.* Cambridge, U.K.: Cambridge University Press, 1996.

Bristol, R. Curtis. "What Freud Taught Us about Passionate Romantic Love." In *The Psychoanalytic Century: Freud's Legacy for the Future,* edited by David E. Scharff, 215–30. New York: Other Press, 2001.

Brodsky, Vivien. "Widows in Late Elizabethan London: Remarriage, Economic Opportunity and Family Orientations." In Bonfield, Smith, and Wrightson, *The World We Have Gained,* 122–54.

Brown, Anthony. *The Darwin Wars: The Scientific Battle for the Soul of Man.* London: Touchstone, 2000.

Brown, Donald E. *Human Universals.* New York: McGraw-Hill, 1991.

Bryan, Margaret B. "Volumnia: Roman Matron or Elizabethan Huswife." *Renaissance Papers* (1972): 43–58.

Bullough, Geoffrey. *Narrative and Dramatic Sources of Shakespeare.* Vol. 7. London: Routledge, 1973.

Burton, Robert. *The Anatomy of Melancholy 1621.* Edited by Thomas C. Faulkner, Nicolas K. Kiessling, and Rhonda L. Blair. Oxford: Clarendon, 1994.

Buss, David. *The Dangerous Passion: Why Jealousy Is as Necessary as Love and Sex*. New York: Free Press, 2000.

Cahill, Larry. "Why Sex Matters for Neuroscience." *Nature Reviews Neuroscience* 7 (June 2006): 1–8. Available online at www.nature.com/nrn/journal/v7/n6/full/nrn1909.html.

Calderwood, James L. "Appalling Property in *Othello*." *University of Toronto Quarterly* 57, no. 3 (1988): 353–75.

Campbell, Anne. *A Mind of Her Own: The Evolutionary Psychology of Women*. Oxford: Oxford University Press, 2002.

Campbell, David A. *Greek Lyric I: Sappho and Alcaeus*. Loeb Classical Library 142. 1982. Reprinted with corrections. Cambridge, Mass.: Harvard University Press, 1990.

Carroll, Joseph. "The Ecology of Victorian Fiction." *Philosophy and Literature* 25 (2001): 295–313.

———. *Evolution and Literary Theory*. Columbia: University of Missouri Press, 1995.

———. "Evolutionary Psychology and Literature." In *Handbook of Evolutionary Psychology*, edited by David Buss, 931–52. New York: Wiley, 2005.

———. *Literary Darwinism: Evolution, Human Nature, and Literature*. London: Routledge, 2004.

———. "Organism, Environment and Literary Representation." *Isle* 9, no. 2 (2002): 27–45.

Casey, James. *The History of the Family*. New Perspectives on the Past. Edited by R. I. Moore. Oxford: Basil Blackwell, 1989.

Cavell, Stanley. *Disowning Knowledge in Six Plays of Shakespeare*. Cambridge, U.K.: Cambridge University Press, 1987.

Charnes, Linda. "Near-Misses of the Non-Transcendent Kind: Reply to Richard Levin." *Textual Practice* 7, no. 1 (1993): 56–59.

———. "What's Love Got to Do With It? Reading the Liberal Humanist Romance in Shakespeare's *Antony and Cleopatra*." *Textual Practice* 6, no. 1 (1992): 1–16.

Charney, Maurice. *Shakespeare on Love and Lust*. New York: Columbia University Press, 2000.

Cook, Ann Jennalie. *Making a Match: Courtship in Shakespeare and His Society*. Princeton: Princeton University Press, 1991.

Cornelius, Randolph R. *The Science of Emotion: Research and Tradition in the Psychology of Emotions*. Upper Saddle River, N. J.: Prentice-Hall, 1996.

Cosman, Bard C. "*All's Well That Ends Well*: Shakespeare's Treatment of Anal Fistula." *Diseases of the Colon and Rectum* 41 (1998): 914–24.

Cotterill, Rowland. "Shakespeare and Christianity." In *The Discerning Reader: Christian Perspectives on Literature and Theory*, ed. David Barratt, Roger Pooley, and Leland Ryken, 155–76. Leicester: Apollos, 1995.

Cowhig, Ruth. "The Importance of Othello's Race." *The Journal of Commonwealth Literature* 12, no. 2 (1977): 153–61.

Crane, Mary Thomas. *Shakespeare's Brain: Reading with Cognitive Theory.* Princeton: Princeton University Press, 2000.

Cressy, David. "Foucault, Stone, Shakespeare and Social History." *English Literary Renaissance* 21, no. 2 (1991): 121–33.

Crews, Frederick C. "Confessions of a Freud Basher." *Times Higher Education Supplement,* March 3, 1995. Available online at http://human-nature.com/freud/crews.html.

Crick, Brian. "Lear and Cordelia's Tragic Love Revisited." *Critical Review* 37 (1997): 61–80.

Culler, Jonathan. *Literary Theory: A Very Short Introduction.* Oxford: Oxford University Press, 2000.

Cunningham, John. "*King Lear:* The Opening Scenes." In *"King Lear": William Shakespeare,* Longman Critical Essays, edited by Linda Cookson and Bryan Loughrey, 20–29. Harlow: Longman, 1988.

Danby, John F. *Shakespeare's Doctrine of Nature: A Study of "King Lear."* London: Faber and Faber, 1949.

Darwin, Charles. *The Autobiography: 1809–1882.* Edited by Nora Barlow. London: Collins, 1958.

———. *The Descent of Man: Selection in Relation to Sex.* London: John Murray, 1871.

Dennett, Daniel C. *Darwin's Dangerous Idea: Evolution and the Meanings of Life.* London: Penguin, 1995.

———. *The Expression of Emotions in Man and the Animals.* 1872. Reprint, edited and with an introduction by Paul Ekman. London: HarperCollins, 1998.

Dennis, Carl. "*All's Well That Ends Well* and the Meaning of Agape." *Philological Quarterly* 50, no. 1 (1971): 75–84.

Desens, Marliss C. *The Bed-Trick in English Renaissance Drama: Explorations in Gender, Sexuality, and Power.* Newark: University of Delaware Press, 1994.

De Waal, Frans. *Good Natured: The Origins of Right and Wrong in Humans and Other Animals.* Cambridge, Mass.: Harvard University Press, 1996.

Diamond, Lisa. "What Does Sexual Orientation Orient? A Biobehavioral Model Distinguishing Romantic Love and Sexual Desire." *Psychological Review* 110, no. 1 (2003): 173–92.

Dickemann, Mildred. "Paternal Confidence and Dowry Competition: A Biocultural Analysis of Purdah." In Betzig, *Human Nature,* 311–28.

Dilman, Ilham. *Love: Its Forms, Dimensions and Paradoxes.* London: Macmillan, 1998.

Dion, Kenneth L., and Karen K. Dion, "Romantic Love: Individual and Cultural Perspectives." In Sternberg and Barnes, *Psychology of Love,* 264–89.

Dissanayake, Ellen. *Art and Intimacy: How the Arts Began.* Seattle: University of Washington Press, 2000.

Dodd, William. "Impossible Worlds: What Happens in *King Lear*, Act 1, Scene 1?" *Shakespeare Quarterly* 50, no. 4 (1999): 477–507.

Donne, John. "An Anatomy of the World." In *The Norton Anthology of English Literature*. 5th ed. Edited by M. H. Abrams, vol. 1, 1091–97. New York: W. W. Norton, 1986.

Dover, Gabriel. "Human Nature: One for All and All for One?" In Wells and McFadden, *Human Nature*, 82–102.

Drakakis, John. "The Engendering of Toads: Patriarchy and the Problem of Subjectivity in Shakespeare's *Othello*." *Shakespeare Jahrbuch* 124 (1988): 62–80.

Dreher, Diane Elizabeth. *Domination and Defiance: Fathers and Daughters in Shakespeare*. Lexington: University Press of Kentucky, 1986.

Dryden, John. "Of Dramatic Poesy, an Essay." 1668. *Essays*, ed. W. P. Ker, vol. 1, 21–108. New York: Russell and Russell, 1961.

Eagleton, Terry. *After Theory*. London: Allen Lane/Penguin, 2003.

Easterlin, Nancy. "'Loving Ourselves Best of All': Ecocriticism and the Adapted Mind," *Mosaic* 37: 3 (2004), 1–18.

———. "Making Knowledge: Bioepistemology and the Foundations of Literary Theory." *Mosaic* 32, no. 1 (1999): 131–47.

Ehrlich, Paul R. *Human Natures: Genes, Cultures, and the Human Prospect*. Westport, Conn.: Praeger, 1997.

Ekman, Paul. "An Argument for Basic Emotions." *Cognition and Emotion* 6 (1992): 169–200.

Elster, Jon. *Alchemies of the Mind: Rationality and the Emotions*. Cambridge, U.K.: Cambridge University Press, 1999.

Elton, William. *"King Lear" and the Gods*. San Marino, Calif.: Huntington, 1966.

Erickson, Peter, ed. *Making Trifles of Terrors: Redistributing Complicities in Shakespeare*. Introduction by Peter Erickson. Stanford: Stanford University Press, 1997.

Evans, Mary. *Love: An Unromantic Discussion*. Cambridge, U.K.: Polity, 2003.

Fausto-Sterling, Anne. "Beyond Difference: Feminism and Evolutionary Psychology." In Rose and Rose, *Alas, Poor Darwin*, 174–89.

———. *Myths of Gender: Biological Theories about Men and Women*. 2nd rev. ed. New York: Basic, 1992.

———. *Sexing the Body: Gender Politics and the Construction of Sexuality*. New York: Basic Books, 2000.

Fernie, Ewan. *Shame in Shakespeare*. London: Routledge, 2002.

Findlay, Alison. *A Feminist Perspective on Renaissance Drama*. Oxford: Blackwell, 1999.

———. *Illegitimate Power: Bastards in Renaissance Drama*. Manchester, U.K.: Manchester University Press, 1994.

Fisher, Helen E. *Anatomy of Love: A Natural History of Mating, Marriage, and Why We Stray*. New York: Columbine, 1994.

Fisher, Helen, Arthur Aron, and Lucy L. Brown. "Romantic Love: An fMRI Study of a Neural Mechanism for Mate Choice." *Journal of Comparative Neurology* 493 (2005): 58–62.

Fisher, Helen, Arthur Aron, et al. "Defining the Brain Systems of Lust, Romantic Attraction, and Attachment." *Archives of Sexual Behavior* 31, no. 5 (2002): 413–19.

Foakes, R. A. Introduction to *Troilus and Cressida*. The New Penguin Shakespeare. London: Penguin, 1987.

Ford, Jane M. *Patriarchy and Incest from Shakespeare to Joyce*. Gainesville: University Press of Florida, 1998.

Foyster, Elizabeth. *Manhood in Early Modern England: Honour, Sex, and Marriage*. London: Longman, 1999.

French, Marilyn. *Shakespeare's Division of Experience*. London: Jonathan Cape, 1981.

French, Peter, and Howard K. Wettstein, eds. *Philosophy of Emotions*. Midwest Studies in Philosophy 22. Notre Dame, Ind.: University of Notre Dame Press, 1998.

Friedman, Marilyn. "Romantic Love and Personal Autonomy." In French and Wettstein, 162–81.

Fromm, Erich. *The Art of Loving*. 1957. Reprint, London: Allen and Unwin, 1979.

Frye, Northrop. "King Lear." In *Northrop Frye on Shakespeare*, edited by Robert Sandler, 101–21. Ontario: Fitzhenry and Whiteside, 1986.

Fudge, Erica. *Perceiving Animals: Humans and Beasts in Early Modern English Culture*. London: Macmillan, 2000.

Fudge, Erica, Ruth Gilbert, and Susan Wiseman. *At the Borders of the Human: Beasts, Bodies and Natural Philosophy in the Early Modern Period*. Basingstoke, U.K.: Macmillan, 1999.

Gadamer, Hans-Georg. *Truth and Method*. 2nd rev. ed. Translated by Joel Weinsheimer and Donald G. Marshall. New York: Continuum, 1989.

Geary, David C. *Male, Female: The Evolution of Human Sex Differences*. Washington, D. C.: American Psychological Association, 1998.

Gillis, John R. *For Better, for Worse: British Marriages, 1600 to the Present*. Oxford: Oxford University Press, 1985.

Girard, René. "The Politics of Desire in *Troilus and Cressida*." In *Shakespeare and the Question of Theory*, 188–209. New York: Methuen, 1985.

———. *A Theater of Envy: William Shakespeare*. Oxford: Oxford University Press, 1991.

Glass, Jay D. *Soldiers of God: Primal Emotions and Religious Terrorists*. Corona del Mar, Calif.: Donnington Press, 2003.

Gottschall, Jonathan. "Literary Studies, Universals, and the Sciences of the Mind." *Philosophy and Literature* 28, no. 1 (2004): 202–17.

————. *The Rape of Troy: A Darwinian Perspective on Conflict in Homer.* Forthcoming, Cambridge University Press, fall 2007.

Gottschall, Jonathan, and Marcus Nordlund. "Romantic Love: A Literary Universal?" *Philosophy and Literature* 30 (2006): 432–52.

Gottschall, Jonathan, and David Sloan Wilson, eds. *The Literary Animal: Evolution and the Nature of Narrative.* Evanston, Ill.: Northwestern University Press, 2005.

Gowing, Laura. *Domestic Dangers: Women, Words, and Sex in Early Modern London.* Oxford: Clarendon, 1996.

Grady, Hugh. "Shakespeare Studies, 2005: A Situated Overview." *Shakespeare* 1, no. 1 (2005): 102–20.

Grene, Nicholas. *Shakespeare's Tragic Imagination.* London: Macmillan, 1992.

Griffiths, Paul E. *What Emotions Really Are: The Problem of Psychological Categories.* Chicago: University of Chicago Press, 1997.

Gross, Alan C. *The Rhetoric of Science.* Cambridge, Mass.: Harvard University Press, 1990.

Gross, Kenneth. *Shakespeare's Noise.* Chicago: University of Chicago Press, 2001.

Gurr, Andrew. "*Coriolanus* and the Body Politic." *Shakespeare Survey* 28 (1975): 63–69.

Hacking, Ian. *The Social Construction of What?* Cambridge, Mass.: Harvard University Press, 2000.

Halio, Jay L., ed. *Critical Essays on Shakespeare's "King Lear."* London: Prentice Hall, 1996.

Harmon, A. G. "'Lawful Deeds': The Entitlements of Marriage in Shakespeare's *All's Well That Ends Well.*" *Logos* 4, no. 3 (2001): 115–42.

Harris, Helen. "Rethinking Polynesian Heterosexual Relationships: A Case Study on Mangaia, Cook Islands." In Jankowiak, *Romantic Passion: A Universal Experience?* 95–127.

Harris, Judith Rich. *No Two Alike: Human Nature and Human Individuality.* New York: W. W. Norton, 2006.

————.*The Nurture Assumption: Why Children Turn Out the Way They Do.* 1998. Reprint, London: Bloomsbury, 1999.

Hart, F. Elizabeth. "The Epistemology of Cognitive Literary Studies." *Philosophy and Literature* 25, no.2 (2001): 314–34.

Hatfield, Elaine. "Passionate and Companionate Love." In Sternberg and Barnes, *Psychology of Love,* 191–217.

Hatfield, Elaine, and Richard L. Rapson. "Love and Attachment Processes." In Lewis and Haviland-Jones, *Handbook of Emotions,* 654–62.

————. *Love and Sex: Cross-Cultural Perspectives.* Boston: Allyn and Bacon, 1996.

Hawkes, Terence. "Love in *King Lear.*" *Review of English Studies* 10 (1959): 178–81.

Heelas, Paul. "Emotion Talk Across Cultures." In *The Social Construction of Emotions*, edited by Rom Harré, 234–66. Oxford: Basil Blackwell, 1986.

Hendrick, Susan S., and Clyde Hendrick. "Romantic Love." In *Close Relationships: A Sourcebook*, edited by Clyde Hendrick and Susan S. Hendrick, 203–16. London: Sage, 2000.

Hinton, Alexander Laban. "Outline of a Bioculturally Based, 'Processual' Approach to the Emotions." In *Biocultural Approaches to the Emotions*, edited by Alexander Laban Hinton, 299–328. Cambridge, U.K.: Cambridge University Press, 1999.

Hjort, Mette, and Sue Laver, eds. *Emotion and the Arts*. Oxford: Oxford University Press, 1997.

Hoeniger, F. David. *Medicine and Shakespeare in the English Renaissance*. Newark, Del.: University of Delaware Press, 1992.

Hogan, Patrick Colm. *Cognitive Science, Literature, and the Arts: A Guide for Humanists*. New York: Routledge, 2003.

———. "Literary Universals." *Poetics Today* 18 (1997): 223–49.

———. *The Mind and Its Stories: Narrative Universals and Human Emotion*. Cambridge, U.K.: Cambridge University Press, 2003.

———. "*Othello*, Racism, and Despair." *College Language Association Journal* 41 (1998): 431–51.

Hopkins, Lisa. *The Shakespearean Marriage*. Basingstoke, U.K.: Macmillan, 1998.

Houlbrooke, Ralph. *The English Family 1450–1700*. London: Longman, 1984.

Hrdy, Sarah Blaffer. *Mother Nature: Natural Selection and the Female of the Species*. London: Chatto and Windus, 1999.

Hupka, Ralph B. "The Motive for the Arousal of Romantic Jealousy: Its Cultural Origin." In *The Psychology of Jealousy and Envy*, edited by Peter Salovey, 252–70. New York: Guilford, 1991.

Ide, Richard. *Possessed with Greatness: The Heroic Tragedies of Chapman and Shakespeare*. Chapel Hill: University of North Carolina Press, 1980.

Ingram, Martin. *Church Courts, Sex and Marriage in England, 1570–1640*. Cambridge, U.K.: Cambridge University Press, 1987.

James, Mervyn. *Society, Politics and Culture: Studies in Early Modern England*. Cambridge, U.K.: Cambridge University Press, 1986.

Jankowiak, William, ed. *Romantic Passion: A Universal Experience?* New York: Columbia University Press, 1995.

Jankowiak, William, and Ted Fischer. "A Cross-Cultural Perspective on Romantic Love." *Ethnology* 31 (1992): 149–55. Reprinted in Jenkins, Oatley, and Stein, *Human Emotions: A Reader*, 55–62.

Jenkins, Jennifer M., Keith Oatley, and Nancy L. Stein, eds. *Human Emotions: A Reader*. Oxford: Blackwell, 1998.

Johnson, Samuel. "Preface to Shakespeare." 1765. *The Yale Edition of the Works of Samuel Johnson.* Vol.7. *Johnson on Shakespeare,* 59–113. New Haven: Yale University Press, 1968.

Johnson-Laird, P. N., and Keith Oatley. "Cognitive and Social Construction in Emotions." In Lewis and Haviland-Jones, *Handbook of Emotions,* 458–75.

Johnston, Victor S. *Why We Feel: The Science of Human Emotions.* Cambridge, Mass.: Helix/Perseus, 1999.

Kagan, Jerome. *Galen's Prophecy: Temperament in Human Nature.* New York: Westview, 1994.

Kahn, Coppélia. "The Absent Mother in *King Lear.*" In *Rewriting the Renaissance: The Discourses of Sexual Difference in Early Modern England,* edited by Margaret W. Ferguson, Maureen Quilligan, and Nancy J. Vickers, 33–49. Chicago: University of Chicago Press, 1986.

———. *Roman Shakespeare: Warriors, Wounds, and Women.* London: Routledge, 1997.

Kahn, Paul W. *Law and Love: The Trials of "King Lear."* New Haven: Yale University Press, 2000.

Kastan, David Scott. "*All's Well That Ends Well* and the Limits of Comedy." *English Literary History* 52, no. 3 (1985): 575–89.

Kaula, David. "'Mad Idolatry' in Shakespeare's *Troilus and Cressida.*" *Texas Studies in Literature and Language* 15, no. 1 (1973): 25–38.

Kenrick, Douglas T., Edward K. Sadalla, and Melanie R. Trost. "Evolution, Traits, and the Stages of Human Courtship: Qualifying the Parental Investment Model." In Betzig, *Human Nature,* 213–24.

Kermode, Frank. *Shakespeare's Language.* London: Penguin, 2000.

Kernan, Alvin B. *Shakespeare, the King's Playwright: Theater in the Stuart Court 1603–1613.* New Haven: Yale University Press, 1995.

Kiernan, Victor. *Eight Tragedies of Shakespeare: A Marxist Study.* London: Verso, 1996.

Kirsch, Arthur. *Shakespeare and the Experience of Love.* Cambridge, U.K.: Cambridge University Press, 1981.

Klause, John. "Politics, Heresy and Martyrdom in Shakespeare's Sonnet 124 and *Titus Andronicus.*" In *Shakespeare's Sonnets: New Critical Essays,* edited by James Schiffer, 219–40. New York: Garland, 1999.

Kolin, Philip C., ed. *"Othello": New Critical Essays.* New York: Routledge, 2002.

Konner, Melvin. *The Tangled Wing: Biological Constraints on the Human Spirit.* London: Heinemann, 1982.

Lampert, Ada. *The Evolution of Love.* London: Praeger, 1997.

Laslett, Peter, Karla Osterveen, and Richard Smith, eds. *Bastardy and Its Comparative History.* London: Edward Arnold, 1980.

Lazarus, Richard S., and Bernice N. Lazarus. *Passion and Reason: Making Sense of Our Emotions.* Oxford: Oxford University Press, 1994.

Leach, Edmund. *Social Anthropology.* Glasgow: Collins, 1982.

Leggatt, Alexander. "Madness in *Hamlet, King Lear,* and Early Modern England." In Halio, *Critical Essays on Shakespeare's "King Lear,"* 122–38.

Leites, Edmund. *The Puritan Conscience and Modern Sexuality.* New Haven: Yale University Press, 1986.

Levin, Richard. "Bashing the Bourgeois Subject." *Textual Practice* 3, no. 1 (1989): 76–86.

———. "Feminist Thematics and Shakespearean Tragedy." *Publications of the Modern Language Association* 103, no. 2 (1988): 125–38.

———. *Looking for an Argument: Critical Encounters with the New Approaches to the Criticism of Shakespeare and His Contemporaries.* Madison, Wis.: Fairleigh Dickinson University Press, 2003.

———. "On Defending Shakespeare, 'Liberal Humanism,' Transcendent Love, and Other 'Sacred Cows' and Lost Causes." *Textual Practice* 7, no. 1 (1993): 50–55.

———. "Son of Bashing the Bourgeois Subject." *Textual Practice* 6, no. 2 (1992): 264–70.

Levine, George. "Darwin and Pain: Why Science Made Shakespeare Nauseating." *Raritan* 15, no. 2 (1995): 97–118.

Lewis, C. S. *The Allegory of Love: A Study in Medieval Tradition.* Oxford: Clarendon, 1936.

———. *The Four Loves.* 1960. Glasgow: Collins, 1986.

Lewis, Michael, and Jeannette M. Haviland-Jones, eds. *Handbook of Emotions.* 2nd ed. New York: Guilford, 2000.

Lewis, Thomas, Fari Amini, and Richard Lannon. *A General Theory of Love.* New York: Random House, 2000.

Liebowitz, Michael R. *The Chemistry of Love.* New York: Little, Brown and Company, 1983.

Lippa, Richard. *Gender, Nature, and Nurture.* London: Lawrence Erlbaum, 2002.

Loomba, Ania. "Human Nature or Human Difference?" In Wells and McFadden, *Human Nature,* 147–63.

———. "Sexuality and Racial Difference." In Barthelemy, *Critical Essays on Shakespeare's "Othello,"* 162–86.

Low, Bobbi S. *Why Sex Matters: A Darwinian Look at Human Behavior.* Princeton: Princeton University Press, 2000.

Lyas, Colin. "The Evaluation of Art." In *Philosophical Aesthetics: An Introduction,* edited by Oswald Hanfling, 349–80. Oxford: Blackwell, 1992.

Lyons, Charles. *Shakespeare and the Ambiguity of Love's Triumph.* The Hague: Mouton, 1971.

MacFarlane, Alan. *Marriage and Love in England: Modes of Reproduction 1300–1840.* Oxford: Blackwell, 1986.

Magliola, Robert R. *Phenomenology and Literature: An Introduction.* West Lafayette, Ind.: Purdue University Press, 1977.

Malik, Kenan. *The Meaning of Race: Race, History, and Culture in Western Society.* London: Macmillan, 1996.

Massing, Michael. "America's Favorite Philosopher." *The New York Times Book Review,* December 28, 2003: 7.

McAlindon, Tom. *Shakespeare Minus 'Theory.'* Aldershot, U.K.: Ashgate, 2004.

McCabe, Richard A. *Incest, Drama and Nature's Law 1550–1700.* Cambridge, U.K.: Cambridge University Press, 1993.

McEwan, Ian. *Enduring Love.* London: Random House, 1998.

McFarland, Thomas. "The Image of the Family in *King Lear.*" In *On "King Lear,"* edited by Lawrence Danson, 91–118. Princeton: Princeton University Press, 1981.

———. "Individual and Society in Shakespeare's *Coriolanus.*" In *The Scope of Words: In Honor of Albert S. Cook,* edited by Peter Baker, Sarah Webster Goodwin, and Gary Handwerk, 111–34. New York: Peter Lang, 1991.

McLuskie, Kathleen. "The Patriarchal Bard: Feminist Criticism and *King Lear.*" In Halio, *Critical Essays on Shakespeare's "King Lear,"* 139–48.

Mead, Stephen X. "'Thou Art Changed': Public Value and Personal Identity in *Troilus and Cressida.*" *Journal of Medieval and Renaissance Studies* 22, no. 2 (1992): 237–59.

Middleton, Thomas. *Women Beware Women.* Edited by J. R. Mulryne. The Revels Plays. Manchester, U.K.: Manchester University Press, 1975.

Midgley, Mary. *Beast and Man: The Roots of Human Nature.* 1979. 2nd rev. ed. London: Routledge, 1995.

———. *Science and Poetry.* London: Routledge, 2001.

Miller, Geoffrey. *The Mating Mind: How Sexual Choice Shaped the Evolution of Human Nature.* London: William Heinemann, 2000.

Miola, Robert. *Shakespeare's Rome.* Cambridge, U.K.: Cambridge University Press, 1983.

Mock, Douglas W., and Geoffrey A. Parker. *The Evolution of Sibling Rivalry.* Oxford: Oxford University Press, 1997.

Montaigne, Michel de. *The Essays.* 1603. 3 vols. Translated by John Florio. Edited by W. E. Henley. New York: AMS Press, 1967.

Morgan, D. H. J. *The Family, Politics, and Social Theory.* London: Routledge and Kegan Paul, 1985.

Neely, Carol Thomas. *Broken Nuptials in Shakespeare's Plays.* New Haven: Yale University Press, 1985.

———. "Women and Men in *Othello.*" 1980. Reprinted in Barthelemy, *Critical Essays on Shakespeare's "Othello,"* 68–90.

Newman, Karen. "'And Wash the Ethiop White': Femininity and the Monstrous in *Othello*." In *Shakespeare Reproduced: The Text in History and Ideology*, edited by Jean E. Howard and Marion F. O'Connor, 143–62. New York: Methuen, 1987.

Nordlund, Marcus. "Consilient Literary Interpretation." *Philosophy and Literature* 26, no. 2 (2002): 312–33.

———. *The Dark Lantern: A Historical Study of Sight in Shakespeare, Webster, and Middleton*. Gothenburg Studies in English 72. Gothenburg, Sweden: Acta Universitatis Gothoburgensis, 1999.

———. "Theorising Early Modern Jealousy: A Biocultural Perspective on Shakespeare's *Othello*." *Studia Neophilologica* 74 (2002): 1–15.

Nuttall, A. D. *The New Mimesis: Shakespeare and the Representation of Reality*. London: Methuen, 1983.

O'Hear, Anthony. *Beyond Evolution: Human Nature and the Limits of Evolutionary Explanation*. Oxford: Clarendon, 1997.

Orme, Nicholas. *Medieval Children*. New Haven: Yale University Press, 2001.

O'Rourke, James. "'Rule in Unity' and Otherwise: Love and Sex in *Troilus and Cressida*." *Shakespeare Quarterly* 43, no. 2 (1992): 139–58.

Ovid. *The Art of Love and Other Poems*. Translated by J. H. Mozley. Loeb Classical Library 97. London: Heinemann, 1947.

Palmer, Alan. *Fictional Minds*. Lincoln: University of Nebraska Press, 2004.

Panksepp, Jaak. "Emotions as Natural Kinds within the Mammalian Brain." In Lewis and Haviland-Jones, *Handbook of Emotions*, 137–56.

Panksepp, Jaak, and Jules B. Panksepp. "The Seven Sins of Evolutionary Psychology." *Evolution and Cognition* 6, no. 2 (2000): 108–31.

Patai, Daphne, and Will H. Corral. *Theory's Empire: An Anthology of Dissent*. New York: Columbia University Press, 2005.

Patterson, Annabel. *Shakespeare and the Popular Voice*. Oxford: Blackwell, 1989.

Pearson, Lu Emily. *Elizabethan Love Conventions*. 1933. London: Allen and Unwin, 1966.

Pechter, Edward. *"Othello" and Interpretive Traditions*. Iowa City: University of Iowa Press, 1999.

Person, E. S. "Romantic Love: At the Intersection of the Psyche and the Cultural Unconscious." In *Affect: Psychoanalytic Perspectives*, edited by Theodore Shapiro and Robert N. Emde, 383–412. Madison, Conn.: International Universities Press, 1992.

Platt, Michael. *Rome and Romans According to Shakespeare*. Jacobean Drama Studies 51. Salzburg, Austria: Institut für Englishe Sprache und Literatur, 1976.

Pollock, Linda A. *Forgotten Children: Parent-Child Relations from 1500–1900*. Cambridge, U.K.: Cambridge University Press, 1983.

Postman, Neil. *Building a Bridge to the Eighteenth Century: How the Past Can Improve Our Future.* New York: Alfred A. Knopf, 1999.

Rabkin, Norman. *Shakespeare and the Common Understanding.* New York: Free Press, 1967.

Radcliffe Richards, Janet. *Human Nature after Darwin: A Philosophical Introduction.* London: Routledge, 2000.

Ranold, Margaret. "The Betrothals of *All's Well That Ends Well*," *Huntington Library Quarterly* 26 (1963): 179–92.

Regis, Helen A. "The Madness of Excess: Love Among the Fulbe of North Cameroun." In Jankowiak, *Romantic Passion: A Universal Experience?* 141–51.

Reibetanz, John. *The Lear World: A Study of "King Lear" in its Dramatic Context.* Toronto: University of Toronto Press, 1977.

Rhodes, Clifford. *The Necessity for Love: The History of Interpersonal Relationships.* London: Constable, 1972.

Richmond, Hugh Macrae. "The Audience's Role in *Othello.*" In Kolin, *"Othello": New Critical Essays*, 89–101.

Rogers, Lesley. *Sexing the Brain.* London: Weidenfeld and Nicolson, 1999.

Ronan, Clifford. *"Antike Roman": Power Symbology and the Roman Play in Early Modern England.* Athens, Ga.: University of Georgia Press, 1995.

Rose, Hilary, and Stephen Rose, eds. *Alas, Poor Darwin: Arguments Against Evolutionary Psychology.* London: Jonathan Cape, 2000.

Rose, Mary Beth. *The Expense of Spirit: Love and Sexuality in English Renaissance Drama.* Ithaca: Cornell University Press, 1988.

Rose, Stephen. *Lifelines: Biology, Freedom, Determinism.* London: Penguin, 1998.

Rossiter, A. P. *Angel with Horns: Fifteen Lectures on Shakespeare.* Edited by Graham Storey. London: Longman, 1961.

Rougemont, Denis de. *L'Amour et l'Occident.* Paris: Librairie Plon, 1939.

Rubinstein, Annette T. "Bourgeois Equality in Shakespeare." *Science and Society* 41 (1977): 25–35.

Schlegel, A. W. Excerpt from *Lectures on Dramatic Art and Literature.* In *Shakespeare: "King Lear." A Selection of Critical Essays.* 1969. Reprint edited by Frank Kermode. London: Macmillan, 1973.

Searle, John R. *Speech Acts: An Essay in the Philosophy of Language.* Cambridge, U.K.: Cambridge University Press, 1969.

Sedgwick, Eve Kosofsky. *Between Men: English Literature and Male Homosocial Desire.* New York: Columbia University Press, 1985.

Segerstråle, Ullica. *Defenders of the Truth.* Oxford: Oxford University Press, 2001.

Shakespeare, William. *The Arden Shakespeare: Complete Works.* Edited by Richard Proudfoot, Ann Thompson, and David Scott Kastan. Walton-on-Thames, U.K.: Thomas Nelson, 1998.

————. *All's Well That Ends Well.* The Oxford Shakespeare. Edited by Susan Snyder. Oxford: Clarendon, 1993.

————. *Coriolanus.* Arden, 2nd series. Edited by Philip Brochbank. London: Routledge, 1976.

————. *King Lear.* Arden, 3rd series. Edited by R. A. Foakes. Walton-on-Thames, UK: Thomas Nelson, 1997.

————. *The Winter's Tale.* Arden, 2nd series. Edited by J. H. P. Pafford. London: Methuen, 1963.

Sharpe, J. A. *Early Modern England: A Social History 1550–1760.* London: Edward Arnold, 1987.

Shaver, Phillip, Cindy Hazan, and Donna Bradshaw. "Love as Attachment: The Integration of Three Behavioral Systems." In Sternberg and Barnes, *Psychology of Love,* 68–99.

Sidanius, Jim, and Felicia Pratto. *Social Dominance: An Intergroup Theory of Social Hierarchy and Oppression.* Cambridge, U.K.: Cambridge University Press, 1999.

Singer, Irving. *The Nature of Love.* 3 vols. Chicago: University of Chicago Press, 1984–1989.

Singer, Peter. *A Darwinian Left: Politics, Evolution and Cooperation.* London: Weidenfeld and Nicolson, 1999.

Smallwood, R. L. "The Design of *All's Well That Ends Well.*" *Shakespeare Survey* 25 (1972): 45–61.

Smuts, Barbara. "The Evolutionary Origins of Patriarchy." *Human Nature* 6, no. 1 (1995): 1–32.

Sokol, B. J. *Art and Illusion in "The Winter's Tale."* Manchester, U.K.: Manchester University Press, 1994.

Solomon, Robert C. "The Politics of Emotion." In French and Wettstein, *Philosophy of Emotions,* 1–20.

Spencer, Theodore. *Shakespeare and the Nature of Man.* 1942. 2nd rev. ed. New York: Collier, 1966.

Spiro, Melford E. *Culture and Human Nature.* Edited by Benjamin Kilborne and L. L. Langness. Chicago: University of Chicago Press, 1987.

Stanton, Kay. "All's Well in Love and War." In *Ideological Approaches to Shakespeare: The Practice of Theory,* edited by Robert P. Merrix and Nicholas Ranson, 155–63. Lewiston, N.Y.: Edwin Mellen, 1992.

Stearns, Peter. *Gender in World History.* New York: Routledge, 2000.

————. "History of Emotions: Issues of Change and Impact." In Lewis and Haviland-Jones, *Handbook of Emotions,* 16–29.

Sternberg, Robert J. *Cupid's Arrow: The Course of Love Through Time.* Cambridge, U.K.: Cambridge University Press, 1998.

————. "Triangulating Love." In Sternberg and Barnes, *Psychology of Love,* 119–38.

Sternberg, Robert J., and Michael L. Barnes, ed. *The Psychology of Love*. New Haven: Yale University Press, 1988.

Stevenson, Leslie, and David L. Haberman. *Ten Theories of Human Nature*. Oxford: Oxford University Press, 1998.

Stewart, Frank Henderson. *Honor*. Chicago: University of Chicago Press, 1994.

Storey, Robert. *Mimesis and the Human Animal: On the Biogenetic Foundations of Literary Representation*. Evanston, Ill.: Northwestern University Press, 1996.

Sulloway, Frank. *Born to Rebel: Birth Order, Family Dynamics, and Creative Lives*. London: Little, Brown, 1996.

Swärdh, Anna. *Rape and Religion in English Renaissance Literature: A Topical Study of Four Texts by Shakespeare, Drayton and Middleton*. Studia Anglistica Upsaliensia 124. Uppsala, Sweden: Acta Universitatis Upsaliensis, 2001.

Symons, Donald. "On the Use and Misuse of Darwinism in the Study of Human Behavior." In Barkow, Cosmides, and Tooby, *Adapted Mind*, 137–59, esp. 141.

Tayler, Edward William. *Nature and Art in Renaissance Literature*. 1964. Reprint. New York: Columbia University Press, 1966.

Tennov, Dorothy. *Love and Limerence: The Experience of Being in Love*. New York: Stein and Day, 1979.

Thomas, Keith. *Man and the Natural World: A History of the Modern Sensibility*. New York: Pantheon, 1983.

Thomas, Vivian. *The Moral Universe of Shakespeare's Problem Plays*. London: Croom Helm, 1987.

Tolstoy, Leo. "What is Art?" and "Shakespeare and the Drama." In *Tolstoy on Art*, translated by Aylmer Maude with an introduction by Vincent Tomas, 121–333. 1924. Reprint. New York: Haskell House, 1973. Essays originally published in 1898.

Traub, Valerie. *Desire and Anxiety: Circulations of Sexuality in Shakespearean Drama*. London: Routledge, 1992.

Trivers, Robert L. "Parental Investment and Sexual Selection." In *Sexual Selection and the Descent of Man, 1871–1971*, edited by B. Campbell, 136–79. Chicago: Aldine, 1972.

Vandermassen, Griet. "Sexual Selection: A Tale of Male Bias and Feminist Denial." *European Journal of Women's Studies* 11, no. 1 (2004): 9–26.

Vaughan, Virginia Mason. *"Othello": A Contextual History*. 1994. Reprint. Cambridge, U.K.: Cambridge University Press, 1996.

Veeser, H. Aram. *The New Historicism*. New York: Routledge, 1989.

Vickers, Brian. *Shakespeare, Co-Author: A Historical Study of the Five Collaborative Plays*. Oxford: Oxford University Press, 2002.

Wachterhauser, Brice R., ed. *Hermeneutics and Truth*. Evanston, Ill.: Northwestern University Press, 1994.

Walster, Elaine Hatfield, and G. William Walster. *A New Look at Love.* Reading, Mass.: Addison-Wesley, 1978.

Waters, C. Kenneth. "Causal Regularities in the Biological World of Contingent Distributions." *Biology and Philosophy* 13 (1998): 5–36.

Wells, Robin Headlam. *Shakespeare on Masculinity.* Cambridge, U.K.: Cambridge University Press, 2000.

———. *Shakespeare's Humanism.* Cambridge, U.K.: Cambridge University Press, 2005.

Wells, Robin Headlam, Glenn Burgess, and Rowland Wymer, eds. *Neo-Historicism: Studies in Renaissance Literature, History and Politics.* Cambridge, U.K.: D. S. Brewer, 2000.

Wells, Robin Headlam, and Johnjoe McFadden, eds. *Human Nature: Fact and Fiction.* With a foreword by A. C. Grayling. London: Continuum, 2006.

Wiederman, Michael W., and Erica Kendall. "Evolution, Sex, and Jealousy: Investigation with a Sample from Sweden." *Evolution and Human Behavior* 20 (1999): 121–28.

Wilson, Edward O. *Consilience: The Unity of Knowledge.* London: Abacus, 1998.

———. *On Human Nature.* Cambridge, Mass.: Harvard University Press, 1978.

———. *Sociobiology: The New Synthesis.* Cambridge, Mass.: Harvard University Press, 1975.

Wilson, Margo, and Martin Daly. "The Man Who Mistook His Wife for a Chattel." In Barkow, Cosmides, and Tooby, *Adapted Mind,* 289–322.

Wilson, Richard. "Against the Grain: Representing the Market in *Coriolanus.*" *The Seventeenth Century* 6, no. 2 (1991): 111–48.

Winslow, J. T., et al. "A Role for Central Vasopressin in Pair Bonding in Monogamous Prairie Voles." *Nature* 365 (1993): 544–48.

Wright, Thomas. *The Passions of the Mind in General.* 1601/1604. Reprint. Edited by William Webster Newbold. The Renaissance Imagination 15. New York: Garland, 1986.

Yoder, R. A. "'Sons and Daughters of the Game': An Essay on Shakespeare's *Troilus and Cressida.*" *Shakespeare Survey* 25 (1972): 11–25.

Zuk, Marlene. *Sexual Selections: What We Can and Can't Learn about Sex from Animals.* Berkeley: University of California Press, 2002.

About the Author

Marcus Nordlund is an associate professor of English at Göteborg University in Sweden. His previous publications include *The Dark Lantern: A Historical Study of Sight in Shakespeare, Webster, and Middleton* and articles on Shakespeare and literary theory.